# LAWS, CUSTOMS AND RIGHTS

## Charles Hatfield and His Family

## A Louisiana History

Evelyn L. Wilson

HERITAGE BOOKS
2008

# HERITAGE BOOKS
## AN IMPRINT OF HERITAGE BOOKS, INC.

## Books, CDs, and more—Worldwide

For our listing of thousands of titles see our website
at
www.HeritageBooks.com

Published 2008 by
HERITAGE BOOKS, INC.
Publishing Division
100 Railroad Ave. #104
Westminster, Maryland 21157

International Standard Book Numbers
Paperbound: 978-1-58549-942-7
Clothbound: 978-0-7884-7704-1

***Charles Hatfield, Jr.***
(photo courtesy of the family)

To Charles Hatfield
whose courage set a standard for those who would make a difference.

*I want to see the children of the state educated together. I want to see them play together, to study together, to eat their lunch together; and when they grow up to be men they will love each other, and be ready, if any force comes against the flag of the United States, to take up arms and defend it together.*

*Robert H. Isabelle[1]*

1. Member of the Louisiana House of Representatives, 1868-1870, speaking from the floor of the House in 1870, in JAMES G. HOLLANDSWORTH, JR., THE LOUISIANA NATIVE GUARDS 109 (Louisiana State Univ. Press 1995).

# Author's note

While preparing a biographical sketch of Louis Berry, a Howard Law School graduate and former Dean of the Southern University Law Center, I learned of Charles Hatfield's litigation to gain entry into the law school at the Louisiana State University and how that litigation led to the establishment of the law school at Southern University. It seemed appropriate that his act of courage should be commemorated at the celebration of the Fiftieth Anniversary of Southern's Law School and it seemed equally appropriate that his life and his efforts to bring about desegregation in Louisiana should be memorialized.

When I interviewed Charles Hatfield for this biography, he didn't say much about himself. He summed up his life in just a few words, "When I saw that something was wrong, I did what I could to correct it." He didn't look back to recount his accomplishments, but looked forward to what else he could do to improve living conditions for others. Whenever he did look back, he did so to admire his antecedents, their successes, and the challenges they overcame.

Hatfield wanted to attend the Law School at the Louisiana State University. More than wanting to acquire the benefits of a legal education, Hatfield wanted to open LSU's doors and force it to share its bounty. Hatfield felt that he, and others who were raced black, had a right to attend LSU. He risked his life and his future in an effort to exercise that right.

I have written about Charles Hatfield, but also about his family and the Louisiana in which they lived. The Douse-Purnell-Hatfield families were active participants in Louisiana's history. This is their story.

# Acknowledgments

I am exceedingly grateful for all the wonderful people who assisted and encouraged me in this work. Charles Hatfield and his wife were very generous with their time and searched for family documents to share with me. My research assistants, Gary Armstead and Adrian Wilson, students at the Southern University Law Center, were diligent and enthusiastic and greatly increased my knowledge of Internet-based research. The Southern University Law Center supported my research assistants and provided two summer research stipends for me. Glenn Labbe, while a student at the Law Center, took an interest in Charles Hatfield's story and prodded me to write it. He brought me a copy of the case record from the parish courthouse and located Charles Hatfield in New Orleans.

The librarians at all the collections I visited or called were helpful and kind, and, I believe, genuinely interested in assisting me research my topic. The Amistad Research Center, the Southern University Law Center Library, the Louisiana State Library, the Louisiana State Archives, the Louisiana State University Hill Memorial Library, the East Baton Rouge Parish Public Library, the New Orleans Public Library, the Audubon Regional Library in Clinton, Louisiana, and the Cade Memorial Library at Southern University all opened their doors wide for me. Librarians and university staff at other institutions responded to telephone requests and sent information or referred me to web sites. Harold Isadore and Phebe Poydras, research librarians at the Southern University Law Center Library, and Edna Jordan Smith, genealogist at the East Baton Rouge Parish Library, were not only helpful but constant in their support and encouragement. Other Louisiana state employees sent documents and provided insight. Employees at the parish courthouses in West Feliciana and East Baton Rouge parishes sent me in the right directions and steered me when I strayed. Everyone's help is greatly appreciated.

I'd especially like to thank readers of earlier drafts of this work: Judy McMorrow, Avi Soifera and Alfred Brophy at Boston College Law School; J. Clay Smith, Jr. at Howard University School of Law; Charles Vincent, at Southern University, Washington Marshall at the Southern University Law Center, Adisa Makalani and Columbus Brown, friends of many years, and Clara Satterfield, my mother, all of whom shared their thoughts and suggestions and meticulously proofread. Any remaining errors are due to my stubbornness in not taking their advice. I thank all the unnamed people in my life who encouraged me to finish this work or who offered to help or did help, and I thank my family, Charles, Charles II and Jeremy Shropshire, who agreed to go to the movies without me so that I could complete this work.

# CONTENTS

**Introduction**     **3**

**Part I**     The Family

    Chapter 1.    The Douses    9
    Chapter 2.    The Civil War New Orleans    29
    Chapter 3.    Richard Douse 2nd Regiment
       Louisiana Native Guards    41
    Chapter 4.    The Purnells    59
    Chapter 5.    The Hatfields    73
    Chapter 6.    The *Gaines* case    87
    Chapter 7.    The Army    99

**Part II**     Spawning a Law School

    Chapter 8.    Challenging an Institution    107
    Chapter 9.    Litigating in Louisiana    123
    Chapter 10.   The Louisiana State University and
       Agricultural and Mechanical College
       133
    Chapter 11.   Louisiana *Gaines* School    143
    Chapter 12.   Part of a Larger Movement    153
    Chapter 13.   Creating Opportunities    167

**Part III**     Moving On

    Chapter 14.   Graduate School and Teaching    189
    Chapter 15.   Activism    197

**Bibliography**     **205**

# FAMILY TREE

Arab woman m. Senegalese man
?-?      ?-?

Former Slave m. Cherokee woman
?-?      ?-?

George Douse m. Eliza Pukett
1790 -1843      ?-?

Thomas Purnell - Mary Martin
1798-1861      1802-1884

Daughter - Faucheaux
?-?      ?- c. 1863

Richard McKennon Douse m. Ann Maria Purnell
1834-1921    1872    1836-1917

Alice Stevens - Charles Hatfield
1858-1908      ?-?

Mary Elizabeth Douse
1879-1953

m.
1912

Charles Hatfield
1878-1931

Charles J. Hatfield, Jr.
1915-2002

# Introduction

*Resolved, That all the rights and immunities of American citizens are justly due to the people of color, who have ever been, and still are, willing to contribute their full share to enrich and to defend our common country.*

Henry Highland Garnet[1]

Charles J. Hatfield, Jr. grew up in Baton Rouge and New Orleans, Louisiana, well aware of segregation. Louisiana's laws prohibited his great-grandfather from marrying his great-grandmother.[2] They forced Hatfield and his family into segregated housing and into segregated schools.[3] They controlled where he could ride, where he could drink and the company he could keep.[4] The disparity between the opportunities open to whites and those open to blacks was glaring.

While growing up Hatfield had heard stories from and about his parents, grandparents and great-grandparents. He knew how their struggles had been more burdensome because of the color of their skin. Louisiana's laws and customs negated their personal choices and limited their freedom. Hatfield wanted to change these laws. Hatfield felt that, as a lawyer, he could help to win the fight against segregation and discrimination. He decided to attend law school.

In 1946, when Hatfield finished undergraduate school at Xavier University, Louisiana had no law school open to persons of color. Tulane

University and Loyola University, both private schools in New Orleans, and Louisiana State University, a state-supported school in Baton Rouge, each offered a law degree program, but all were closed to blacks. Louisiana's black citizens who wanted to attend a law school had to enroll in a school outside of the state. The three black attorneys then licensed to practice law in Louisiana had all studied law at Howard University in Washington, D.C.: Joseph Antonio Thornton, LL.B. 1913, Alexander Pierre Tureaud, LL.B. 1925, and Louis Berry, LL.B. 1941.

As a citizen of Louisiana, planning to practice law in Louisiana, Hatfield wanted to obtain his legal training and his law degree in Louisiana. Adamant that he should not be forced to travel outside of Louisiana to obtain a legal education while whites had a law school conveniently located within the state, Hatfield resolved to attend Louisiana's state-supported law school, the Louisiana State University and Agricultural and Mechanical College in Baton Rouge.

Hatfield was aware that in 1938 the United States Supreme Court had instructed the State of Missouri that if Missouri offered law school training within its borders to any of its citizens, it must offer law school training within its borders to all of its citizens. The Fourteenth Amendment to the United States Constitution prohibited discrimination on the basis of color. Lloyd Gaines "was entitled to be admitted to the law school of the [Missouri] State University in the absence of other proper provision for his legal training within the State."[5] Hatfield believed that the same rule should apply in Louisiana.

Hatfield requested an application for admission to the law school at LSU and was told, "Louisiana State University does not admit colored students."[6] Hatfield then filed a mandamus action against LSU's Board of Supervisors, its President, and its law school dean asking the court to require the school's administrators to admit him into the law school.[7] Instead, the state acted to comply with the *Gaines* decision by creating "a Law School for Negroes at Southern University . . . to be in operation for the 1947-1948 session, . . . "[8]

Hatfield was one of many blacks forced to litigate in pursuit of a measure of equality. Louisiana was one of many states that chose to duplicate its educational facilities rather than admit a black student into a segregated school.

Charles Hatfield was not recruited by outside or Communist agitators to seek admission to LSU. He was motivated to utilize all the advantages of his Louisiana citizenship by the knowledge that he and his

4

family had earned the right to be treated as its citizens. His great-grandparents had lived in Louisiana since shortly after it became a state. His grandfather fought and was wounded in the Civil War. Hatfield, himself, was an Army veteran. He was entitled to enjoy the rights of his Louisiana citizenship, and demanded those rights in his petition.

Charles Hatfield's story begins with his family history. Hatfield's forebears came to Louisiana from Ireland and France, from Maryland and Mississippi, were Native American and African and European. Some were slaves; most were free. Each generation faced setbacks and disappointments; nonetheless, the family moved forward, changing its chartered course when necessary to skirt the obstacles in its path. In each generation his family showed courage and a determination to share in the American Dream of peace and prosperity.

Hatfield's family history, although personal and peculiar in its particulars, was shaped by the history of the State of Louisiana. The character of the man who would demand access to Louisiana's flagship state institution reflects his proud awareness of the struggles and accomplishments of his ancestors: the Douses, the Purnells, and the Hatfields. Their stories, and the story of Louisiana, will help to explain why Charles Hatfield boldly claimed his rights of citizenship and became a catalyst for change in Louisiana.

## Notes

1. Speech delivered at the Seventh Anniversary of the American Anti-Slavery Society, 1840. Earl Ofari, "LET YOUR MOTTO BE RESISTANCE;" THE LIFE AND THOUGHT OF HENRY HIGHLAND GARNET 127 (Beacon Press 1972). Garnet and his family escaped from slavery in Maryland when Garnet was nine years old. They settled in New York City where Garnet excelled in school. Garnet completed Oneida Theological Institute, published a newspaper and was an active abolitionist and activist for equal opportunities for blacks.

2. La. Civ. C. art. 95 (1825), as had La. Civ. C. art 9 (1808), prohibited marriage between free persons and slaves and between free white persons and free persons of color.

3. 1924 La. Acts 118 (Jul. 12, 1924) prohibited whites from establishing a home residence in a black community and prohibited blacks from establishing a home residence in a white community. LA. CONST. of 1898, art. 248 required the establishment of separate schools for blacks and whites.

4. 1916 La. Acts 251, s.2 (Jul. 11, 1918) required segregation in prisons; 1916 La. Acts 118, s. 1 (Jul. 5, 1916) required separate ticket offices and separate entrances for circuses, shows and tent exhibitions; 1894 La. Acts 98 (Jul. 7, 1894) required separate waiting rooms at railway stations. 1890 La. Acts 111 (Jul. 10, 1890) and 1902 La. Acts 64 (Jun. 26, 1902) required segregated railroad cars and street railway cars for blacks and whites. 1908 La. Acts 176, s.6 (Jul. 3, 1908) prohibited bar operators from selling intoxicating liquors for on site consumption to whites and blacks in the same building.

5.*State of Missouri ex rel Gaines v. Canada et al.*, 305 U.S. 337, 352 (1938).

6.Letter from Paul M. Hebert to Charles J. Hatfield, III, (Jan. 24, 1946) (Tureaud Papers, Box 66, Folder 22, Amistad Research Center, Tulane University); *Hatfield v. Bd. of Supv.*, No. 25,520, petition, para X, (19th JDC, Par. of East Baton Rouge, La. Oct. 10, 1946).

7.*State of Louisiana, Ex Rel Charles J. Hatfield v. Bd. of Supv., LSU, W.B. Supv., President, and Paul M. Hebert, Dean of the Law School*, No. 25,520, (19th JDC, Par. of East Baton Rouge, La. Oct. 10, 1946). In a mandamus action, the plaintiff claims a clear legal right to the performance of a particular act and asks the court to order the defendant to perform that act. Hatfield believed that he had a clear legal right to attend the law school at LSU.

8.*Hatfield v. Bd. of Supv.*, No. 25,520, answer para. 22(d), (19th JDC, Par. of East Baton Rouge, La. Dec. 16, 1946).

# Part 1.

# Charles J. Hatfield, Jr.
## of
## Louisiana

# The Douses

George Douse m. Eliza Pukett
1790 -1843        ?-?

Richard McKennon Douse   m.   Ann Maria Purnell
1834-1921        1872        1836-1917

Mary Elizabeth Douse m. Charles Hatfield
1879-1953        1912        1878-1931

Charles J. Hatfield, Jr.
1915-2002

# Chapter 1.

## *The Douses*

*I pledge allegiance to the flag of the United States of America, and to the republic for which it stands, one nation, under God, indivisible, with liberty and justice for all white people.*[1]

Charles Hatfield's roots run deep in Louisiana, but his family's history reaches beyond the shores of the United States. On his mother's side, Hatfield traces his family to the marriage, in France, of an unnamed woman of Arabic origin to an unnamed man from Senegal.[2] Their son, George Douse, was educated in France and, while still a young man, left France for England where he met and married an Irish schoolteacher and dressmaker named Eliza Pukett. The Douses then emigrated from Liverpool, England, to the United States in the early nineteenth century, moving first to Philadelphia, where their two oldest sons were born, John Francis Douse, born 1818, and George P. Douse, born 1819,[3] then to Feliciana Parish, Louisiana.

Feliciana Parish, located along the east bank of the Mississippi River and north of Baton Rouge, remained a part of Spanish West Florida after France acquired the Louisiana Territory from Spain in 1800 then sold it to the United States. In 1810, residents of the area held a two-day convention at Buhler's Plains in New Feliciana to discuss their loyalty to Spain. Napoleon had invaded Spain and forced its King to vacate his throne. Reasoning that they owed no duty to a puppet government controlled by France, the conventioneers captured the Spanish fort in Baton Rouge and declared the area the Free and

Independent State of West Florida. After leaders of the independence movement corresponded with the United States Secretary of State, the area was annexed to the Orleans Territory, the southern part of the Louisiana Territory. Territorial Governor William C. C. Claiborne took possession in December 1810.[4]

The major cities of New Feliciana were Bayou Sarah Landing, on the river, St. Francisville, on a bluff overlooking the river, Jackson, on the east side of Thompson Creek, and Clinton, further east of Jackson. In 1824, the parish was divided into East and West Feliciana Parishes at Thompson Creek.

The Douses settled in St. Francisville and became the parents of three more sons and a daughter: Richard McKennon Douse, born August 12, 1834, Michael William Douse, born July 27, 1836, Mary Elizabeth Douse, born March 3, 1838, and Daniel Turnbull Douse, born in 1840.[5] George Douse worked as a steward on the steamer, *Brilliant*, a passenger boat that traveled weekly between Bayou Sarah Landing and New Orleans.

On May 27, 1831, Douse purchased three *arpents* of land from Doctor Henry Baines.[6] An *arpent* is a French unit of land measurement roughly equivalent to an acre. Two and one-half weeks later, on June 14, 1831, Douse enrolled in the office of the parish judge, John B. Dawson, declaring his presence in the parish as required by an 1830 statute that prohibited free blacks from entering the state after 1824.[7]

The 1830 enrollment requirement was a part of Louisiana's continuing response to a concern that freed or enslaved blacks emigrating from the French or English Antilles would spread abolitionist sentiment among enslaved blacks in Louisiana. As early as 1786, Don Esteban Miro', Spanish Governor of Louisiana, ordered slave merchants to stop bringing blacks born in the Antilles into Louisiana. In 1790, free blacks who had fled from French colonies were forbidden to enter Louisiana. Free blacks in Haiti, numbering 30,000 compared to 35,000 whites in 1791, owned approximately one-fourth of the land and one-third of the slaves in Haiti, but were denied many economic and civic opportunities. Unrest between free blacks and whites had already led to bloodshed. On July 23, 1792, after the start of the Haitian Revolution and after France had abolished slavery in France, Don Francisco Luis Hector, Baron de Carondelet, Governor and Intendant of Louisiana, prohibited former slaves from the French and English Antilles from entering Louisiana and imposed a fine of 400 piasters for violations.

The revolutionary spirit which gave rise to the massive slave revolt in Haiti was believed to be embodied in the blacks of the Caribbean whether they had been enslaved or were free there. It was an ever present threat to slave holders and to colonial authority on the United States mainland.

Slavery in Saint Domingue was especially cruel. The Pearl of the Antilles had accumulated its wealth at the expense of more than a million lives. European colonization in the late 15th and 16th centuries virtually exterminated the indigenous Taino population. Disease, outright murder and Spanish attempts to enslave the Taino proved fatal. Within fifty years of the 1492 landing of Christopher Columbus, more than half a million people and an entire civilization had been destroyed.

Beginning in 1502, African slaves in large numbers were imported into Haiti to provide a labor force that could cultivate a sugarcane crop. Their enslavement was so brutal that a continuous stream of replacements was needed. Men and women were beaten, branded, maimed and killed without restraint. The average life span of a slave in Haiti was only six to ten years. Neither the Roman Catholic Church nor the French Code Noir of 1685 seemed to mitigate this tyranny and its concomitant high mortality rate. Many slaves escaped to the mountains where they formed communities and periodically raided nearby plantations. Called maroons, these former slaves would free slaves and gather foodstuffs and weapons on their raids. Slave uprisings gave voice to the complaints of those who did not or could not escape to join the maroons in the mountains. In 1791, two-thirds of Haiti's half a million black slaves had been born in Africa.

On August 22, 1791, a well-orchestrated show of force led to the end of slavery in Haiti. Across the northern part of the French colony of Saint Domingue, sugarcane fields, woods and plantations were simultaneously set on fire. Flames blown by the wind covered hundreds of miles. Fifty thousand slaves had been organized to revolt against their enslavement by a Voodoo priest named Boukman Dutty who had been brought to Saint Domingue from Jamaica.

Boukman worked as a coachman. Traveling from plantation to plantation, he became familiar with the colony's geography and with the location and defenses of its plantations. He was determined to end slavery in the colony and made contact with like-minded slaves on other plantations and with persons who had escaped slavery and lived as maroons in the mountains throughout the northern portion of the colony.

Boukman killed his owner then spent several years in the mountains of Haiti slowly organizing and training runaway slaves and coordinating with his contacts on the various plantations. He carefully planned his assault upon slavery and its supporters.

Boukman's troops were highly motivated. Men, women and children fought together in this battle for freedom. At Boukman's instruction, slaves on five plantations joined arms and killed their owners and overseers. As news of the rebellion spread, others joined and, eventually, 900 plantations were destroyed. In a matter of days, the former slaves used knives, swords, and guns taken from their former owners to kill 2,000 whites and to destroy millions of dollars in crops and property. Boukman's troops were effective guerilla fighters, setting traps, poisoning water holes, and using whatever resources were at hand. They treated their former masters with the same cruelty they had endured. After Boukman was captured and executed on November 7, 1791, the revolution continued.

Boukman's death, and the subsequent display of his head on a pole, incited blacks to be unremitting in their struggle in his honor. The whites of Saint Domingue retaliated, indiscriminately slaughtering 15,000 to 20,000 blacks and mulattos over the next few weeks although mulattos had played no role in Boukman's uprising. The slaves fighting for their freedom did not give up. By May 1793, the capital city of Cap Francois was captured. After this victory, Toussaint L'Ouverture emerged as Boukman's successor.

Thin and sickly as a child, Francois Dominique Toussaint was comparatively well treated. He was taught to read and write, knew mathematics, and was an excellent swimmer and horseman. He learned, among other things, to use plants and herbs as medicines and was known personally or by reputation across much of the island. He was often seen riding from plantation to plantation with his father or asked to apply his medical remedies to slave and free persons alike. His studies of Julius Caesar and other military leaders, an interest he developed in his youth, provided him with a wealth of information about military tactics and strategies.

Toussaint was initially appointed Physician in Chief of the Army. As his command over troops increased, he trained his revolutionary forces to be professional soldiers, to march in formation and to follow orders without challenge. He was well loved and well respected by his troops and willingly accepted the challenge left by Boukman's death. For his prowess in battle, Toussaint acquired an additional name, L'Ouverture, the opening. An admiring Frenchman declared, "Cet homme fait L'ouverture." "This man makes an opening."[8]

Toussaint L'Ouverture initially joined forces with Spanish troops who were willing to fight against the French on the island. Spain and France were perennially at war and the French forces were quickly defeated. On September 28, 1791, the French Assembly abolished slavery in France and then on February 4, 1794, France abolished slavery in its colonies. As France no longer supported slavery, Toussaint was willing to fight local slave holders in the name of France. He abandoned his allegiance to Spain which continued to protect slavery. Slave holders in Haiti then sought support from Great Britain and Spain who sent more troops to the island. This time the Spanish would fight against Toussaint.

Both the British and the Spanish governments feared that a successful revolution in Haiti would inspire similar revolts among the slaves in their possessions. These fears were not unfounded. An April 1795 revolt on the Poydras Plantation in Pointe Coupee Parish, Louisiana, then a Spanish possession, was directly attributed to the revolution in Haiti. Slaves who had been removed from Haiti to Pointe Coupee Parish invoked the name of Boukman to inspire their forces. A second revolt in March 1796, also in Pointe Coupee Parish and also attributed to Haitian influence, was frustrated when the plot was disclosed. A female slave abused by her master retorted that she would soon get her revenge. She was asked what she meant by that threat and was tortured into disclosing what she knew about the planned insurrection. All of the central planners of that uprising were executed.

In Haiti, Toussaint defeated the forces sent by Great Britain in May 1798 and defeated the Spanish forces in 1801, conquering Santo Domingo for the French. He then declared the colony free of slavery. As he had fought in the name of France, Toussaint did not declare the colony independent of France. His revolutionary purpose was to free Haiti from slavery, not to free it from France. Toussaint restored order on the island and was conciliatory toward whites, inviting those who had left to return and reclaim their plantations. The French named Toussaint General in Chief of the St. Domingue armies and Toussaint became the island's governor. He appointed a committee to draft a constitution for his government and insisted that it include a guarantee of religious as well as personal freedom. He encouraged international trade. He discharged his armies, instructing his soldiers to return to the farms where they had worked, this time as free men.

Napoleon, however, would not leave Toussaint in peace. Perhaps he was embarrassed by Toussaint defeating the French forces early in the Revolution. Perhaps he was insulted by correspondence from Toussiant with the salutation, "The first of the blacks, to the first of the whites." Newspapers had called Toussaint "The Black Napoleon." Perhaps Napoleon was afraid of the thousands of republican soldiers adrift within France and sought to occupy their idle hands.[9] Whatever his reason, in 1802, Napoleon sent more than 30,000 men to restore slavery to the island. Napoleon's effort was futile. Toussaint's army would not be defeated. As Napoleon's army advanced, Toussaint withdrew into the interior of Haiti, and Napoleon's army was decimated by malaria and fatigue and by confrontations with small bands of Toussaint's soldiers.

Reduced to a force of 8,000 men, the French resorted to trickery. Toussaint was invited by the French to negotiate a truce aboard a French ship. Once aboard, Toussaint was placed in chains and carried to France where he was imprisoned in an unheated Alpine dungeon, the Chateauz de Joux. The single window in his 12 x 12 cell overlooked Switzerland's snow-covered mountains. Toussaint was starved until his death on April 7, 1803.

As with Boukman, Toussaint's absence from the fighting did not bring the revolution to an end. On December 31, 1803, Jean Jacques Dessalines and Henri Christophe, who assumed the leadership of the revolution after Toussaint's kidnaping, declared Haiti the second independent nation in the Americas. The victors chose to call their nation Haiti, the name given to it by the native Taino Indians. Haiti means mountainous. Freedom in Haiti had come from the mountains.

By the time the fighting ended, more than 350,000 people had died, 200,000 of them blacks and mulattos. Nearly all of the whites, and many of the blacks and mulattos, left the island during the years 1798-1804, taking their slaves with them when they could. They sought refuge in Santo Domingo, the Spanish side of the island, and in France, Cuba, Jamaica, New Orleans and the coastal cities of the United States: Savannah, Charleston, Norfolk, Baltimore, Philadelphia, and New York. Haitians who had migrated elsewhere eventually settled in New Orleans where they joined the large body of French-speaking people already there. After years of intercourse between the two French colonies, many Haitians had family or business associates in New Orleans.

Spain transferred ownership of the Louisiana Territory to France in 1800, then France sold it to the United States in 1803. The United States divided the territory into two parts: The Orleans Territory, south of the 33$^{rd}$ degree north latitude, which included the city of New Orleans, and the district of Louisiana, north of that latitude.

Concerned that disquiet would result should the revolutionary spirit successful in Haiti take hold in the Orleans Territory, the United States Congress prohibited all persons from importing slaves into the territory from outside of the United States and banned from the territory all slaves who had entered the United States after May 1, 1798. No slaves could be brought into the territory, "except by a citizen of the United States, removing into said territory for actual settlement, and being at the time of such removal bona fide owner of such slave or slaves; . . ."[10] Settlers could bring in their seasoned slaves, but slave traffic was otherwise forbidden.

Territorial Governor William C. C. Claiborne reported a total of 52,998 persons under his jurisdiction in 1806.[11] Within the population of 23,574 slaves, 3,355 free persons of colour, and 26,069 whites in the Orleans Territory, only 13,500 were natives of Louisiana. More than 10% of the population, 1,979 slaves, 1,977 free persons of color, and 1,798 whites, had moved into the territory to escape from the fighting in Haiti. Claiborne counted these 5,754 persons; an unknown number entered the territory without formalities.

Not satisfied that prohibiting the importing of slaves would protect the territory from a slave revolt, the territory of Orleans prohibited the emigration of free people of color from Hispaniola (the name of the island Haiti shares with the Dominican Republic) and the other French Islands of the Caribbean into the territory of Orleans. The prohibiting act instructed that no free man of color from any of the formerly French territories in America should be admitted into the territory. Free women of color and young people under fifteen years of age were permitted to enter the state, as they were presumed "to have left the island above named, to fly from the horrors committed during its insurrection."[12] Black women and children did not engender the fear evoked by free black men. Those persons of color from Hispaniola who were now in Louisiana were required to prove to a justice of the peace or a mayor of a city that they were not the slaves of anyone and to obtain a certificate from that official attesting to their free status.

The following year, 1807, the Legislative Council replaced that law with a more general statute prohibiting all free persons of color from entering the territory to settle from anywhere outside of it. Any free black or mulatto, who recently moved to the territory and remained there for more than two weeks after being asked to leave, could be assessed a fine of twenty dollars per week.[13] This statute apparently had little effect. Claiborne noted in his Executive Journal that, "the colored people who had been ordered to depart continued to evade the order, and remained in New Orleans."[14]

In 1809, Haitian immigrants who had settled in Cuba were rudely expelled. After France invaded Spain and deposed its King, the Cubans felt that Frenchmen within their borders could not be trusted. Between May 1809 and January 1810, thousands of Haitians left Cuba and entered Orleans Territory through the port at New Orleans. Records show 3,102 free persons of color, 3,226 slaves and 2,731 whites entering New Orleans from Cuba in just these few months.

Federal law prohibited these Haitians from bringing their slaves with them into the United States. As permitted by the United States Constitution, Congress had prohibited the importation of slaves into the jurisdiction of the United States effective January 1, 1808.[15] At the request of representatives from Orleans Territory, however, Congress authorized the President to allow "persons who shall have been forcibly expelled from the island of Cuba" to bring their slaves into the United States without being subject to the penalties imposed on other importers of slaves.[16] Louisianians feared the revolutionary spirit of the Caribbean slaves, but sympathized with the French-speaking Haitians who, having taken refuge in Cuba, were now forcibly evicted. They had lost their land in Haiti and the bulk of their remaining wealth was in the form of the slaves they held captive.

These representatives of the territory may have soon regretted their compassion. Participants in a January 1811 revolt led by Charles Deslondes claimed to have received spiritual encouragement and material support from slaves who had been brought into the territory by slave holders fleeing Haiti and then Cuba. Beginning in St. John the Baptist Parish, near its juncture with St. James and Ascension Parishes, slaves armed with agricultural implements and a few stolen guns liberated themselves and marched southward toward New Orleans. Their plan was to meet with an organized group there and seize the federal arsenal. Armed with weapons, the former slaves could capture New Orleans and drive slave holders from the land, as had been done in Haiti.

Blacks along the Mississippi River, drums pounding, flags

waving and voices singing, covered twenty-five miles in eleven days, burning and killing and freeing slaves. They gathered more than 500 former slaves and free blacks into their army before the revolt was crushed. The heads of those who had joined the revolt were displayed on poles for sixty miles along the road to New Orleans.

After Louisiana became a state in 1812, it continued to prohibit free blacks from entering the state. In 1830, the state legislature authorized the arrest and prosecution of "any free negro, [sic] mulatto, or other free person of colour, . . . come into this state, [in violation of the 1807 act] since the first day of January of 1825."[17] Once convicted of illegally entering the state after January 1, 1825, free persons of color were to leave within sixty days. Those who failed to leave could be sentenced to imprisonment, at hard labor, for life. By its explicit language, the statute placed on Louisiana's free black citizens the burden of proving that they had been in Louisiana prior to January 1, 1825: "the presumption shall always be, that they have actually come into the same in violation of this act."[18]

To avoid accusation and conviction under this statute, George Douse enrolled in the office of the parish judge where he resided "setting forth [his] age, sex, colour, trade or calling, place of nativity and the time of their arrival in the state . . ."[19] In his statement of enrollment, Douse declared himself a free man of colour, "of yellow complexion, a mariner by trade, born in the City of Philadelphia in the State of Pennsylvania in the year Ninety."[20] It was in George's best interest to declare that he was American born rather than foreign born given the anti-immigrant legislation enacted in Louisiana. His story was plausible as Pennsylvania had begun to abolish slavery in 1780.[21]

Some ten years later, in November 1840, Douse attested to the free status of twenty-eight-year-old William Jones, stating that he was well acquainted with William Jones, a free man of color born of free parents in New York City. Douse reported that Jones had been living with George Douse since 1821, shortly after Douse moved to Feliciana Parish.[22]

In 1831, George Douse was a rural landowner and slave holder. On July 5, 1831, Douse purchased "1 Negro Boy Named Simon . . . to be a Slave for Life."[23] On March 6, 1832, he purchased a "Negro man named Mike, aged about 50 years, slave for life."[24] In 1835 he paid cash for five *arpents* of land adjacent to land that he already owned.[25]

Douse used his land to construct an inn and "house of

entertainment frequented by plantation gentry."[26] Douse's land was located approximately three and one-half miles north of St. Francisville on Woodville Road. Woodville Road, now U.S. Highway 61, is part of a scenic parkway along the Mississippi River that runs from Baton Rouge in Louisiana, to St. Paul, Minnesota.[27] Anyone traveling from Baton Rouge or St. Francisville would pass Douse's property on their way to Natchez or Port Gibson or Vicksburg.

Douse's *Orange Hill* offered three meals a day with champagne, ice cream, Havana cigars, and brandy. It offered lodging, and boarding for horses.[28] *Orange Hill* was a favored site for dinners, parties and balls. A February 1836 letter to Lewis Sterling, Jr., the owner of Wakefield Plantation, mentions two parties at Douse's, one of which was well attended and one which was forthcoming.[29] The Feliciana Volunteers Fire Department held a July 4th dinner there in 1836.[30] Bennet Barrow noted in his diary that he attended parties and balls given at Douse's in 1839, 1840 and 1841, and described one as "verry [sic] pleasant."[31]

In 1837, Douse purchased an additional 26.93 *arpents* of land. This time he mortgaged property he already owned and bought the new land on credit.[32] Douse renovated and enlarged *Orange Hill*, placing 88 feet of brick pillars beneath it and adding a double brick chimney 31 and ½ feet high. His bricklayer charged him for 3,850 bricks and three barrels of lime.[33] Douse spent more than $400 at the firm of Barclay and Tenney, lumber salesmen in Bayou Sarah Landing, for flooring plank, weather boards, shingles and other building materials.[34]

Douse's investment was not profitable. He failed to pay all that he owed for the land and McMicken, his vendor, brought suit to collect. On May 7, 1839, Douse admitted that he owed McMicken $1,579.75, plus interest, and judgment in that amount was rendered against Douse. *Orange Hill* was seized by the sheriff and sold at auction on March 28, 1842.[35] Douse's property had been appraised at $5,000 and Charles McMicken purchased Douse's land and his two slaves, Simon and Mike, at the sheriff's sale. Douse remained at *Orange Hill* even after the sale. On April 2, 1842, Douse sent a note from *Orange Hill* to a Mr. Sidney Flowers, Jr. asking that Flowers pay Douse the $2.50 that he owed for a bottle of Madera wine. He sent the note by his son, Richard Douse, Charles Hatfield's grandfather.[36]

Douse was not the only landowner to suffer an economic setback in 1842 Louisiana. A financial crisis in the state caused seven banks in New Orleans to go out of business that year, while the remaining nine were greatly limited in their ability to provide services because of a general lack of confidence in their operations. Barrow notes in his diary in February 1842 that, "nearly every House in the city has failed or will fail . . . should these times continue 2 Months great many planters must be broken up . . ."[37] The issue of the *Louisiana Chronicle* dated February 11, 1843, lists 21 bankruptcies and 14 Sheriff's sales in West Feliciana Parish.[38] George Douse was one among many who lost property in 1842.

No longer landowners, George and Eliza arranged for Brisbane Marshall, who bought and sold lots in the New Valencia subdivision of the Town of Bayou Sarah,[39] formerly Bayou Sarah Landing, to execute for them an affidavit of their freedom. Douse probably met Marshall on the Mississippi River where Douse worked as a steamboat steward. Marshall may have been Douse's employer at one time as Marshall had helped to organize the Bayou Sarah Steam Boat Company in June 1830.[40]

George and Eliza wanted documentation of their long term Louisiana residency and wanted proof of their free status. Louisiana had enacted yet another statute designed to prevent free persons of color from entering the state.[41] The new law posed a threat to all free blacks in Louisiana as it authorized the arrest and prosecution of free persons of color who had entered the state after January 1, 1825. Under the 1830 statute, any free black convicted of entering the state after January 1, 1825, was required to leave the state within 60 days. Under the 1842 statute, any free black who came into the state aboard any vessel or steamboat whether as an employee or a passenger was subject to imprisonment while the ship was in port and was forced to leave the state with the ship that brought them in or by other means.

Free blacks were seen as a source of instability in the south as pressure to eliminate slavery grew in the nation. George and Eliza Douse, aware of the state's desire to rid itself of free blacks and aware of the ease by which they could be reduced to slavery, did not want themselves or their children to become victims of a mistake in identification.

In his affidavit, Marshall swore that he "became acquainted with George Douse, a free man of color + his wife Eliza Douse, a free woman of color, in the year 1824, in the State of Louisiana, where they then resided; ..."[42] The date of 1824 was prophylactically prior to January 1, 1825, and protected the Douses from prosecution under these statutes. Marshall swore that George and Eliza were, in 1824, reputed to be free, and "have since been so considered," that he met John and George, their children, in 1824, and that he knows Richard, Mary and Daniel, who have been born since 1824. Each family member could carry a copy of this document as proof of his or her free status and proof of birth in Louisiana or residency in Louisiana before January 1, 1825.

It is curious that Eliza, who was white and Irish, should be described in Brisbane's affidavit as a free woman of color. Perhaps, after exposure to Louisiana's sun, her skin color was not so very different from that of her husband who was of a yellow complexion. It may be, instead, that Eliza was considered black by association. While a person with any known origin in a group native to Africa is often raced "black" regardless of skin color or phenotypical characteristics, a person whose ancestry is unknown in a given community can declare themselves black or white, whichever they choose. One's appearance as black or white is, at times, of far less importance than one's claimed or known lineage.[43] The color line could be crossed in both directions.

Given that marriage between whites and blacks was prohibited in Louisiana, Eliza may have preferred her designation as a woman of color rather than bring the mixed nature of her marriage to the attention of the authorities. Pinkney and Sarah Ross, a black man and a white woman lawfully married in South Carolina in May 1873, moved to Charlotte, North Carolina, and were indicted for fornication and adultery, as North Carolina laws forbid a white person to marry a black person. Their South Carolina marriage was recognized as valid and they were found not guilty.[44] They later returned to South Carolina and, at a time when South Carolina would prohibit their marriage, the 1900 Census of Cherokee County shows both Pinkney Ross and his wife Sarah to be black.[45] The Census taker may have indicated a designation without asking.

In 1842, free persons of color were not required by law to carry with them proof of their free status. Louisiana's law required free persons to carry a certificate from a Justice of the Peace attesting to their freedom only if they carried arms or were from the island of Hispaniola.[46] Slaves, in contrast, had to carry written permission from their owner any time they were any distance from their work station stating how far they were permitted to travel and for what purposes.[47] An unescorted slave found away from his owner's plantation or other place of work without written permission could be seized and violently subdued by whoever apprehended him.[48] Skin color linked a free black to slavery and a free black bore the burden of proving he was not a slave traveling without papers. Whether carrying a firearm or not, the prudent free black carried documentation of his or her free status. Blacks believed that a free black who lost these papers, or who could not produce them or a white person to speak on their behalf on demand, would be put up for auction without hesitation.

Slave-catchers and slave-traders were known to capture free blacks who would then be sold as slaves. The practice of selling free blacks as slaves was so pervasive that legislation was enacted to impose a fine on kidnappers: "[W]hoever shall knowingly bring or cause to be brought into this State, any free person of color as a slave, shall, upon conviction thereof, be fined one thousand dollars, one-half to go to the informer. He shall also be liable to such free person of color for damages."[49] The purchaser who believed he had paid for a slave could try to seek compensation from the slave trader.

Richard Douse explained to Hatfield that he and his brothers believed it was vitally important to carry identification papers. Richard's brother, John Francis Douse, had been born with blonde hair and blue eyes and looked as white as any person raced "white." Richard resented his brother's white features but took pleasure in noting that John also felt obliged to carry papers documenting his free status. John Douse's white skin color, blonde hair and blue eyes were not enough to protect him from the threat of slavery.

George Douse died September 6, 1843, only a year and a half after he lost his property. His children, John, George, Richard, Mary, and Daniel, moved from West Feliciana Parish to New Orleans. Michael had apparently died sometime before September 1842 as his name does not appear in the Brisbane affidavit. Eliza may have stayed in West Feliciana parish as her name does not appear in the New Orleans register of free blacks or in the U.S. Census records.

In New Orleans, the Douses found a large community of free blacks. The first records of free persons of color in New Orleans date from the 1720s, early in the city's history. By 1830, free blacks in New Orleans had organized *La Societe e' Economie* among professional men and *La Societe des Artisans* among the craftsmen. They had erected the Economy Hall and the Artisans Hall for their societies' use. The 1850 census shows 9,961 free black persons living in Orleans Parish.

Some owned their homes and businesses, while others worked for wages or by the job and rented rooms that they shared with family, friends or strangers. Most had been born in Louisiana, but many had come from other states or from the Caribbean, or from outside of the Americas despite the laws that hampered their immigration.[50] Many had never known slavery, while others had bought their freedom with their earnings or with the earnings of family members. Some had been freed by their owners. Others had escaped from slavery and managed, once in New Orleans, to escape detection.

Slaves who were skilled laborers were often allowed to work in New Orleans and to retain any money they earned over and above that demanded by their owner. Louisiana's Black Code, approved June 7, 1806, instructed slave holders to "leave to their slaves the free enjoyment of Sundays, and . . . pay them for their labour on said day . . ."[51] Slaves routinely worked on Sundays and would save these earnings to purchase their freedom and that of their family members and friends.

In 1850, an overwhelming majority of the free Negro men in New Orleans were skilled laborers. Many black immigrants, whether slave or free, were skilled laborers before they came to New Orleans and brought their skills with them. Others learned their skills after they arrived. The free adult Negro males listed in the 1850 census in New Orleans were engaged in fifty-four different occupations, working as carpenters, masons, cigar makers, shoemakers, clerks, mechanics, coopers, barbers, draymen, painters, blacksmiths, butchers, cabinetmakers, cooks, stewards, or upholsterers. Others worked as architects, bookbinders, brokers, engineers, doctors, jewelers, merchants, undertakers, real estate brokers, tailors, grocers, importers, poets, and musicians. Fewer than 10 percent of the free adult black males in New Orleans in 1850 were unskilled laborers. John and Richard were craftsmen: bricklayers, plasterers, and stonemasons.

The Douses, who were literate, opened a school for the children of free blacks. They were not allowed to teach whites at their school, nor were they allowed to teach slaves, as slaves were forbidden by law to learn to read.[52] Both adults and children were anxious to decipher the written word. By 1860, 87.8% of the free blacks in Louisiana over 20 years of age were literate.[53]

John, Richard's blued eyed brother, moved to Iberville Street, (then known as Custom House Street) between Claiborne and Derbigny Streets and worked as a steward on a steamboat, as had his father.[54] John died of yellow fever on October 26, 1856, at age 38 and is buried in the St. Louis Cemetery #2.[55] He left behind him a wife, Adele Murry Douse, and two children, Emma, a schoolteacher, and John, a cooper.[56]

Epidemics of yellow fever frequently plagued New Orleans. It suffered its worst recorded yellow fever epidemic in 1853 when the Saffron Scourge, as it has been called, killed approximately 8,400 people.[57] Conditions in the city were perfect for a yellow fever epidemic that summer. New Orleans had experienced frequent rains, which alternated with blistering heat, encouraging disease-carrying mosquito populations to spread their cargo across the city. Culverts, already filled with stagnant water, overflowed with filth. In August, death rates reached as high as 250 people per day.

In the following years, 1854 and 1855, deaths from yellow fever continued, reaching 2,500 and 2,670, respectively. In 1858, another 4,855 people were killed. In 1856, when John Douse died of yellow fever, only 73 deaths were attributed to that pestilence. John, may have been exposed to the disease by a passenger traveling on a steamboat with him.

In 1859, Louisiana passed yet another act authorizing the arrest of free persons of color who had recently entered the state.[58] Although their father had registered the family at the courthouse in West Feliciana Parish, Richard, Mary Elizabeth, and Daniel were obliged to register themselves at City Hall in New Orleans to create a local record of their free status. They presented the affidavit by Brisbane Marshall as proof. Richard, a plasterer, was 5 feet 5 inches and 24 years old. Mary, at 5 foot 2 inches and age 22, was a seamstress. Daniel, at 5 feet 3½ inches and age 19, was a cabin boy on a steamboat.[59]

Richard left New Orleans soon thereafter. By 1860, he was living with the family of Edward Murry in East Baton Rouge Parish.[60] Murry's sister, Adele, was the widow of Richard's brother, John, who had died of yellow fever in 1856.[61] Like Richard, Murry was a plasterer. In September 1862, Richard Douse left Murry's house to join the U.S. Army. He would become a part of the Second Regiment, Louisiana Native Guards. George P. Douse, who like his father and his brother, John, worked as a steward on a steamboat, died in New Orleans on December 22, 1863, at age 44.[62]

## Notes

1.The Pledge of Allegiance to the United States of America, as uttered under their breath by discerning black school children.

2.This story, and other family history appearing without citation, was provided by Charles J. Hatfield, the subject of this biography, in interviews held at his home on October 29, 1998, December 11, 1998, October 15, 1999 and by correspondence and telephone conversations on various dates between October 1997 and the completion of this biography. Where information provided by Mr. Hatfield has been verified, a citation appears.

3.The 1856 Certificate of Death for John Douse states that he was born in Louisiana, 32 Orleans Deaths Indices 1804-1885 325, while that of George Douse says he was born in Philadelphia. 22 Orleans Death Indices 1804-1885 363.

4.FORTIER, ALCEE, III A HISTORY OF LOUISIANA 64-70 (Goupil & Co, Manzi, Joyant & Co., Successors 1904).

5.Affidavit of Freedom of George + Eliza Douse and their children by Brisbane Marshall, Book H, Page 244, Conveyance Records, West Feliciana Parish, La. (Sept. 1, 1842); Affidavit of Elizabeth Townsend (Sept. 24, 1904), Pension File of Richard Douse, File #C 2536643, Civil War and Later Pension Files, Records of the Veterans Administration, Record Group 15, National Archives, Washington, D.C.; Orleans Deaths Indices 1804-1885.

6.Sale to George Douse by Henry Baines, Book D, Page 233, Conveyance Records, West Feliciana Parish, La. (May 27, 1831).

7.1830 La. Acts at 90 (Mar. 16, 1830). "AN ACT to prevent free persons of colour from entering into this State, and for other purposes. Section 1st. Be it enacted by the senate and house of representative of the State of Louisiana in general assembly convened, That all free negroes; [sic] mulattoes, or other free persons of colour, who have come into this state since the first day of January of 1825, in violation of an act of the Territory of Orleans, passed on the 14th of April 1807, entitled 'An act to prevent the emigration of free negroes [sic] and mulattoes into the Territory of Orleans,' shall and may be arrested and proceeded against by warrant, before any judge, justice of the peace, or mayor in this state."

8.N.B. Wood, *Fathers to the Race*, in A NEW NEGRO FOR A NEW CENTURY 349 (J.E. MacBrady, ed. American Publ. House 1900).

9.Wood, *Fathers to the Race*, in A NEW NEGRO FOR A NEW CENTURY 353.

10."An Act erecting Louisiana into two territories, and providing for the temporary government thereof." 2 Stat. 283, Chap. 38, s. 10 (Mar. 26, 1804)

11.Letter from William Claiborne to Secretary of State, Washington, D.C., 4 Executive Journal 82 (May 18, 1808) in CHARLES GAYARRE, IV, HISTORY OF LOUISIANA 212 (Pelican Publishing Co., 5th ed. 1974).

12.1806 La Acts XXX (Jun. 7, 1806) "An Act to prevent the introduction of Free People of Color from Hispaniola and the other French Islands of America, into the Territory of Orleans."

13.1807 La. Acts XXVIII (Apr. 14, 1807) "An Act to prevent the emigration of Free Negroes and Mulattoes into the Territory of Orleans."

14.Letter to Mr. Anderson, American Consul at Havana, from William Claiborne, 4 Executive Journal 121 (1808) in CHARLES GAYARRE, IV HISTORY OF LOUISIANA 219.

15.*An Act to prohibit the importation of Slaves into any port or place within the jurisdiction of the United States, from and after the first day of January, in the year of our Lord one thousand eight hundred and eight,* (Mar. 2, 1807) ch.22, 2 Stat. 426 (1861).("That from and after the first day of January, one thousand eight hundred and eight, it shall not be lawful to import or bring into the United States or the territories thereof from any foreign kingdom, place, or country, any negro, [sic] mulatto, or person of colour, with intent to hold, sell, or dispose of such negro, [sic] mulatto, or person of colour, as a slave, or to be held to service or labour.") U.S. CONST. art. I, s. 9. ("The Migration or Importation of such Persons as any of the States now existing shall think to admit, shall not be prohibited by the Congress prior to the Year one thousand eight hundred and eight,...")

16.*An Act for the remission of certain penalties and forfeitures, and for other purposes,* (Jun. 28, 1809) ch. 8, 2 Stat. 549 (1861). The slaves admitted into the state under this act had to enter into U.S. Territory in the same vessel with the immigrant claiming ownership.

17.1830 La. Acts at 90 s.1 (Mar. 16, 1830). "An Act to prevent free persons of colour from entering into this State, and for other purposes."

18.1830 La. Acts at 90 s. 2, 17.

19.1830 La. Acts at 90 s. 12.

20.Statement of enrollment in compliance with 1830 La. Acts (Mar. 16, 1830), Book D, Page 235, Conveyance Records, West Feliciana Parish, La. (Jun. 22, 1831). The census taker who interviewed Richard Douse's family in 1880, reported that George was born in England and that Eliza was born in Philadelphia. 1880 Census of East Baton Rouge Parish, Louisiana 51. Douse was born March 9, 1790.

21.1780 Pa. Laws (Mar. 1, 1780). ("[A]ll persons as well negroes [sic] and mulattoes as others, born after passage of this act within this state shall be free, and that servitude for life in consequence of the slavery of the mother is forever abolished. ... [A]ny negro [sic] or mulatto children born after the passage of this act, who would otherwise have been slaves, shall be servants to the owners until twenty-eight years of age...") *Id.,* s. 3 and 4.

22."Proof of the Freedom of William Jones," Book G, Page 169, Conveyance Records, West Feliciana Parish, La. (Nov. 6, 1840).

23.Sale to George Douse by William Massingill, Book D, Page 267, Conveyance Records, West Feliciana Parish, La. (Jul. 5, 1831).

24.Sale to George Douse by Edward H. Barton, Book D, Page 374, Conveyance Records, West Feliciana Parish, La. (Mar. 6, 1832).

25.Sale to George Douse by Charles McMicken, Book E, Page 348, Conveyance Records, West Feliciana Parish, La. (Mar. 6, 1835)

26.Elisabeth Kilbourne Dart, *Douse, George, planter, taverner* in A DICTIONARY OF LOUISIANA BIOGRAPHY VOL. 1 254 (Glenn R. Conrad, ed., La. Hist. Asso. 1988)

27.Transportation Equity Act, Pub. L. No. 105-178. S. 1219; La. R.S. 56: 1948.5 (16).

28.Statement of Account dated at Orange Hill, Nov. 28, 1838, submitted by George Douse in the Succession of Robert Haile, Claim #56, Probate Box 43, Succession Records, West Feliciana Parish, La. (Jan. 30, 1844).

29.Letter from Anne M. Lobdell to Lewis Stirling, Jr. (Feb. 1836), Stirling Papers, Hill Memorial Library, LSU.

30.Succession of Robert Haile, Claim #56, Probate Box 43, Succession Records, West Feliciana Parish, La. (Jan. 30, 1844).

31.EDWIN ADAMS DAVIS, PLANTATION LIFE IN THE FLORIDA PARISHES OF LOUISIANA, 1836 - 1846 AS REFLECTED IN THE DIARY OF BENNET H. BARROW (AMS Press, Inc. 1967). (at 145, "Went to a Ball last night. Given at Douces" (Apr. 10, 1839); at 202, "preparations for great doings at Douces to day" (Jul. 4, 1840); at 218, "Went to a Party Given by John Harbour at Douces. Great many there, verry pleasant..." (Dec. 23, 1841).)

32.Sale to George Douse by Charles McMicken, Book F, Page 208, Conveyance Records, West Feliciana Parish, La. (Feb. 18, 1837). Charles McMicken was a resident of Hamilton County, Cincinnati, Ohio.

33.*William Cooke vs. George Douse*, No. 1707, note attached to petition in suit to collect debt, (3rd JDC, Par. of West Feliciana, La. Jul. 26, 1837). The note is dated April 19, 1837, and totaled $171.35. This suit was dismissed at Cooke's request on December 25, 1837.

34.*Barclay & Tenney vs. George Douse*, No. 1708, record of account attached to petition in suit to collect a debt, (3rd JDC, Par. of West Feliciana, La. Jul. 26, 1837). The record of account is dated June 10, 1837, and shows purchases from March 24 to May 23, 1837, totaling $411.55. This suit was dismissed at the request of Barclay and Tenney on December 25, 1837.

35.*Charles McMicken vs. George Douse*, No. 1951 (3rd District Court, West Feliciana Parish, La. 1839).

36.Original note in possession of Elisabeth Kilbourne Dart, St. Francisville, La.

37.DAVIS, PLANTATION LIFE IN THE FLORIDA PARISHES 251 (entry is dated Feb. 19, 1842).

38.Louisiana Chronicle, St. Francisville, La., Feb. 11, 1843, at 3-4.

39.*See*, generally, Vendor and Vendee Indexes to Conveyances H to O, from 1811 to June 30, 1974, Conveyance Records, West Feliciana Parish, La. *See*, for example, Book D, Page 142 (Oct. 4, 1830) and Book E, Page 4 (Jan. 21, 1833).

40.Incorporation of Bayou Sarah Steam Boat Company, Book D, Page 364, Conveyance Records, West Feliciana Parish, La. (Act of Jun. 16, 1830 recorded Apr. 5, 1832).

41.1830 La Acts "An Act to prevent free persons of colour from entering into this State, and for other purposes." (Mar. 16, 1830). 1842 La. Acts 123 (Mar. 16, 1842). "An Act more effectually to prevent free persons of color from entering into this state, and for other purposes."

42.Brisbane Marshall, "Freedom of George & Eliza Douse + John F., George P., Richard McK, Mary E. & Daniel T. Douse" Book H, Page 244, Conveyance Records, West Feliciana Parish, La. (Sept. 1, 1842).

43.*See* Taunya Lovell Banks, *Colorism: A Darker Shade of Pale*, 47 UCLA L.REV. 1705, 1710 - 1712 (2000).

44.*N. Carolina v. Pink Ross and Sarah Ross*, 76 N.C. 242 (1877).

45.1900 Census of Cherokee County, S.C., Roll 1522, p. 95. Mark Jones and John Wertheimer, *Pinkney and Sarah Ross: The Legal Adventures of an Ex-Slave and His (Originally) White Wife on the Carolina Borderlands During Reconstruction*, 103-4 SOUTH CAROLINA HISTORICAL MAGAZINE (October 2002).

46.1856 La. R.S. (Phillips) Black Code art. 94.

47.1856 La. R.S.(Phillips) Black Code art. 69; 1855 La. Acts 308, s. 88 (Mar. 15, 1855).

48.1856 La. R.S.(Phillips) Black Code art. 71.

49.1855 La. Acts 308, s. 91.

50.U.S. BUREAU OF THE CENSUS, NEGRO POPULATION IN THE UNITED STATES 1790-1915 64. (8,123 born in Louisiana, 378 in Virginia, 571 in other states, 647 in West Indies, 121 in Africa, 121 in other countries. Free Colored Black and Mulatto Population of Selected Areas Classified by State and Country of Birth: 1850.)

51. Black Code: An Act prescribing the rules and conduct to be observed with respect to Negroes and other Slaves of this territory. s.1 in L. MOREAU LISLET, A GENERAL DIGEST OF THE ACTS OF THE LEGISLATURE OF LOUISIANA: 1804-1827 Vol. II. (Benjamin Levy 1828).

52. 1830 La. Acts at 96, s. 3 (Mar. 16, 1830). ("That all persons who shall teach, or permit or cause to be taught, any slave in this state, to read or write, shall, on conviction thereof, before any court of competent jurisdiction be imprisoned not less than one month nor more than twelve months.")

53. MONROE N. WORK, NEGRO YEAR BOOK 1937-1938 161 (Tuskegee Institute 1937).

54. Gardner's New Orleans Directory 143 (Charles Gardner 1861).

55. 32 Orleans Deaths Indices 1804-1885 325, Sworn to by Elyzabeth Townsend (Apr. 10, 1866).

56. 1870 Census of New Orleans, La. Roll 521, Page 765. A cooper makes or repairs wooden casks or tubs. WEBSTER'S NEW COLLEGIATE DICTIONARY 250 (G. & C. Merriam Co. 1974).

57. JO ANN CARRIGAN. THE SAFFRON SCOURGE: A HISTORY OF YELLOW FEVER IN LOUISIANA 1796-1905 59-63, 80 (Center for Louisiana Studies, Univ. of Southwest Louisiana 1974).

58. 1859 La Acts 87 (Mar. 15, 1859). ("That any free person of color coming into the State on board of any vessel,...shall, upon the arrival of said vessel,... be forthwith lodged in the parish jail, and shall remain therein until the vessel,... shall be ready to leave port.") 1859 La Acts 87 s.1.

59. REGISTER OF FREE COLORED PERSONS: 1840-1864, 59 and 79 (State Archives, Baton Rouge, La.).

60. 1860 Census of East Baton Rouge Parish, La. 477; 1870 Census of East Baton Rouge Parish, La. 18.

61. 32 Orleans Deaths Indices 1804-1885 325.

62. 22 Orleans Deaths Indices 1804-1885 363.

# Chapter 2.

## The Civil War
## New Orleans

*To the Free Colored Inhabitants of Louisiana:*

*Through a mistaken policy, you have heretofore been deprived of a participation in the glorious struggle for national rights in which our country is engaged. This no longer shall exist.*
*As sons of freedom, you are now called upon to defend our most inestimable blessing. As Americans, your country looks with confidence to her adopted children for valorous support, as a faithful return for the advantages enjoyed under her mild and equitable government. As fathers, husbands, and brothers, you are summoned to rally around the standard of the Eagle, to defend all which is dear in existence ...*

*General Andrew Jackson*[1]

In December 1860, the Louisiana legislature authorized Governor Thomas Overton Moore to convene a state convention that would determine if and when Louisiana would join South Carolina in seceding from the Union. Delegates to the convention were selected on January 7, 1861. The voters of Louisiana chose eighty secessionist delegates who wanted Louisiana to secede from the Union immediately; forty-four

29

cooperationists who questioned the wisdom of leaving the Union impetuously and were willing to negotiate with the Union before deciding to leave it; and only six doubters who spoke against secession.

Anticipating the outcome of the Convention scheduled for January 23, 1861, on January 10th, Governor Moore sent state troops to seize United States military installations in and around New Orleans. Three months before the April 12$^{th}$ Confederate attack on Fort Sumter, Louisiana militia seized the Barracks and Arsenal in Baton Rouge, Forts Jackson and St. Philip south of New Orleans, Fort Pike on Lake Pontchartrain northeast of New Orleans, and several smaller forts guarding water approaches to New Orleans.

Forts Jackson and St. Philip stood facing each other on either side of the Mississippi River seventy miles south of New Orleans at Plaquemines Bend in Plaquemines Parish, Louisiana. Merely ten months earlier, the Louisiana State Legislature had asked its Congressional delegation to urge the federal government to improve these fortifications defending New Orleans. U.S. Army Major P.G.T. Beauregard, who would later gain notoriety as a General for the Confederacy, had been assigned to strengthen these forts.

Neither Beauregard nor any significant number of Federal troops were present at these facilities when the state units took possession. The forts were staffed with caretakers only. Facing the large number of state militiamen sent to seize their duty stations, the caretakers at each site surrendered the forts without violence. These forts remained under Confederate control for slightly more than a year. The Federal fleet successfully passed between Forts Jackson and St. Philip on the night of April 24, 1862, and took possession of them four days later.

Fort Pike was situated such that its garrisons could guard the nine-mile-long Pass Rigolets which connected Lake Pontchartrain to Lake Borgne and the Mississippi Sound. Like Forts Jackson and Philip, Fort Pike had no large force present; only an Ordnance Sergeant was in charge when the state troops seized the fort.

The Baton Rouge Arsenal Complex, Governor Moore's final major target, was located ninety miles north of New Orleans, on a bluff overlooking the Mississippi River, near the site where the Spanish fort, San Carlos, had stood. The Arsenal had been built over the period 1819 to 1822 to quarter an infantry regiment. The eleven building complex included the largest ordnance depot in the south, yet only twenty men of the Ordnance Corps occupied the Arsenal when an overwhelming force of Governor Moore's troops forced its surrender on January 10, 1861. Another sixty federal artillerymen occupied the Arsenal barracks.

With the late afternoon seizure of the Arsenal Complex, Governor Moore's occupation of strategic U.S. military posts surrounding New Orleans was complete. From the Arsenal, the state seized fifty thousand stands of small arms, four howitzers, three hundred barrels of powder, cannons and ammunition, some of which was sent to Mississippi to help in that state's war effort. When the Arsenal was recovered by Union forces in May 1862, most of what had been there was gone.

Governor Moore had acted before the scheduled convention and without the approval of the state legislature. He explained to the legislature, "I decided to take possession of the military posts and munitions of war within the state . . . in order to prevent a collision between Federal troops and the people of the state."[2] That collision was not prevented, but it was delayed for a year. The delegates to the succession convention began their deliberations on January 23, 1861, and, by January 26th, had decided by an overwhelming majority that Louisiana would leave the Union.

Citizens across the state formed voluntary military units to fight for their state. Nearly 20,000 troops enlisted during the first nine months of 1861. By June 1861, Louisiana had sent 16,000 troops to fight out of state. Free blacks joined the war hysteria, forming militia companies in Baton Rouge, Pointe Coupee Parish and New Orleans. By early 1862, more than 3,000 free men of color throughout the state were members of military organizations loyal to Louisiana and ready to fight against the Union should it attack.

Participation by blacks, both slave and free, in defensive military action was not new to Louisianians. Since the first settlements in the Louisiana territory, Spanish, French, and American forces turned to black militiamen to fight for the territory's security. Blacks fought both with and against the French, who were battling indigenous populations in the 1700s. They fought against the British in the Revolutionary War under the flag of Spain, and fought the British again in the War of 1812, under the United States flag. Whenever Louisiana was threatened, whether as a colony, province, territory, or state, black troops were called upon and responded.

Nearly fifty years earlier, in the very year in which Louisiana became a state, Louisiana authorized its free blacks to form a fighting battalion to participate in the War of 1812.[3] Governor Claiborne recommended these troops to General Andrew Jackson, writing that:

> Among the militia of New Orleans there is a battalion of chosen men of color, organized under a special act of the Legislature . . . Under the Spanish Government the men of color of New Orleans were always relied on in times of difficulties, and on several occasions evinced in the field the greatest firmness and courage.[4]

Jackson accepted this battalion of men and encouraged their participation, telling them, "As sons of freedom, you are now called upon to defend our most inestimable blessing. As Americans, your country looks with confidence to her adopted children for a valorous support, as a faithful return for the advantages enjoyed under her mild and equitable government."[5] Jackson could not anticipate the rancorous debate that took place fifty years later over whether or not the U.S. Army should enlist black troops to fight in the Civil War.

Jackson promised the troops that, although all officers would be white, "noncommissioned officers will be appointed from among yourselves."[6] He promised them, "the same bounty in money and lands now received by the white soldiers of the United States . . . (and) the applause and gratitude of your countrymen." Whether or not Jackson was sincere when he presumed to speak for his countrymen when promising their gratitude, and whether or not these black soldiers believed his promises, they fought admirably with Andrew Jackson, and he praised them, noting, "I expected much from you, . . . but you surpass my hopes."[7]

Black veterans of the War of 1812 helped to organize the black units formed in 1861 in New Orleans. Jordan Noble, the drummer boy from the 1815 Battle of New Orleans, issued a call for militiamen to form the First Native Guard Louisiana Militia. Black troops numbered 1,500 in New Orleans alone by the time the Union Army arrived in April 1862. Although Governor Moore officially enrolled the Native Guard as part of the state militia, the Native Guard received neither arms nor orders from the Confederacy. They provided their own uniforms, rifles, and equipment.

To protect New Orleans from a naval attack, state militiamen constructed a raft of cypress trees, chains and large timber across the

Mississippi River, closing the river where Fort Jackson stood across from Fort St. Philip. Only one vessel at a time could pass between the forts. Any enemy vessel coming up the river would get caught in crossfire just as it turned a bend, affording New Orleans formidable protection from the sea. New Orleans was just as easily defended against land forces. The swamps and waterways that surrounded the city would disrupt any troop travel. With the river closed and the swamps impeding troop movement, the Confederates believed New Orleans was secure. The Confederacy was so confident that New Orleans was safe from Union attack that it withdrew all but 3,000 of its infantry troops from the city.

Commodore David G. Farragut's federal naval forces could not cause sufficient damage to Forts Jackson and St. Philip to force them to surrender and could not travel up the river between them to New Orleans because of the obstructing raft. On the night of April 20, 1862, Captain Bell of Farragut's fleet broke the chain of debris between the forts and the two pieces fell away. Farragut bombarded Forts Jackson and St. Philip over the following few days and, on April 24th, the Union fleet passed between the forts at around 3:30 a.m. Federal ships poured more shells into the forts as they passed and only one union ship was lost. By one o'clock on the afternoon of April 25, 1862, the Federal fleet had anchored with its guns pointed directly at the city of New Orleans.

When General Mansfield Lovell, Commander of the Department of Louisiana for the Confederacy, learned that the Federal fleet had passed between the forts south of the city, he ordered the remaining Confederate troops and state militia to evacuate the city and move north of New Orleans to Camp Moore,[8] leaving the city without any military defense. This retreat avoided a bombardment of the city. Lovell had his troops pack whatever they could carry, loading it onto wagons and into railroad freight cars, forcing his soldiers to ride on top of the cars. He instructed that any property left behind that might be of value to the enemy should be either hidden or destroyed. New Orleans officials and residents joined in a frenzy of looting and destruction. Lumberyards and coal yards were set afire; factory machinery was smashed; dry docks were sunk; ships were burned with their cargo; warehouses were opened and their contents -- cotton, rice, bacon, sugar, tobacco, molasses -- were carried away, burned, dumped into the river or thrown out into the street.

Before he left the city, Lovell had suggested that the ships under construction for the Confederate Navy be moved further up the

Mississippi River. He believed they could be made safe from Union forces and could be used by the Confederacy sometime in the future. Instead, the nearly completed ships were set afire then sent adrift down the river in an effort to slow the Union Navy's advance. As the city's would-be defenders rode away on the evening of April 24th, the night sky was lit with flames. This deliberate destruction of foodstuffs left the residents of New Orleans only a few weeks away from starvation.

The Louisiana state flag flew above the City Hall and Confederate flags flew over the United States Mint and Customhouse when the Federal Navy entered New Orleans. Neither New Orleans Mayor John T. Monroe nor General Lovell, its ranking military officer, would surrender the city and strike the flags. Mayor Monroe argued that he was not in charge because the city was under martial law; General Lovell explained that his troops had already withdrawn from the city so he no longer had authority.

New Orleanians were in shock at having lost what they thought was an impregnable city. This Union victory came much too early in the war and came without a good showing by Confederate defenders. The city had not surrendered, yet it was occupied by the enemy. New Orleanians believed that the Union presence in their beloved city was a temporary mishap of the war, and convinced themselves that they would be rescued by the Confederates at any moment.

On April 26, 1862, Captain Morris of the Federal Navy sent a landing party ashore to replace the Confederate flag flying over the United States Mint with the flag of the United States. Once the Union flag was flying, W.B. Mumford, a common gambler in New Orleans, climbed onto the roof of the Mint and pulled it down, to the cheers of his fellow city dwellers. He tore the flag to bits and wore a piece of it in his buttonhole. No further attempt to fly the United States flag was made that day. On April 28, having heard that New Orleans had fallen, the militiamen in the forts surrounding the city surrendered. When Union troops returned to New Orleans on April 29, 1862, they were able to raise the United States flag without incident. Lieutenant Albert Kautz "simply cut the halyards."[9]

General Benjamin F. Butler took command of New Orleans on May 1, 1862. He was a coarse man and, for that reason alone, was unlikely to be made welcome among the genteel people of a cosmopolitan city like New Orleans. To make matters worse, Butler's reputation had preceded him.

In May of 1861, three of many runaway slaves arrived at Fortress Monroe, Virginia. Customarily, when slaves sought refuge with the U.S. Army, federal officers restored them to their former owners when those owners appeared or sent someone to claim them. General Butler, in command of Fortress Monroe, refused to return these runaways.

Under rules of war, any government could seize property that had been used in a war effort against it. These runaways claimed that they had been forced to dig a Confederate battery position. They had been used by the Confederates in their war effort and were contraband subject to confiscation by the Union.

Butler's decision established a precedent eagerly followed by other Union officers in need of laborers. That following August, 1861, Congress legitimized Butler's act when it authorized the seizure of all Southern property used in aid of the rebellion.[10] Given Butler's treatment of runaways at Fortress Monroe, New Orleanians feared that Butler would not respect their property rights in slaves and hated Butler long before he was put in charge of their city.

They waged a psychological battle against Butler's occupying army from the North. They were outwardly resistant to the army of occupation and openly expressive of their pro-Confederate sentiment. Butler's troops were laughed at, cursed at, and spat upon by civilians, both males and females. Shopkeepers refused to sell to Union soldiers, and church congregations prayed for a Confederate victory. Public school teachers allowed their students to sing pro-Confederate songs. One man threatened to kill another for leasing his house to the Federals and a bookseller displayed a skeleton that he claimed once belonged to a Union soldier. Although deserted by Confederate troops as the Northern fleet advanced, the people of New Orleans wanted to show their conquerors that, "in spite of their humiliating, soul-searing defeat, their spirits were still unbroken."[11]

Butler attempted to run the city in cooperation with the existing governing structure, but was met with obstinate resistance and abuse. Newspapers refused to publish Butler's orders and foreign consuls aided the Confederacy by importing guns and exporting cotton on behalf of Louisiana residents who would not swear loyalty to the United States. Butler was frustrated in his efforts to appease New Orleans' citizens and responded to their opposition with brashness. Butler ruled the city under martial law. He ordered offending newspapers to cease publication and forced churches openly supporting the Confederacy to close. He imprisoned both men and women for refusing to obey his orders or for insulting his officers.

Women loyal to the Confederacy were particularly irritating to General Butler and his troops. They continually showed disrespect for the Union. They wore black crepe to mourn the loss of their city and taught their children to spit upon Union officers. They taught anti-Union songs in the schoolhouses and stepped off of the sidewalk when Union soldiers approached. They left the streetcars when soldiers got on and moved out of church pews when soldiers sat down. They taunted Union officials as if hoping to be abused so that their abuse would spark a revolt against Butler.

On one occasion, a group of women whom Butler was addressing turned their backs to him. He commented that they knew which end of them looked better. On another occasion a chamber pot was emptied onto the heads of two Union officers who were on their way to church. To Butler, this dumping was more than an insult to his officers; it was an insult to the uniform of the United States Army. This act exhausted Butler's patience. He adapted an old London statute that sought to control prostitution to address the behavior of these protestors and issued his General Orders Number 28 on May 15, 1862:

> As the officers and soldiers of the United States have been subject to repeated insults from the women (calling themselves ladies) of New Orleans, in return for the most scrupulous noninterference and courtesy on our part, it is ordered that hereafter when any female shall, by word, gesture, or movement, insult or show contempt for any officer or soldier of the United States, she shall be regarded and held liable to be treated as a woman of the town plying her avocation.[12]

General Butler had authorized his soldiers to arrest any woman who disrespected them just as the police arrested prostitutes who plied their trade. Any arrested women would be held in jail overnight then, the next morning, be brought before a magistrate who, if they were found guilty, could assess a fine.

The response to this order was impassioned. Butler was accused of labeling all the women of New Orleans prostitutes. His order was widely reported as a grant of permission for Butler's troops to rape and ravish any and all females in the city. In a letter to General Butler, New Orleans Mayor Monroe called the order a license for soldiers to commit outrages upon defenseless women. General P.G.T. Beauregard read it aloud at his campgrounds to inflame his troops. The English House of Commons sent an official protest to the United States Secretary of State concerning the order. More than one hundred years later, it is widely believed and frequently repeated in Louisiana that Butler called all the ladies of New Orleans prostitutes.

In contrast to the uproar, there is no report of any soldier relying on this order to commit any abomination. In fact, Butler's soldiers were so well disciplined that even his most ardent critics have not complained that his soldiers committed any offenses against the citizenry. Butler, himself, hanged four of his men after learning that they had plundered houses in New Orleans. Butler's General Orders Number 28 gave a rallying advantage to the rebel cause, but it also served its intended purpose. It succeeded in ending the widespread disrespect shown to Union soldiers.

On June 7, 1862, Butler hanged Mumford, the zealot who tore the U.S. flag into pieces, for his treason. Butler considered relenting, but the threats to Butler's life and the general feeling that, "Butler won't dare to hang him," persuaded him against any show of weakness.[13]

While many recount the firm hand General Butler exercised during the short time he was in charge of New Orleans, little is said of the good that he did. In this city close to starvation, Butler allowed civilians to purchase food shipped into New Orleans for his troops. To those without money, he distributed massive amounts of food at no cost. On September 1, 1862, Butler reported that he was distributing about $50,000 in food and money per month to whites in New Orleans and that his commissary distributed twice as much in rations to nonwhites as was used by his troops. Butler fed nearly one-quarter of the city's population. He organized the public school system and set food prices to protect against profiteers. He gave the city's hospital $5,000 per month.

Managing the city's infrastructure, Butler ordered that the levees around New Orleans be repaired and that its wharves be rebuilt. This provided jobs for the unemployed as well as flood protection for the city. To support his relief efforts, and to punish his enemies, Butler taxed those firms and individuals who had supported the cause of the Confederacy. He assessed them each one-quarter of whatever they had contributed to defend New Orleans from Union forces. He was able to raise more than $340,000 in this manner.

Butler's biggest morale problem came from the threat of yellow fever. Caused by a virus and spread by a mosquito, yellow fever can lead to delirium, coma, and death. It is believed to have originated in Africa and to have been brought to Europe and the Americas with the slave trade in the 1800s,[14] and was the cause of death for at least one of Richard Douse's brothers. New Orleans had suffered serious yellow fever epidemics between 1853 and 1858 in which more than 18,000 people died out of a population that ranged between 154,000 and 166,000 in those years. Epidemics were frequent and visitors to the city were disproportionately susceptible to the disease.

Confederate sympathizers had hoped that the yellow fever would drive the Yankees out of the city, making the use of Confederate military force unnecessary. New Orleans children teased the Union soldiers about their vulnerability to yellow jack, one of the nicknames for yellow fever, and New Orleans adults included this topic in every conversation with the Yankees. Butler's soldiers asked for transfers and for extended leaves to get away from this source of death.

General Butler recognized the seriousness of the disease and the effect that its mention had on his troops. He set about to understand how it worked, reading books on the subject and studying the maps of earlier outbreaks. He developed the theory that putrid animal matter produced typhus fever, and that rotting vegetable matter produced congestive fevers. According to his theory, yellow fever required that putrid animal matter and decaying vegetable matter, together or separately, support and encourage some imported element that, in this environment, would give rise to the disease.[15]

Butler embarked on a campaign of sanitation and quarantine. He hired two thousand men to clean the city's streets, public squares, and unoccupied lands. He ordered the city's waterworks to flush the streets. All ships approaching New Orleans were inspected for passengers carrying the disease. Ships containing infected persons were held for forty days, seventy miles below New Orleans, then were reinspected before they could enter the city. On October 24, 1862, Butler was able to report an absence of the epidemic.[16]

Without knowing it, Butler had taken precisely the steps most effective for combating that disease. The yellow fever virus was, indeed, an imported element. By inspecting every ship and enforcing a forty-day quarantine of infected persons, Butler stopped the virus from coming

38

into the city. By keeping the streets and gutters clear, Butler eliminated mosquito breeding grounds.[17] Only nine deaths from yellow fever were reported for New Orleans civilians for the three years of Union occupation, 1863-1865, although the Federal river fleet, not protected by the quarantine, experienced 300 cases during this period. Yellow jack returned after the Union Occupation ended claiming 3,000 lives in 1867.

Despite the successes of his administration of New Orleans and the humane treatment of its citizens, when Louisianians recall the rule of General Butler, they revile him for his General Orders Number 28, and the insult to women it allegedly embodied. When Butler left New Orleans in December 1862 he left behind a healthy but ungrateful city filled with an animosity toward him and glad to see him go.

Charles Hatfield recalled hearing stories of the Civil War years in New Orleans. He heard disparaging references to carpetbaggers and comments that the Union Army wasn't particularly "decent" to New Orleans people during the occupation. He believes that, if the residents of New Orleans were at all mistreated, such treatment was necessary until the Louisiana people "corrected themselves."

In Hatfield's opinion, Louisiana had lost possession of New Orleans, and Butler had the right to treat its citizens as a conquered people. He did not have to tolerate insults and abuse and was entitled to punish behavior that frustrated his efforts to retain possession of the city. Residents of New Orleans channeled the shame they felt for losing their city so early in the war to an effort to undermine their occupation. Hatfield believed that Butler did only what was necessary to keep a rebellious people under control.

### Notes

1.Proclamation. Mobile, Ala. (Jan. 21, 1815). GERALD ASTOR, THE RIGHT TO FIGHT: A HISTORY OF AFRICAN AMERICANS IN THE MILITARY 17 (Presidio 1998).

2.JOHN D. WINTERS, THE CIVIL WAR IN LOUISIANA 11 (Louisiana State Univ. Press 1963).

3.1812 Acts of Louisiana XXIII (Sept. 6, 1812). "Be it enacted by the Senate and House of Representatives of the State of Louisiana, in general assembly convened, That the governor of the State of Louisiana is authorized by virtue of the present act, to organize in a corps of militia ... certain free men of colour, to be chosen from among the creoles... owners or sons of owners of landed property of at least the value of three hundred dollars."

4.Letter from Claiborne to Jackson, Aug.12, 1814 in CHARLES GAYARRE, IV HISTORY OF LOUISIANA 335 (Pelican Publ. Co., 5th ed. 1974).

5.Jackson's second proclamation to the people of New Orleans addressed to free black males. (Mobile, Ala. Jan. 21, 1815.) in GAYARRE, IV HISTORY OF LOUISIANA 355.

6.Jackson's second proclamation to the people of New Orleans addressed to free black males. (Mobile, Ala. Jan. 21, 1815.) GAYARRE, IV HISTORY OF LOUISIANA 355.

7.GAYARRE, IV HISTORY OF LOUISIANA 408.

8.Camp Moore is located in Tangipahoa Parish, about 78 miles north of New Orleans. It was built in May 1861 to accommodate the large number of volunteers who responded to Governor Moore's call, and was named after him. POWELL A. CASEY, ENCYCLOPEDIA OF FORTS, POSTS, NAMED CAMPS, AND OTHER MILITARY INSTALLATIONS IN LOUISIANA 1700-1981 122 (Claitor's Publ. Div. 1983).

9.EDWIN ADAMS DAVIS, LOUISIANA: A NARRATIVE HISTORY 255 (Claitor's Publ. Div., 3rd ed. 1971).

10.12 Stat. 319 (Aug. 6, 1861). *An Act to confiscate Property used for Insurrectionary Purposes.*

11.EDWARD LAROCQUE TINKER, CREOLE CITY ITS PAST AND ITS PEOPLE 78-80 (Longmans, Green & Co. 1953).

12.GERALD MORTIMER CAPERS, OCCUPIED CITY: NEW ORLEANS UNDER THE FEDERALS 1862-1865 67 (Univ. of Kentucky Press 1965); DAVIS, LOUISIANA: A NARRATIVE HISTORY 262-263.

13.TINKER, CREOLE CITY 90.

14.Yellow Fever Disease Profile (http://entomology.unl.edu/history_bug/yellow_fever.htm visited Aug. 29, 2001).

15.JO ANN CARRIGAN. THE SAFFRON SCOURGE: A HISTORY OF YELLOW FEVER IN LOUISIANA 1796-1905 85 (Center for Louisiana Studies, Univ. of Southwest Louisiana 1974). In 1900, U.S. Army physician James Carroll and Army pathologist Walter Reed determined that mosquitoes transmitted the disease. Http://rs6.loc.gov/ammem/today/aug27.html (visited Aug. 29, 2001).

16.Reports of Major General Benjamin F. Butler, U.S. Army, commanding Department of the Gulf (New Orleans, Nov. 6, 1862) (in LT. COL. ROBERT N. SCOTT, 15 WAR OF THE REBELLION, OFFICIAL RECORDS OF THE UNION AND CONFEDERATE ARMIES, SERIES I 162 (National Historical Society, Washington Government Printing Office 1886).

17.World Health Organization Fact Sheet No. 100 (www.who.int/inf-fs/en/fact 100.html visited Aug. 29, 2001). To prevent yellow fever epidemics, WHO recommends universal vaccination, prompt detection and rapid response, including isolation of the affected population, and mosquito control.

# Chapter 3.

*Richard Douse*
*2ⁿᵈ Regiment*
*Louisiana Native Guards*

*The duty of the colored man is to defend his country,*
*whenever, wherever and in whatever form, is the same*
*with that of white men. It does not depend on, nor is it*
*affected by, what the country pays.*

*Edwin M. Stanton*[1]

When New Orleans fell to Commodore David Farragut and the Union Navy on April 25, 1862, and the Confederate forces hastily left the city, the black troops commissioned by Governor Moore did not accompany them. Instead, shortly after Union Brigadier General Benjamin T. Butler took command of New Orleans, a delegation of Native Guard officers met with him and offered their services. They had enlisted in the militia to protect their homes and to show their loyalty to their state, not to serve the Southern Confederacy.

Butler initially refused their offer. The question of allowing blacks to fight in the Union Army had been raised already and President Lincoln had not approved the recruitment of blacks by the military. In

April 1862, Major General David Hunter had asked the Secretary of War for permission to arm black troops. While waiting for a response from Washington, Hunter declared all the slaves in Georgia, Florida and South Carolina forever free and began to recruit able-bodied men among the former slaves. Rather than wait for volunteers, Hunter and his men impressed newly freed men into service and marched them under guard to a training camp. The First South Carolina Volunteer Regiment, organized by Hunter, was never a part of the U.S. Army and was disbanded by August 1862.

Brigadier General J. W. Phelps suggested to General Butler in June 1862 that escaped slaves be recruited and trained for service in the Union Army. Butler discouraged him, but Phelps nevertheless began training five companies of men. Butler refused to permit them to be trained as soldiers and insisted that the escaped slaves be used only as laborers. In protest, General Phelps resigned.

By August 1862, Butler was desperate for troops. Since the beginning of the occupation of New Orleans, General Butler had repeatedly asked for additional troops. Writing to Major General H.W. Halleck, Butler explained his need:

> I can easily hold this portion of Louisiana, by far the richest, and extend the movement so far as to substantially cut off all supplies from Texas to the enemy this coming winter by this route, if I can receive early re-enforcements [sic] Please therefore send me New England troops. The newspapers assure me there are thousands waiting in Massachusetts . . . I have yet received, with the exception of 60 men, no recruits.[2]

No recruits arrived. General H.W. Halleck advised General Butler, "You are misinformed in regard to there being any troops in New England ready for the field . . . It is hoped that some will be ready to start as soon as the November elections are over."[3] As Butler extended the boundaries of the federally occupied territory, his need for reinforcements became critical. On August 22, 1862, faced with a severe manpower shortage and without authorization from any official source, General Butler invited all former members of the Louisiana Native Guards to enlist in the U.S. Army. Just as Andrew Jackson had before him, Butler promised that the black troops would be treated, paid, equipped, rationed, and armed the same as other United States soldiers.

The First Regiment Louisiana Native Guards, composed of free men of color, many of them French-speaking, was organized in August 1862 and mustered into service on September 27, 1862. During that same period, summer and fall of 1862, Senator James H. Lane of Kansas recruited the 1st Regiment Kansas (Colored) Volunteer Infantry, but that unit would not be made a part of the U.S. Army until January 13, 1863. Thus, the First Regiment Louisiana Native Guards became the first black unit officially enrolled in the Union Army during the Civil War.

The free blacks who had enlisted in the Louisiana militia in 1861 to defend their home state of Louisiana were now ready to fight for the Union. Additional blacks, both free and fugitive, joined the United States Army. Black soldiers filled three regiments in New Orleans by November 24, 1862. By the end of the war, Louisiana had furnished more than 24,000 black soldiers to the Union Army. In 1862, however, Butler did not know if he had done the right thing. On November 6, 1862, he wrote in his report:

> I take occasion to call to the attention of the general commanding in chief that more than seventy days since I called the attention of the War Department to the organization of three colored regiments by my General Orders, No. 63, of August 22, 1862, subject to the approval of the President, and, though I have had many communications directly from the War Department and from the general commanding in chief, no communication disapproving of that organization has been received. I must therefore take it to be approved, but would prefer distinct orders on this subject.[4]

President Lincoln's Emancipation Proclamation, made public on September 22, 1862, gave notice of the Union's intent to use black troops. After declaring that, on January 1, 1863, all persons held as slaves in states then in rebellion against the United States would be free, Lincoln declared that, "such persons of suitable condition will be received into the armed services of the United States . . . "[5] Lincoln had decided to allow blacks to enlist as soldiers, but did not directly approve Butler's preemptive action.

Richard Douse enrolled in the Native Guards under Butler's

command on September 11, 1862, for a period of three years.[6] Douse's enlistment paper shows his occupation as plasterer, his age, 26, and that he was five foot five and one-half inches tall, with black eyes, black hair, and a griffe complexion.[7] The term "griffe" is a part of a taxonomy which existed to describe the proportions of black and white heritage in a person.[8] Skin color was often a proxy for assigning persons to one category or another. Most persons of mixed black and white heritage were simply called mulattos. "The person too black to be a mulatto and too pale in color to be a negro [sic] is a griffe."[9] Douse was undoubtedly darker than his blue-eyed brother, John.

Douse mustered into the Army on October 12, 1862, as First Sergeant, Company C, 2nd Regiment Louisiana Infantry, Native Guards, Free Colored. His regiment was subsequently known as the 2nd Regiment Infantry, Corps de Afrique, U.S. Colored Volunteers, and then, after April 4, 1864, as the 74th Regiment U.S. Colored Troops.[10] The War Department renumbered all the black military units in April 1864.

Douse reported to duty at the Judah Touro Building on the corner of Front and Levee Streets in New Orleans. After the three regiments had been formed, the black troops were moved to Camp Strong at the Louisiana Race Track. Visitors to the camp commented on the high level of competency of the black troops. A *New York Times* correspondent wrote, "Their conduct could not have been better. I have seen older white regiments with more regimental drills, that are not their equal."[11]

Douse's line officers and noncommissioned officers were all African-Americans and included such notables as Captain P.B.S. Pinchback, delegate to the 1868 state Constitutional Convention, state senator 1868-1871, School Director of New Orleans 1871-1877, Lieutenant Governor of Louisiana 1871-1872, after the death of Oscar Dunn, and Acting Governor during the impeachment hearings of Henry Clay Warmoth 1872; Lieutenant Octave Rey, Captain of the Metropolitan Police in New Orleans 1868-1877; Captain Arnold Bertonneau, delegate to the 1868 state Constitutional Convention, and Radical Republican club leader; Major Francois Ernest Demas, member of the state House of Representatives 1870-1876, who lost the Republican nomination for Governor in 1868 to Henry Clay Warmoth by only two votes; Captain Robert H. Isabelle, delegate to the 1868 state Constitutional Convention, member of the state House of Representatives 1868-1870, who was a strong supporter of integrated education; and Charles S. Sauvinet, elected Civil Sheriff of Orleans Parish in 1870, who brought the first lawsuit to enforce Louisiana's Civil Rights Act of 1869. In January 1871, Sauvinet ordered a drink at the Bank Saloon, 6 Royal Street, New Orleans. The owner refused to serve him, so he sued, demanding damages and the revocation of the owner's liquor license. Judge Henry C. Dibble awarded Sauvinet $1,000 in exemplary damages plus all legal costs.

Douse's 2nd Regiment also included two privates recently transported from the Congo River region of Africa. Wimba Congo and August Congo had been brought to Louisiana in 1858 aboard the *Wanderer,* an illegal slave ship. When Butler issued his call to recruit black troops, they escaped their enslavement and enlisted to fight for the Union.

Douse's Regiment received marching orders on October 29, 1862, at 12:00 midnight. It was assigned to march out as far as Raceland, Louisiana, to guard the New Orleans, Opelousas and Great Western Railroad from Algiers to Lafourche, a distance of forty miles. The Regiment headquarters was located at the Boutte Station, 23 miles from New Orleans. Douse's Company C guarded the westernmost end of the forty miles near the Raceland Station.[12] General Butler wanted to protect the railroad to allow inland planters loyal to the Union to ship their sugar and cotton to New Orleans and to allow the Union Army to ship men and supplies to its military units in western Louisiana.[13] Company C marched the four miles from Camp Strong to Gretna, then traveled by railroad to Raceland Station.

In January 1863, Douse's Company C was relieved from guarding the railroad by a company of white soldiers from New York and was sent to Algiers where it boarded the steamer, *Northern Light,* bound for Ship Island, off the coast of Mississippi. The Company was assigned to "guard prisoners, erect fortifications, and defend the post."[14] Most of Butler's black troops guarded bridges, military installations, fortifications, prisoners, railroads and strategic bayous. They built dams, repaired roads and levees, and were so constantly at work that they had little time to drill. On Ship Island, Douse's regiment constructed batteries, mounted nine inch guns, built bombproof magazines, guarded Confederate prisoners and worked to maintain the post. Despite its laborers' workload, the regiment continued daily artillery and infantry drills.[15] An aide from the Office of the Inspector General reported that "the Second Corps was fair at battalion drill, good at handling heavy guns, and had weapons in excellent order."[16]

On April 8, 1863, Company C, along with Companies B and G

of Douse's Regiment were sent to confront the enemy in East Pascagoula, Mississippi. Carried by the transport, *General Banks*, the men arrived by 9:00 a.m. the next morning. While twenty men under the command of Captain Charles Sauvinet secured the wharf, others entered a large frame hotel and unfurled a United States flag on its roof. The raised flag provoked the more than 300 Confederate infantry and cavalry nearby to attack and Douse's 2nd regiment became the first black Union Army troops to engage Confederate forces during the Civil War.[17]

The Company C report describes the battle:

> Had a sharp engagement of two hours in which we repulsed the enemy consisting of a superior force of infantry and cavalry. We were forced to retire in consequence of the arrival of a largely superior reinforcement to the enemy. We had sixty-four rank and file engaged in the action, commanded by Captain Hannibal Carter. There was one killed and three wounded of the members of this company.[18]

Colonel Nathan W. Daniels, in charge of the assault, praised his troops:

> for their unflinching bravery and steadiness under their first fire, exchanging volley after volley with the coolness of veterans; for their determined tenacity in maintaining their position, and taking advantage of every success that their courage and valor gave them; and also to their officers who were cool and determined throughout the action.[19]

Daniels lost two killed and five wounded in several hours of fighting with the Confederates, then lost four killed and five seriously wounded in an instant when sailors on the Federal ship assigned to assist the infantry troops, the *John P. Jackson*, threw a shell which landed in the midst of a group of Daniel's men.[20] After that engagement, Company C returned to Ship Island to maintain guard duty and saw no further combat.

Seven weeks later, other units of Louisiana Native Guards were engaged in combat. The First and Third Louisiana Native Guards, although not the Second to which Richard Douse was attached, participated in the Union siege of Port Hudson. Located on a high bluff, and protected on one side by the Mississippi River, Port Hudson was a formidable installation, one of the strongest natural positions along the line held by the Confederates. In addition to its natural advantages of river, woods, ravines and marshes, the Confederates had added a semicircle of felled trees with sharpened branches pointed toward the Union soldiers and a fifteen-foot ditch at the base of their fortress.

On May 27, 1863, barely more than 1,000 black troops were ordered to attack at Port Hudson. Clearly visible, and protected only by willow trees, these Union troops faced cannon and rifle fire from the bluffs above them. Of the 500 men who bore the bulk of the action, there were 308 casualties. "Their conduct surprised their worst critics in the Union ranks, and their bravery and dash more than pleased their strongest supporters."[21]

Port Hudson, unlike New Orleans, proved impenetrable. Despite repeated attempts to capture the fort, Union troops could only hold their positions until the Confederate commanders surrendered the fort on July 8, 1863, four days after Vicksburg fell to General Grant. By the time of their surrender, the defenders of Port Hudson had been reduced to mule rations and twenty rounds of ammunition. Their mission, to engage the enemy to prevent the reinforcement of Grant's troops at Vicksburg, had been accomplished, and they had given the black troops at Port Hudson an opportunity to demonstrate their courage.

The valor of black troops in the field changed the minds of many skeptics and critics. Commenting that the gallantry of the Native Guards at Port Hudson should silence concern about the wisdom of recruiting blacks into the federal army, Secretary of State William Henry Seward wrote that, "The newly raised regiments exhibited all necessary valor and devotion in the military assaults which were made, with desperate courage, and not without fearful loss . . . "[22]

Closer to the battlefield, however, their sacrifice was not always rewarded. At Port Hudson, Union and Confederate forces called a truce on May 28, 1863, the day following the decimation of the 1st Regiment, Louisiana Native Guards. The remains of white troops were retrieved and buried, while the bodies of the Native Guardsmen were left to rot and be eaten by turkey buzzards. The stench was so unbearable that Confederate troops offered to help retrieve and bury the bodies. General Banks, when asked about retrieving the bodies of black troops from the battlefield, replied that he had no dead there. The bodies of the Louisiana Native Guards were not removed until after the surrender of Port Hudson. They had festered on the battlefield for 42 days.

Richard Douse was promoted to Sergeant Major on June 9, 1863. Upon his promotion, he was transferred out of Company C and onto the roster of the Regimental Non-Commissioned Staff stationed on Ship Island.[23] Shortly thereafter, Douse and his regiment received their first paychecks, almost a full year after they joined the Army.

Douse's regiment was paid only seven dollars per month, after waiting almost a year for any pay at all, while white troops were given thirteen dollars per month.[24] General Butler's recruiting promise to his Native Guards that they would be treated, paid, equipped, rationed, and armed the same as other United States soldiers had not been kept. The Army had reluctantly accepted them and then deliberately paid them as military laborers rather than as soldiers.

After the Union occupation of New Orleans, there was such an influx of escaped slaves into New Orleans that General Butler required blacks who had been free before the war to carry papers documenting their free status so that they could be readily distinguished from blacks who had recently escaped slavery and come into the city. Black residents not carrying passes from their owners, or papers attesting that they were free before the war began, were arrested as vagrants and taken to work on abandoned plantations that had been seized by Union forces or on the plantations of Southerners who took an oath of allegiance to the United States.

Planters or overseers were to pay their workers ten dollars per month, but could withhold one-half of the pay until the end of the year. These "employees" were not allowed to leave their assigned place of employment without a pass from their employer.

Blacks whose families had been free for generations complained bitterly that this Union-imposed requirement to carry passes was worse treatment than the prewar Black Code. Unlike the old law, this new law made no distinction between educated and highly skilled blacks prominent in their communities and recently escaped field hands who had been denied education or training to prepare them for other labor. All men of the darker hue who were found without papers were transported to plantations to work in the fields.

When General Nathaniel P. Banks replaced General Butler, he

continued Butler's labor plan and made it more burdensome. Blacks were forced to agree to one year contracts with their plantation employers, contracts that would be enforced by Banks' troops. Frederick Douglass described this labor policy as a re-institution of slavery, protesting that, "[W]hen any individual or combination of individuals undertakes to decide for any man when he shall work, where he shall work, at what he shall work, and for what he shall work, . . . [that man] is a slave."[25]

The status of blacks who had been free before the Civil War became even more precarious in early 1863 when General Daniel Ullman arrived in Louisiana to raise troops among blacks. He was given thirty days to raise four regiments and impressed into service any able-bodied blacks that he found without a pass. Blacks were marched to recruitment depots at gunpoint where armed guards prevented these "volunteers" from escaping.

Whether enrolled in the Army or forced to work on plantations, former slaves were paid ten dollars per month. Douse and his comrades, many of whom had been free before the Civil War and all of whom enlisted as soldiers, not laborers, were paid ten dollars per month, then the Army deducted three dollars per month for their uniforms.

By the summer of 1863, many units of black troops had been formed across the country, both north and south. Blacks troops complained about the inequality of their pay. A soldier from the Fifty-fourth Massachusetts Volunteers wrote:

> We have fought like men; we have worked like men; we have been ready at every call of duty, and thus have proved ourselves to be men: but still we are refused the thirteen dollars per month. Oh, what a shame it is to be treated thus! ... We have offered our lives a sacrifice for a country that has not the magnanimity to treat us as men.[26]

They were serving as loyally and risking their lives as bravely as whites in Union uniforms. They were deserving of equal pay.

The state legislature in Massachusetts took steps to mitigate this insult for their recruits. It agreed to use monies from the state treasury to pay black troops in Massachusetts units the difference between what white soldiers were paid and what black soldiers received. The soldiers of the 54th Massachusetts, organized in early 1863, declined to accept the money offered by the state and refused to accept less than what was due to them from the Army. They told their benefactors, "Tis the principle, not the money, that we contend for: we will either be paid as soldiers, or fight without reward."[27] They continued to fight without pay. Soldiers of the 55th Massachusetts wrote to officials in Washington that they would rather be discharged from service than be paid less than their white counterparts.

Soldiers in Company A, 3rd South Carolina Colored Troops, the 21st USCT, stacked their arms before their captain's tent and demanded to be paid on an equal basis. When ordered to retrieve their arms and report for duty, Company A refused. On November 19, 1863, Sergeant William Walker, who had led the nonviolent protest, was convicted of mutiny and executed by firing squad in Jacksonville, Florida. His martyrdom prompted Congress to act. Black soldiers recruited into the Army to dig ditches and guard prisoners because white soldiers were in short supply would be paid as soldiers, not as laborers.

The United States Congress voted, on June 15, 1864, to pay persons of color in military service the same as it paid other soldiers, retroactive to January 1, 1864. For persons who were free on April 19, 1861, at the start of the war, the appropriations act allowed full pay from their date of enlistment.[28] Douse's September 1864 Muster Roll includes the remark that Douse was free before April 19, 1861, and, thus, entitled to the higher pay from his 1862 enlistment date. The unpaid portion of the monthly salary due the soldiers in Douse's regiment finally was paid some time late in 1864.

Opposition to the use of black troops was widespread and black soldiers were well aware and frequently reminded of the disdain whites felt for them. Even concerning matters other than pay, few received the equal treatment promised by Butler. Some black troops went into battle with unserviceable arms and with flintlock muskets which had been twice condemned by Army inspectors. They faced hostility from their comrades and loathing from their enemies.

On November 5, 1862, Brigadier General G. Weitzel wrote to Major George C. Strong, Assistant Adjutant General, Department of the Gulf, "I cannot command those negro [sic] regiments."[29] At Fort Wagner in South Carolina, July 18, 1863, Major General Truman Seymour decided to "put those damned niggers from Massachusetts (Colonel Robert Gould Shaw's 54th Massachusetts) in the advance; we may as well get rid of them one time as another."[30] At Fort Jackson, south of New

Orleans, a chaplain complained of officers striking and kicking black enlisted men and imposing severe punishment for minor infractions. One lieutenant colonel was so abusive to blacks that his fellow white officers demanded that he be punished.

The 3rd Regiment, Louisiana Native Guards, was badly treated when it arrived in Baton Rouge on January 24, 1863. The post commander, Brigadier General Cuvier Grover, refused to issue clothing, blankets or pay to the regiment. When a black captain reported for duty as officer of the day, the white soldiers in the guard refused to acknowledge him as their superior officer. They threatened to kill him if he tried to enforce his rank. Rather than punish the white soldiers, Department Commander Nathaniel Banks, recommended that the black officers of the 3rd Regiment resign.

Commander Banks felt that black officers were a source of embarrassment and annoyance to the United States Army. White soldiers who disrespected black officers created a discipline problem Banks had to address. Even New England soldiers refused to give black officers the proper military courtesies. Banks decided to rid himself of his black officers. He established a competency examination board, then excused white officers from appearing before it. The August 1863 examining board for officers from the 2nd Regiment was composed of white officers from the same regiment, all junior in rank to those they were to examine. The junior officers sitting on the board would receive promotions to replace any senior officers they found to be unfit.

Through resignations and dismissals, all but one of the black officers left the 2nd Regiment by August 1864. Only Charles Sauvinet served until the end of the war. Many of the resignations cited prejudice and disrespect as reasons for leaving. Similarly, all but one black officer of the 1st Regiment resigned or were dismissed. By March 22, 1864, only Captain Louis A. Snaer remained. All of the officers of the 3rd Regiment resigned, as encouraged by Banks. In their letter of resignation, they expressed their hopes and regrets:

[W]e did most certainly expect the Privileges, and respect due to a soldier who had offered his service and his life to his government, ever ready and willing to share the common dangers of the Battle field. This we have not received, on the contrary, we have met with scorn and contempt, from both military and civilians.[31]

51

To add insult to injury, some of the officers who had been pressured to resign had not served two full years in the Army and were drafted back into military service as privates.

The treatment of black soldiers by the Confederates was even worse. The official Confederate position was that black soldiers were not soldiers at all but slaves fighting against their masters. As death was the customary punishment for slaves who used force against their masters,[32] killing black military prisoners or selling them as slaves was an acceptable consequence for their taking part in the war effort.

In 1863, in Jackson, Louisiana, Confederate cavalrymen captured twenty-one black enlisted men and their black officer. Fearing that they might effect an escape, the cavalry men shot them all. At Fort Pillow, on April 12, 1864, Confederate General Nathan Bedford Forrest, who would become, in 1867, the first Grand Wizard of the Order of the Ku Klux Klan,[33] allowed his troops to shoot black and white soldiers and civilians after they had put down their weapons in surrender.

Fort Pillow, located on a bluff overlooking the Mississippi River forty miles above Memphis, Tennessee, had been established by the Confederates. Union soldiers captured it in 1862. Commanding one thousand five-hundred troops, Forrest was determined to recapture the fort. He placed sharpshooters in the hills overlooking the fort preventing its defenders from shooting at his advancing army. The Union troops could not position themselves atop the four-foot wide walls of the fort without being shot and could not otherwise see outside of the fort. Forrest placed his men in a circle around the fort and, under a flag of truce, demanded that the Union soldiers surrender, warning them, "Should my demand be refused, I cannot be responsible for the fate of your command."[34]

The fort was manned by 557 Union officers and men, consisting of soldiers of First Battalion, 6th Colored Heavy Artillery unit, Company D, 2nd Colored Light Artillery, and First Battalion, 13th Tennessee Cavalry (white). Its commanding officer refused to surrender, expecting support from a Union gunboat in the river behind it. The Union gunboat was of little assistance and, after a brief and almost bloodless battle, Confederate troops entered the fort.

Once the fort was captured, Forrest's men engaged in an indiscriminate slaughter of men, women and children, black and white. Black troops experienced a mortality rate of 64%; the rate for white troops was between 31 and 34%. A subcommittee of the Congressional Joint Committee on the Conduct of the War investigated the incident and reported that the Confederates had set tents on fire, roasting the wounded in their beds, and had buried persons still alive with the dead. The story circulated that Forrest ordered his men to lock their black prisoners of war inside a house, then set the house on fire.[35] While this is an exaggeration, stories of the horrendous conduct at Fort Pillow were not fabricated out of whole cloth.

An officer of the Thirteenth Tennessee Cavalry reported that men were shot down without mercy and without regard to color from 4:00 p.m., when the fort was taken, until dark. "This horrid work of butchery . . . was renewed again in the next morning, when numbers of our wounded were basely murdered after a long night of pain and suffering . . ."[36] Confederate Sergeant Achilles V. Clark wrote in a letter home, the "slaughter was awful. Words cannot describe the scene. The poor deluded negroes [sic] would run up to our men fall upon their knees and with uplifted hands scream for mercy but they were ordered to their feet and then shot down. The whitte [sic] men fared but little better."[37] When a badly wounded soldier asked to be spared, he was told, "No: damn you! You fight withe [sic] niggers!"[38] Blacks were killed because they were black; whites were killed because they had fought alongside black soldiers.

Union Lieutenants Francis A. Smith and William Cleary reported that Confederate soldiers "employed themselves in shooting down negro [sic] troops as fast as they made their appearance."[39] They described the death of Lieutenant J.C. Ackerstrom, acting regimental quartermaster. Ackerstrom surrendered, then was severely wounded, and nailed to the side of a house. The house was set on fire, burning him to death. George Shaw, Company B, 6th Colored Heavy Artillery unit, testified that three young boys, civilian employees of the Army aged fifteen or sixteen, were shot in the forehead by Confederate soldiers. Daniel Tyler of Company B was shot three times, struck on the head and buried alive. He and another soldier dug themselves out.

The mania of Forrest's troops at Fort Pillow might have been stirred by their recent defeat at Fort Anderson, located west of Paducah, Kentucky. On March 25, 1864, Colonel S. G. Hicks, commanding 665 men at Fort Anderson, including 120 from the 122nd Illinois Infantry (white), 271 from the Sixteenth Kentucky Cavalry (white), and 274 from the First Kentucky Heavy Artillery (Colored), repelled three attacks from

Forrest before Forrest's troops withdrew around midnight. Colonel Hicks reported that his black troops "fought as bravely as any troops in the fort."[40] Hicks lost 14 killed and 46 wounded and estimated that Forrest lost 300 killed, including one of his two Generals, and one thousand wounded. At Fort Anderson, Forrest's rebels had faced and been soundly beaten by a force that included black troops. They exacted their revenge at Fort Pillow.

Douse remained stationed at Ship Island, a member of the Regimental Non-Commissioned staff, for the remainder of the war while companies of his regiment moved between Fort Pike, Louisiana, and Ship Island, Mississippi. Although his muster-out-date was October 11, 1865, Douse remained in service and on duty until November 14, 1865.[41] He had received a glancing gunshot wound during his service and carried a one and one-half inch scar on his right hand as evidence.[42]

After completing his military service in November 1865, Richard Douse returned to his brother in law's house in Baton Rouge and to his occupation as a plasterer.[43] He became a deputy collector for the United States Internal Revenue Service on April 1, 1872, when B.T. Beauregard, Collector of Internal Revenue for the Second Collection District in Louisiana, appointed him to collect revenue in Avoyelles and East and West Feliciana Parishes located north and northwest of Baton Rouge.[44] Douse had grown up in West Feliciana Parish.

B.T. Beauregard had been recommended to the position of Collector by, among others, Oscar J. Dunn, the first black Lieutenant Governor of Louisiana (1868-1871).[45] Beauregard resigned the position effective May 19, 1873, ending Douse's tenure as deputy.[46] On August 20, 1874, Douse, still politically connected, was appointed by William P.H. Kellogg, Governor of Louisiana (1873 to 1877), to serve as Clerk of Supervisor of Registration, Parish of West Baton Rouge.[47] Douse continued to live with his brother-in-law in East Baton Rouge Parish until he married Ann Maria Purnell, the daughter of Thomas and Mary Purnell.

Notes

1. United States Secretary of War Edwin M. Stanton defending his decision to pay black soldiers less than what was paid to white soldiers in GERALD ASTOR, THE RIGHT TO FIGHT: A HISTORY OF AFRICAN AMERICANS IN THE MILITARY 29 (Presidio 1998).

2. Report of Major General Benjamin F. Butler, U.S. Army, commanding Department of the Gulf (New Orleans, October 24, 1862) in LT. COL. ROBERT N. SCOTT, 15 WAR OF THE REBELLION, OFFICIAL RECORDS OF THE UNION AND CONFEDERATE ARMIES, SERIES I 158, 159-

160 (National Historical Society, Washington Government Printing Office 1886).

3.Letter from H.W. Halleck, General-in-Chief, to Maj. Gen. Benjamin F. Butler (Washington, D.C., Nov. 3, 1862) in SCOTT, 15 WAR OF THE REBELLION 589.

4.Reports of Major General Benjamin F. Butler, U.S. Army, commanding Department of the Gulf (New Orleans, November 6, 1862) in SCOTT, 15 WAR OF THE REBELLION 162.

5.Abraham Lincoln, Emancipation Proclamation, 12 Stat. Appendix 17, p. 1268, 1269 (Jan. 1, 1863).

6.Company and Field and Staff Muster Rolls, St. Louis Archives, (Hatfield Papers, Amistad Research Center, Tulane Univ.).

7.Enlistment Paper, Richard Douse Service Record, United States Colored Troops, 74th Infantry, General Records, Old Army, Record Group 94, National Archives, Washington, D.C.

8.A mulatto was the child of a white and a Negro; a quadroon, of a white and a mulatto; an octoroon, of a white and a quadroon; a tierceron, of a mulatto and a quadroon; a griffe, of a Negro and a mulatto; a marabon, of a mulatto and a griffe; and a sacatron, of a Negro and a griffe. A similar taxonomy existed for a person of mixed black and Native American heritage. HARNETT T. KANE, QUEEN NEW ORLEANS; CITY BY THE RIVER 185 (Bonanza Books 1949).

9.State v. Treadaway, 126 La. 300, 323 (1910).

10.Company and Field and Staff Muster Rolls, St. Louis Archives, (Hatfield Papers, Amistad Research Center, Tulane Univ.)

11.JAMES G. HOLLANDSWORTH, JR., THE LOUISIANA NATIVE GUARDS; THE BLACK MILITARY EXPERIENCE DURING THE CIVIL WAR 23 (Louisiana State Univ. Press 1995).

12.Company C, Record of Events for Seventy-fourth United States Colored Infantry, October 1862-June 1865, 78 SUPPLEMENT TO THE OFFICIAL RECORDS OF THE UNION AND CONFEDERATE ARMIES, Ser. No. 90, Part II - Record of Events 546 (Janet B. Hewett, ed. Broadfoot Pub. Co. 1998). Company K, Record of Events for 74th USCI 558.

13.Report of Major General Benjamin F. Butler, U.S. Army, commanding Department of the Gulf (New Orleans, Oct. 24, 1862) (SCOTT, 15 WAR OF THE REBELLION 159.)

14.Company C, Record of Events for 74th USCI 547.

15.Field and Staff Record, Record of Events for 74th USCI 539.

16.C. PETER RIPLEY, SLAVES AND FREEDMEN IN CIVIL WAR LOUISIANA 118-119 (Louisiana State Univ. Press 1976).

17. Lane's1[st] Regiment Kansas (Colored) Volunteer Infantry was the first black military unit to engage the Rebels. After leaving Fort Lincoln in Eastern Kansas, that unit fought Missouri bushwhackers at Island Mound, Missouri, on October 29, 1862. This unit did not become a part of the Union Army until January 13, 1863. JAMES G. HOLLANDSWORTH JR., THE LOUISIANA NATIVE GUARDS; THE BLACK MILITARY EXPERIENCE DURING THE CIVIL WAR 46-47 (Louisiana State Univ. Press 1995).

18.Company C, Record of Events for 74th USCI 547.

19.NOAH ANDRE TRUDEAU, LIKE MEN OF WAR; BLACK TROOPS IN THE CIVIL WAR 1862-1865 32 (Little, Brown and Co. 1998).

20.TRUDEAU, LIKE MEN OF WAR 32. Army inquiries could not determine whether the shelling was accidental or intentional. Trudeau cites to Daniel's Diary. The Regiment's Field and Staff Record reported two killed and seven wounded. Record of Events for 74th USCI 539. Company B reported two of its company killed, two mortally wounded and six others wounded. Record of Events for 74th USCI 544-545. Company C reported one killed and three wounded. Record of Events for 74th USCI 547. Company G reported one killed and two wounded. Record of Events for 74th USCI 554.

21. JOHN D. WINTERS, THE CIVIL WAR IN LOUISIANA 253 (Louisiana State Univ. Press 1963).

22. William H. Seward, *Review of Recent Military Events*, quoted in ASTOR, THE RIGHT TO FIGHT 38.

23. Company Muster Roll, Richard Douse Service Record, United States Colored Troops, 74th Infantry, General Records, Old Army, Record Group 94, National Archives, Washington, D.C.

24. Field and Staff, Record of Events for 74th USCI 539.

25. JAMES M. MCPHERSON, THE NEGRO'S CIVIL WAR: HOW AMERICAN NEGROES FELT AND ACTED DURING THE WAR FOR THE UNION 128-129 (Pantheon Books 1965).

26. WILLIAM WELLS BROWN, THE NEGRO IN THE AMERICAN REBELLION 250-251 (Citadel Press 1971).

27. BROWN, THE NEGRO IN THE AMERICAN REBELLION 253.

28. 38 U.S. Stat. 124, s. 2-4 (Jun. 15, 1864) ("That all persons of color who were free on the nineteenth day of April, eighteen hundred and sixty-one, and who have been enlisted and mustered into the military service of the United States, shall, from the time of their enlistment, be entitled to receive the pay, bounty, and clothing allowed to such persons by the laws existing at the time of their enlistment." s. 4.)

29. SCOTT, WAR OF THE REBELLION 171.

30. Quoted in testimony of Nathaniel Paige of the New York *Tribune* before American Freedman's Inquiry Commission, 15 May 1864, *The Negro in the Military Service of the United States, 1639-1886*, Microfilm M858, National Archives, Washington, D.C., in BERNARD C. NALTY AND MORRIS J. MACGREGOR, BLACKS IN THE MILITARY, ESSENTIAL DOCUMENTS 32-33 (Scholarly Resources Inc. 1981).

31. HOLLANDSWORTH, JR., THE LOUISIANA NATIVE GUARDS 44 quoting a letter from sixteen black officers of the 3rd Regiment, Louisiana Native Guard, to Banks (Sept. 19, 1863).

32. 1855 La. Acts 308 (Mar. 15, 1855). (Sec. 3 "That any slave who shall wilfully and maliciously strike his master or mistress ... so as to cause a contusion or shedding of blood, shall be punished with death or imprisonment at hard labor..." Sec. 4 "That if a slave shall shoot at or stab any person with intent to kill, such slave, on conviction of either of said offences, shall suffer death." Sec. 9 "That if any slave shall strike a white person, ... but for the third offense the said slave shall suffer death...")

33. The Ku Klux Klan, or the Invisible Empire, organized in 1867 as a multi-state group committed to preventing blacks from exercising political or economic power. JOHN HOPE FRANKLIN, RECONSTRUCTION: AFTER THE CIVIL WAR 155 (Univ. of Chicago Press 1961).

34. SHELBY FOOTE, THE CIVIL WAR, A NARRATIVE: RED RIVER TO APPOMATTOX 108-109. (Vintage Books 1974).

35. *See*, for example, WILLIAM LOREN KATZ, BREAKING THE CHAINS 163 (Atheneum 1990). ("At Fort Pillow, on April 12, 1864, Confederate General Nathan Bedford Forrest's troops massacred black prisoners by locking them in houses that were then set on fire.")

36. HONDON B. HARGROVE, BLACK UNION SOLDIERS IN THE CIVIL WAR 172 (McFarland & Co., Inc. 1988).

37. TRUDEAU, LIKE MEN OF WAR 168.

38. BROWN, THE NEGRO IN THE AMERICAN REBELLION 239.

39. HARGROVE, BLACK UNION SOLDIERS IN THE CIVIL WAR 173.

40. HARGROVE, BLACK UNION SOLDIERS IN THE CIVIL WAR 169.

41. Company and Field and Staff Muster Rolls, St. Louis Archives, (Hatfield Papers, Amistad Research Center, Tulane University.)

42. Surgeon's Certificate, Pension File of Richard Douse, File #C 2536643, Civil War and Later Pension Files, Records of the Veterans Administration, Record Group 15, National Archives.

43. 1870 Census of East Baton Rouge Parish, La. 18.

44. An Act to provide Internal Revenue to support the Government, to pay Interest on the Public Debt, and for other Purposes. 38th Cong., Sess. 1, Ch. 173, s. 10 (June 30, 1864) permits the employment of Collectors and Deputy Collectors to collect the revenue due the United States under the act. Certificate of appointment (Hatfield papers, Amistad Research Center, Tulane University.)

45. Undated letter to President U.S. Grant from O.J. Dunn, James F. Casey, Stephen B. Packard, and John Ray, Record Group 56, Treasury Dept., Entry 258, Records of Division of Appointments, Applications for Positions as Internal Revenue Collectors and Assessors, 1863-1910, Box 109, Application of B.T. Beauregard.

46. Undated letter of resignation to J.W. Douglass, Commissioner, from B.T. Beauregard, Record Group 56, Treasury Dept., Entry 258.

47. Certificate of appointment (Hatfield papers, Amistad Research Center, Tulane University); 1868 La. Acts 92, An Act to facilitate the registry of voters..., authorized the appointment of clerks to assist the supervisors of registration in the parishes of Louisiana to "effect the complete registration of all those who are entitled thereto." (Sept. 7, 1868).

# The Purnells

Thomas Purnell - Mary Martin
1798-1861          1802-1884


Ann Maria Purnell  m. Richard McKennon Douse
1834-1921      1872          1836-1917


Mary Elizabeth Douse  m.  Charles Hatfield
1879-1953          1912      1878-1931


Charles J. Hatfield, Jr.
1915-2002

# Chapter 4.

## *The Purnells*

*There is a certain affinity between individuals of opposite colors. The fascination of the unknown is so alluring . . .*

*George Schuyler*[1]

Thomas R. Purnell, born in 1798 into a prominent white family in Snow Hill, Worcester County, Maryland, moved to Louisiana in 1817 to buy land for and act as agent and overseer for Thomas Robins Purnell Spence of Snow Hill, Worcester County, Maryland. Generations of Purnells had lived in Snow Hill and were slave holders and owners of large estates there. Immigrant records show a Thomas Purnell entering Maryland in 1663 and another entering in 1673.[2] Land records show a Worcester County land patent of 325 acres by a Thomas Purnell dated December 15, 1683, and a land patent of 360 acres by a Thomas Purnell dated November 5, 1695.[3] Census records show a land and slave owning Thomas Purnell as a head of household in Worcester County in the very first Census of the United States Population in 1790.[4] The 1800 Census of that county shows three land and slave holding households headed by a Thomas Purnell,[5] and the 1810 Census shows four.[6] Thomas Spence was probably a cousin of Purnell, given the overlap of their names.

Purnell, as agent for Thomas Spence, purchased three tracts of land for $5,000 on November 13, 1822. The land, amounting to 778 and 3/4 *arpents,* was in Feliciana Parish, on the west side of Little Bayou Sara, fronting the Bayou.[7] Purnell continued to buy and sell land and slaves in West Feliciana Parish, as agent for Spence and for himself, until

1860 when he moved to Baton Rouge.[8]

Mary Ann Martin, the mother of Purnell's children, had been born into slavery in Maryland in 1802.[9] It is likely that she was a slave of the Purnells and moved to Louisiana with Thomas in 1817; her obituary states that she had lived in Louisiana since 1817.[10] Purnell had two female slaves between the ages of sixteen and twenty-five in his household in 1820, one of which was probably Mary. For that census, he reported 13 persons as slaves, and no free colored persons, attached to his household.[11]

By an act dated July 27, 1829, Thomas R. Purnell emancipated Mary Martin and their children, Matilda, John, and Edward Purnell. [12] Under Louisiana's 1807 statute, a slave was eligible for emancipation only if over thirty years of age and of good conduct. When those conditions were met, the local parish judge could issue a judgment of emancipation. If those conditions were not met, as when someone wanted to emancipate a child, the slave holder could petition the legislature which could grant the emancipation. Besieged by special requests for emancipations, in 1827, the legislature enacted a new statute which allowed the emancipation of persons under age 30 upon the approval of the parish judge and a three-fourths vote of the parish police jury.[13]

Purnell filed his petition of emancipation with the parish judge and placed the following notice of his intent to emancipate Mary and her three children in the *Florida Gazette* to appear on June 27, 1829:

> TAKE NOTICE - Whereas Mr. Thomas R. Purnell, of the Parish of West Feliciana, State of Louisiana, has applied to the Parish Judge to emancipate a Negro Woman named MARY and her three children Matilda, John and Edward. Now, all persons having any sufficient reason to offer why the said slaves shall not be emancipated will file their objections in thirty days from the date hereof, or the act of emancipation will be passed. M. Courtney, Sheriff[14]

The 1830 U.S. Census reflects this emancipation and lists Purnell's emancipated family as: two free colored males, both under age 10, and two free colored females, one under age 10 and one between 24 and 36 years of age.[15] Mary and Thomas' children born after Mary's emancipation would not need to be emancipated as the children of a free woman would be born free.

Mary and Thomas lived together and raised their family until Thomas' death,[16] but they would never marry. Louisiana law prohibited marriage between free people of color and free white persons, just as it prohibited marriage between free persons and slaves.[17] This prohibition was removed in 1870 when the Louisiana Civil Code was revised, but was reinstated in 1894.[18] Despite the absence of a legally celebrated marriage, Mary was known in her community and among her acquaintances as Mary Purnell.[19]

Mary and Thomas parented eight children: Matilda, born 1823, John, born 1825, Edward, born 1829, Sally or Sarah E., born 1832, Alexander, born 1834, Ann, born 1836, William, born 1840, and Eugene, born 1843.[20] William died of brain fever at age ten on July 21, 1850.[21] John, Edward, and Alexander became carpenters; Ann became a school teacher.[22] Although Purnell freed his children and their mother, he continued to own and to buy and sell other persons held as slaves.[23] The Purnell household owned fifteen slaves in 1840.[24]

Thomas and Mary's open miscegenation was not unusual in West Feliciana Parish. Bennet Barrow, a plantation owner in that area, complained that:

There is a great deal of talk through the Country about abolition &c. Yet the people submit to Amalgamation in its worse Form in this Parish, Josias Grey takes his mulatto children with him and to public places &c. and receives simalar [sic] company from New Orleans . . . Greys son with two of his visitors from the City had the impudence to pass here & through my Quarter, on a visit to see Purnells family.[25]

Barrow was outraged in 1839 when a member of his party invited "T Purnells Molatto [sic] boy" to eat dinner with them.[26] He observed with dismay that not everyone objected to treating the offspring of blacks and whites as equals. In 1841, Barrow noted, "(O)ur District Attorney, (W.D. Boyle) made a beggininng [sic] towards enforcing the Law, in removing free negros [sic] from the Parish, came to old Greys family, saw the Law in a different Light, . . ."[27]

Thomas Purnell filed the 1829 act emancipating Mary and her children in the West Feliciana Parish conveyance records on July 18,

1842.[28] Just as George Douse was motivated to protect his family members from enslavement by filing proof of their free status in the conveyance records at the parish courthouse in 1842, so was Thomas Purnell. Both acted in response to continuing state legislation intended to prevent free persons from entering the state but, in fact, jeopardizing the freedom of free blacks already in the state.

Louisiana's 1830 statute allowed a slave to leave Louisiana to be emancipated with the consent of his or her owner and to return to Louisiana as a free person.[29] Louisiana's 1842 statute forbid an inhabitant to take a slave from Louisiana into any state or country where slavery was prohibited, although free persons of color who resided in Louisiana before January 1825 were free to leave and return to Louisiana.[30]

Perhaps fearing that the late filing of the emancipation document would raise doubts as to its validity, Purnell filed a second document that same day confirming his intent to emancipate Mary and her seven living children. In it he declared:

> his intention to authorise and permit his slaves, as follows to wit: Woman, named "Mary" aged about forty years, of a Yellowish complexion, + her seven children, all mulattos, named + aged as follows to wit: Girl "Matilda" aged nineteen years; Boy "John" aged seventeen years; Boy "Edward" aged about fourteen years; Girl "Sally" aged about nine years; Boy "Alexander" aged about six years; Girl "Ann Mariah" aged about four years; Boy "William" aged about two years; to go to the City of Cincinnati, in the State of Ohio, for the purpose of residing there + enjoying the benefit of the laws of said State of Ohio, which confer freedom on all Slaves, who are allowed by their owners to live in said State or to return to the State of Louisiana at their pleasure, or the pleasure of their Mother Mary, who is fully authorised to take all said children to said City of Cincinnati - the said Thomas R. Purnell declaring that it is fully + absolutely his intention by this act, to emancipate all his aforesaid Slaves.[31]

Purnell also recorded the documents expressing his intent to free Mary and their children in the Court of Common Pleas, Hamilton

County, State of Ohio. He then recorded, in West Feliciana Parish, the certification from the Hamilton County Clerk noting that Purnell's "Certificate of the Emancipation of 'Mary' + her seven children" was recorded in the Hamilton County Records, Book No. 5, pages 764-765, Negro Records.[32] By recording the emancipation papers in an Ohio courthouse, Purnell sought to protect his family against the possibility of courthouse fires in Louisiana or other mishaps or intentional acts which might lead to the destruction or disregard of the record of emancipation filed in West Feliciana Parish. By filing the Ohio document in the West Feliciana Parish records, Purnell gave notice of its existence and suggested the futility of any intentional act meant to defeat his family's freedom. Purnell's second document allowed his family to travel to Cincinnati, Ohio, to be free there, should they be forced to leave Louisiana. Like Douse, Purnell took every measure to protect his children and their mother from slavery.

On February 2, 1833, Purnell, purporting to act as the agent for Thomas Spence, purchased 120.1 acres of land from Mrs. Maria Clark. Purnell paid seven hundred dollars cash for the land located about eight miles north of St. Francisville.[33] Purnell moved onto this land with his family and purchased land to the north and east of this estate in his own name.[34] On July 15, 1843, again purportedly acting as agent for Spence, Purnell conveyed the 120.1 acres on which he and his family lived to Mary Martin for six hundred dollars cash.[35] The act of sale describes the land as "The same land on which the said Thomas R. Purnell now resides and the same which was heretofore to wit on the second day of February, Eighteen hundred and thirty-three conveyed by Mrs. Maria Clark to said Spence . . ."[36] Thomas had arranged for Mary to become a landowner to protect her in her status as a free woman. As a landowner, she was less likely to be "mistaken" for a slave.

Thomas probably provided the cash for the sale, if any cash exchanged hands, as Mary was a housewife with no apparent source of cash income. Thomas could not have bought the land in his own name and then given the land to Mary as Louisiana law prevented Thomas and Mary from marrying each other, and prevented them from giving gifts of immovable property to one another because they were living together as a married couple but were not married to each other.[37] The legal prohibition against Thomas and Mary's marriage continued until after Thomas' death. While Purnell's other lands were used for farming or were sold to his sons or to others, Mary remained the record owner of this 120.1 acre tract where she and Purnell lived until the property was sold and they moved to Baton Rouge.

By 1845, Thomas Purnell had abandoned any plans he may have had to return to Maryland. In January of that year he appointed William M. Purnell, of Worcester County, Maryland, his agent for any property he owned in Maryland.[38] He then sold his last tract of land in West Feliciana Parish to John and Edward Purnell, his sons, on June 14, 1851.[39]

On March 15, 1860, Mary sold the land on which she and Thomas lived to John J. Barrow for $1,600.[40] That same day, Thomas sold his livestock, and the security brand he used to mark his livestock, also to Barrow.[41] Two weeks later, on March 29, 1860, Mary Martin purchased a 64 by 90-foot lot on the corner of Royal and Europe Streets, Lot 10, Square 37, Beauregard Town, Baton Rouge, Louisiana.[42] Sarah and Ann, still living at home in 1860, moved with their parents to Baton Rouge.[43]

The Beauregard Town subdivision of Baton Rouge, braced by North and South Boulevards and East Boulevard and St. Phillip Street, a few blocks from the Mississippi River, was laid out by Arsene LaCarriere LaTour for Elias Beauregard around 1805. In accordance with French tradition, it had a public square at its center and four streets, Grandpre, Beauregard, Penalver and Somerulos, radiated diagonally outward from the corners of the inner square to the corners of the outer square. The *Place d'Armes* was on its east side and a market stood on the river end of North Boulevard. The street names included St. Louis, St. Ferdinand, St. Charles, Royal, Napoleon, St. Joseph, Maximilian, America, Louisiana, Spain, France, Europe and Mayflower.

The neighborhood around Royal and Europe Streets, where the Purnells bought, included persons of many shades of skin color from various nationalities living as neighbors. Couples of mixed ethnicity could feel comfortable in that neighborhood. Thomas lived there with Mary until his death on April 23, 1861.[44] By 1870, Sarah had left home and Alexander, Mary's son, had moved in with his mother and his sister, Ann.[45]

On December 31, 1872, Richard Douse, tax collector and former military clerk, married Ann Maria Purnell, daughter of Thomas and Mary Purnell, in the parlor of her mother's home, Lot 10, Square 37, Beauregard Town, 522 Europe Street, Baton Rouge. It is very likely that Richard had known Ann Maria when they were children. Thomas and

***Ann Maria Purnell*** *c. 1870*
(photo courtesy of the family)

Orange Hill April 2nd 1842

Mr. Sidney Flowers Dr. to
George Douse
one bottle Madera Wine 2 – 6

As you was so kind as to say you
would pay me the other Day. I would
thank you kindly if you would it
with the barer My Son Richard

Mr. James Flowers                George Douse

*Bill sent by George Douse from Orange Hill*

Mary Purnell had lived close enough to George and Eliza Douse in West Feliciana Parish that their families were listed on the same page of the 1840 Census of the U.S. Population.[46]

The Purnells regularly attended St. Joseph's Roman Catholic Church, 405 Main Street, Baton Rouge, and Rev. Father E.M. Loponarn, Assistant Priest at St. Joseph's, officiated at Ann's wedding.[47] Catholic churches, although not their schools, remained racially integrated in those years immediately following the Civil War. Richard Douse was not Catholic, but "made the promises required by the Catholic church" and married Ann in a Catholic ceremony.[48]

St. Joseph's Roman Catholic Church, now Cathedral, was built on land donated by Don Antonio Gras at the corner of Fourth and Main Streets in Baton Rouge. Organized in the 1790s, the church was chartered by the State of Louisiana on March 17, 1820.[49] Don Gras' marriage in that church, on January 15, 1793, is the first recorded marriage to take place in Baton Rouge.[50] The church extant in 1872 was constructed between 1853 and 1856, replacing structures built in 1792 and 1831.[51]

Richard and Ann lived in the house in which they were married, on the corner of Royal and Europe Streets, for the rest of their lives, except for a very brief period when, after Ann's death, Richard moved temporarily to New Orleans.[52] When Ann's mother, Mary Martin Purnell, died on April 12, 1884, at the age of 83,[53] a newspaper article noting her death stated that she was a native of Snow Hill, Maryland, but had lived 67 years in Louisiana, 24 of them in Baton Rouge. Her obituary included the comment that, "No name, among our free colored citizens, stands higher than that of Purnell."[54] Richard and Ann Douse remained in her home after her death, raising their children there.

They had three children. John T. Dudley Douse was born January 9, 1876, married March 13, 1895, and had 13 children with his wife, Ada. Richard Charles Douse was born Thursday, September 27, 1877, and died unmarried and childless on July 12, 1900, at age 22 years, 10 months.[55] Their only daughter, named Mary Elizabeth Douse after her aunt, was born December 19, 1879, and married Charles Hatfield, a chef.

When not working as a deputy tax collector or as an election registration clerk, Richard Douse worked as a plasterer. In September 1895, scaffolding on which Richard Douse was working gave way and he fell about eight feet to the floor.[56] He was sixty years old at the time and his left arm and shoulder were broken. Four years later, in 1899, Douse applied to the Bureau of Pensions, Department of the Interior, for an Invalid Pension. Federal Act 634 of June 27, 1890, allowed a Civil War veteran honorably discharged after serving ninety days or more, and currently suffering from a permanent physical or mental disability, to receive an invalid pension in an amount between six and twelve dollars a month, "proportioned to the degree of inability to earn a support . . ."[57] After examinations by three physicians, Douse received a pension of six dollars per month, although his Surgeon's Certificate recommended a rate of $10 per month.[58]

In 1898, Mary Elizabeth Douse was graduated from Holy Family Academy, an elementary school located on St. Charles St. in Baton Rouge, within walking distance of her home. The school was run by the Congregation of the Sisters of the Holy Family, an order of nuns founded in 1842 by Henriette DeLille and her childhood friend, Juliette Gaudin.[59] DeLille, born in 1813, was the daughter of a white merchant, Jean Baptiste DeLille Sarpy, and a free woman of color, Marie Joseph Dias. As a child, DeLille wanted to become a nun but the convents in New Orleans were closed to persons of color. Juliette Gaudin shared her ambition. Gaudin, born in Cuba, had come to New Orleans at age nine.

On August 15, 1836, DeLille and Gaudin drew up rules for a religious order. They pledged themselves to serve the poor and ignorant and prayed daily at St. Mary's Church that their order would come into being. Their prayers were answered in 1842 shortly after Mademoiselle Marie Jeanne Aliquot arrived in New Orleans.

Mademoiselle Aliquot, also an aspiring nun, had sailed from France to join her sister who was already serving as a nun in the Ursuline Convent in New Orleans. When her ship docked, Aliquot tried to go ashore before the gangway was firmly attached and she fell into the Mississippi River. She was rescued by a black man and, in gratitude, vowed to devote her life to helping blacks and instructing former slaves. She purchased the former site of the College of Orleans, a square bounded by St. Claude, Bayou Road, Liberty and Ursuline Streets, and opened a school.

Often visiting St. Mary's Church, she noticed the two women who came to pray each night and eventually asked them about the object of their prayer. DeLille and Gaudin explained their intent to form a religious order and Aliquot advised them to talk to Reverend Father Etienne Rousselon, vicar-general of the diocese. Pere Rousselon, as he was known, had shown great sympathy for the plight of blacks, especially the elderly, and had greatly aided Aliquot with her school. Rousselon agreed to help DeLille and Gaudin. On November 21, 1842, Rousselon rented a small house on St. Bernard Street to serve as both a convent and a home for aged women. DeLille, Gaudin, and two elderly women moved in. They soon moved to a larger house on Bayou Road, between Rampart and St. Claude Streets, to accommodate the growing number of elderly served by the home. DeLille was able to purchase this house for the order in 1851.

Josephine Charles, the daughter of a prominent family of free blacks, joined DeLille and Gaudin in 1843. She was a popular seamstress at the fashionable D.H. Holmes department store in downtown New Orleans, and her family opposed her decision to work among the poor. She was determined and left home without her family's knowledge. Her assistance allowed DeLille and Gaudin to offer catechism classes for children and adults.

In 1850, DeLille was allowed to attend noviate training at Saint Michael Convent in Saint James Parish, Louisiana, and, within the year, she returned to tutor her co-workers. Srs. DeLille, Gaudin and Charles took their first vows on October 15, 1852. The childhood dreams of DeLille and Gaudin had been fulfilled. The Congregation of the Sisters of Holy Family had come into being and was serving the poor and the untutored. The order owned a convent, taught catechism, and operated a home for the elderly on Bayou Road. Henriette DeLille died November 17, 1862, at age fifty, but her work was continued.

A girl's secondary school, St. Mary's School, was founded in 1867 and renamed St. Mary's Academy in 1882. In 1872, Reverend Father Jean Francois Raymond invited the order to open a school in Opelousas, Louisiana. St. Joseph School, which the order opened in August 1873, was the first of many schools that would be operated by the order outside of the City of New Orleans. The Sisters of Holy Family established schools for blacks in Mandeville, Lafayette, Madisonville, Covington, Donaldsonville, and Baton Rouge, Louisiana; Stann Creek, British Honduras (now Belize); Galveston, Ames, Houston, Corpus Christi, and San Antonio, Texas; Pine Bluff, Arkansas; Pritchard, Alabama; Tulsa, Oklahoma; and Apalachicola, Florida.

In 1881, the former Orleans Ballroom, built in 1817 at 717 Orleans Street in the French Quarter of New Orleans, became available for sale. The order was able to purchase the property, situated between Orleans, St. Ann, Royal, and Bourbon Streets, by exchanging properties owned by the order, or owned by the three founding Sisters, as a down payment, then agreeing to pay the remaining cost within ten years at six per cent interest. The walls were cleaned and the floors repaired. A part of the dance hall was converted into a chapel and the order was able to house their convent, a boarding school, a day school, and an orphanage in that building.

Also in 1881, Father Cyril Delacroix, pastor of the St. Joseph's Church in Baton Rouge, convinced the Sisters of Holy Family to open the St. Mary's School for Negroes on Florida Street. That school closed within the year. Undeterred, the Sisters of Holy Family returned to Baton Rouge in 1895 to operate Holy Family Academy, the school attended by Mary Douse. The Sisters of Holy Family operated the Holy Family Academy until 1919 when the Josephite Fathers purchased the school and convent and continued its operation as St. Francis Xavier Catholic School.

When Mary Douse was graduated from Holy Family Academy on June 29, 1898, she moved to Iberville Street in New Orleans where she stayed with her aunt Elizabeth Douse, a teacher and dressmaker. In New Orleans, Mary Douse attended the Sisters of Holy Family Teacher's Normal School in the former Orleans Ballroom. After graduation, she taught for a number of years at a private school for Creoles near New Roads, Louisiana, and in the Catholic schools in East Baton Rouge Parish until 1912 when she married Charles Hatfield in Baton Rouge.

### Notes

1. KATHRYN TALALAY, COMPOSITION IN BLACK AND WHITE: THE LIFE OF PHILIPPA SCHUYLER 18 (Oxford Univ. Press 1995).

2. THE EARLY SETTLERS OF MARYLAND - AN INDEX TO NAMES OF IMMIGRANTS COMPILED FROM RECORDS OF LAND PATENTS, 1633-1680, IN THE HALL OF RECORDS, ANNAPOLIS, MARYLAND 377 (Gust Skordas, ed., Baltimore Genealogical Publ. Co. 1968).

3. RUTH T. DRYDEN, LAND RECORDS OF WORCESTER COUNTY, MD. 1666-1810 119, 105 (Family Line Publications 1992).

4. 1790 Census of Worcester Co., Md. 126.

5. 1800 Census of Worcester Co., Md.195, 197, 204.

6. 1810 Census of Worcester Co., Md. 560, 591, 599, 602.

7. Book B, Page 557, Conveyance Records, West Feliciana Parish, La. (Nov. 13, 1822).

8. *See*, generally, Conveyance Records, West Feliciana Parish, La., Books B-N (Nov. 13, 1822 - Mar. 15, 1860).

9. 1850 Census of West Feliciana Parish, La. 276

10. Undated newspaper clipping found in Charles Hatfield's Family Bible.

11.1820 Census of Feliciana Parish, La. 45.

12.Act of Emancipation, Book H, Page 230, Conveyance Records, West Feliciana Parish, La. (Jul. 27, 1829 recorded Jul.18, 1842). 1807 La Acts Ch. x p. 82 allowed the emancipation of slaves who were over age thirty and had displayed good conduct for four years, or who had saved the life of their owner, his wife or children. 1827 La. Acts p. 12 allowed slaves under the age of thirty to be emancipated upon application to the parish judge and the local police jury where three fourths of the members would have to vote in favor of emancipation.

13.1807 La. Acts X (Mar. 9, 1807)(An Act to regulate the conditions and forms of the Emancipation of Slaves.); 1827 La. Acts (Jan. 31, 1827)(An Act to determine the mode of emancipating Slaves who have not attained the age required by the Civil Code for their emancipation).

14.26 Florida Gazette, St. Francisville, La., June 27, 1829, at 1, col. 5.

15.1830 Census of West Feliciana Parish, La. 241.

16.Census of West Feliciana Parish, 1830-1860.

17.La. Civ. Code art. 95 (1825), ("Free persons and slaves are incapable of contracting marriage together; the celebration of such marriage is forbidden, and the marriage is void; there is the same incapacity and the same nullity with respect to marriages contracted by free white persons with free people of colour.")

18.1870 Revised Civil Code art. 94. 1894 La. Acts no. 54, "Marriage between white persons and persons of color is prohibited..."

19.Book M, Page 343, Conveyance Records, West Feliciana Parish, La. (May 23, 1857). ("Be it known that on this third day of May in the year 1857 Mary Martin appeared better known as Mary Purnell ...")

20.1850 Census of West Feliciana Parish, La. 276.

21.Burial records of Grace Episcopal Church, St. Francisville, La. (Jul. 21, 1850). His brother John died in Baton Rouge, La. Oct. 1, 1894. CIVIL BIRTH AND DEATH REGISTERS FOR THE CITY OF BATON ROUGE 1874-1918 Book I, Page 101 (Judy Riflel, et al, La Comite' des Archives de la Louisiane Baton Rouge 2001).

22.1850 Census of West Feliciana Parish, La. 276.

23.Book L, Page 245 Conveyance Records (Feb. 28, 1854); Probate Sales Book E 1848-1873 (Apr. 12, 1851)West Feliciana Parish, La.

24.1840 Census of West Feliciana Parish, La. 210

25.EDWIN ADAMS DAVIS, PLANTATION LIFE IN THE FLORIDA PARISHES OF LOUISIANA, 1836 - 1846 AS REFLECTED IN THE DIARY OF BENNET H. BARROW 206 (AMS Press, Inc. 1967). (entry is dated Aug. 3, 1840). William H. Grey and Matilda Purnell, both children of white fathers and black mothers, married one another. Book M, Page 343, Conveyance Records, and General Index of Marriage Licenses 371 West Feliciana Parish, La. (Aug. 24, 1848).

26.DAVIS, PLANTATION LIFE IN THE FLORIDA PARISHES 169 (entry is dated Nov. 6, 1839).

27.DAVIS, PLANTATION LIFE IN THE FLORIDA PARISHES 239 (entry is dated Aug. 15, 1841). 1830 La Acts 90 required the District Attorney of each parish to enforce the law that free persons of color resident in Louisiana before January 1, 1825, must enroll in the office of the parish judge where they live, and that free persons of color who entered the state after January 1, 1825, leave within 60 days.

28.Act of Emancipation, Book H, Page 230, Conveyance Records, West Feliciana Parish, La. (Jul. 27, 1829 recorded July 18, 1842).

29. 1830 La. Acts 90, s. 16 (Mar. 16, 1830).

30. 1842 La. Acts 123, s. 8-9. (Mar. 16, 1842, to take effect six months later)

31. Book H, Page 230, Conveyance Records, West Feliciana Parish, La. (Jul. 18, 1842).

32. Book H, Page 240, Conveyance Records, West Feliciana Parish, La. (Aug. 5, 1842 recorded Aug. 29, 1842).

33. Book E, Page 35, Conveyance Records, West Feliciana Parish, La. (Feb. 28, 1833).

34. Book F, Page 333, Conveyance Records, West Feliciana Parish, La. (Dec. 18, 1837).

35. Book H, Page 443, Conveyance Records, West Feliciana Parish, La. (Jul. 19, 1843).

36. Book H, Page 444, Conveyance Records, West Feliciana Parish, La. (Jul. 19, 1843).

37. "Those who have lived together in open concubinage are respectfully incapable of making to each other, whether inter vivos or mortis causa, any donations of immovables; and if they make a donation of moveables, it can not exceed one-tenth of the whole value of their estate." La. Civ. Code art. 1481 (West 1987), repealed 1987 La. Acts 468 (Jul. 9, 1987); La. Civ. Code art. 1468 (1825).

38. Book I, Page 177, Conveyance Records, West Feliciana Parish, La. (Jan. 3, 1845).

39. Book K, page 279, Conveyance Records, West Feliciana Parish, La. (Jun. 17, 1851).

40. Book N, Page 296, Conveyance Records, West Feliciana Parish, La. (Mar. 15, 1860).

41. Book N, Page 297, Sale of Stock and Security Brand, Conveyance Records, West Feliciana Parish, La. (Mar. 15, 1860).

42. Book S, Folio 233, Conveyance Records, East Baton Rouge Parish, La. (Mar. 29, 1860).

43. 1860 Census of East Baton Rouge Parish, La. 466.

44. Petition of John and Mary Douse, para. VII, *Succession of Richard Douse and Ann M. Douse*, Probate No. 3,364, (22nd JDC, Par. of East Baton Rouge, La., Jul. 29, 1922).

45. 1870 Census of East Baton Rouge Parish, La. 45.

46. 1840 Census, West Feliciana Parish, La. 210.

47. Copy of Original Record of Marriage, *Succession of Richard Douse and Ann M. Douse* 9.

48. Marriage Certificate, a true copy of original prepared by D. Blanco, Assistant Pastor, St. Joseph Catholic Cathedral (Jan. 25, 1922), *Succession of Richard Douse and Ann M. Douse* 9, Probate No. 3,364, (22nd JDC, Par. of East Baton Rouge, La. Jul. 29, 1922).

49. 1820 La Acts "An Act to incorporate the Roman Catholic Inhabitants of East Baton Rouge." (Mar. 17, 1820).

50. Historical Marker at 405 Main Street, Baton Rouge.

51. Plaque located inside the church sanctuary.

52. Affidavit of Eliza Turnbull Connor, *Succ. of Richard Douse and Ann M. Douse* 14.

53. Register of Deaths, City of Baton Rouge 32 (Apr. 13, 1884), cause of death apoplexy.

54. Undated newspaper clipping found in Charles Hatfield's Family Bible.

55. Form 3-173, Pension File of Richard Douse, National Archives, (Jun. 30, 1901).

56. General Affidavit of Richard Douse, (Mar. 11, 1901), Pension file, National Archives.

57. 1890 USC 634, s. 2.

58. Surgeon's Certificate, (Sept. 12, 1900), Pension file.

59.SISTER MARY FRANCIS BORGIA HART, SSF, VIOLETS IN THE KING'S GARDEN; A HISTORY OF THE HOLY FAMILY OF NEW ORLEANS 6-10 (self-published Aug. 1976).

# The Hatfields

Former Slave m. Cherokee woman
?-?                    ?-?

Daughter - Faucheaux
?-?          ?- c. 1863

Alice Stevens - Charles Hatfield
1858-1908              ?-?

Mary Elizabeth Douse m. Charles Hatfield
1879-1953      1912      1878-1931

Charles J. Hatfield, Jr.
1915-2002

# Chapter 5.

## *The Hatfields*

*The welfare of our nation demands that all its citizens
be convinced of the superiority of American democracy
over other forms of government, but to appreciate its
blessings and liberty one must be permitted the
opportunity to experience them.*

*Sister M. Gonzaga*[1]

Charles Hatfield, born May 1878, was the son of Alice Stevens of Baton Rouge and Charles Hatfield, a native of Massachusetts.[2] Alice Stevens' grandfather had been a slave in the Feliciana Parishes north of Baton Rouge or in nearby Southern Mississippi. When he escaped from slavery, he joined with Cherokee Indians in Baton Rouge and married a young Cherokee woman. Marriage between Indians and blacks was not an uncommon practice in the South. Although many Native Americans owned slaves themselves, runaway slaves often found refuge and freedom with local tribes. This runaway slave and the Cherokee woman he married had only one child, a daughter, before he died.

The Cherokee wife, Alice's grandmother, supported herself and her child by making and selling rugs and eventually became attached to a French family in Baton Rouge by the name of Faucheux, probably as servants. One of the Faucheux' sons, who was later killed in the Civil War, became Alice's father. Alice, part Cherokee, part African, and part European, was born in January 1858. She was considered by many to be one of the most beautiful women in Louisiana. Ms. Alma, a close friend of the Hatfield family, used to say so all the time.[3]

When Charles Hatfield of Massachusetts first arrived in Baton Rouge, he boarded with the Faucheux family. Family gossip labeled Hatfield as a snob and an aristocrat. When he later moved to his own house in the Spanish Town section of Baton Rouge, he asked Alice to move there with him to care for his household. Alice and Hatfield had one child born in May 1878 who they named after his father, Charles Hatfield. Hatfield soon left Baton Rouge to move to Oregon, but left money with Alice to educate his son and namesake.

Alice Stevens had four more children, three boys and a girl.[4] Two of her sons, Leon and Duplantier, moved to Chicago, Illinois, and later sent for their sister, Maryann. All three "crossed the color line," marrying white spouses and providing no evidence of their nonwhite heritage. [5] Hatfield's siblings were of the African race by Louisiana's standards. In Louisiana, anyone with any appreciable degree of Negro blood was considered a member of the African race in 1878.[6] Hatfield's siblings, however, were light skinned enough to pass for white. The French speakers of New Orleans use the phrase, *passe a blanc*, for such persons. Alice's children wrote to their mother and other family members from time to time, always regretting that they could not invite them to come to visit in Chicago.

A *passe a blanc* tries to avoid contact with all family and friends after deciding to pass as white. "Total separation was necessary for secrecy. . . . Any . . . contact would arouse suspicion, and with suspicion comes demotion and a return to 'colored' status."[7] Hatfield's wife, Mary, often laughed about her in-laws who didn't want their darker family members to expose their ethnic history.

When Charles Hatfield, Jr., the subject of this biography, was asked whether he wanted to be called "Negro" or "black" or "African-American," he expressed the concern that no words can capture the mix that was his ethnicity. "If I claim to be an African-American, I disclaim all the others involved in getting me here. The Native American, the French, the Irish, the African are all a part of me. Whatever they call me, I know what they mean."[8]

In 1894, Alice Stevens bought a lot at 201 Spanish Town Road, on the corner of West Street, lot one, square one, Aubert Town, in Baton Rouge.[9] She built a house on the land and lived there until her death on June 30, 1908.[10] In February 1907, more than a year before her death, she sold her house and land to her eldest son, Charles Hatfield.[11]

Charles Hatfield became a chef. He studied under both French and German chefs in Baton Rouge and New Orleans, and worked in country clubs and restaurants. He was an excellent cook, but not a businessman. Hatfield invested his earnings in real estate and overextended himself. He mortgaged land that he owned to invest in other property and in various business deals, and eventually lost everything.

The wonderful chef but unsuccessful real estate investor married Mary Elizabeth Douse, the school teacher, in 1912. According to Mary's father, Richard Douse, Charles Hatfield was the only man good enough to marry his daughter. Charles and Mary had waited for each other. Charles was thirty-four and Mary was thirty-three years old. Charles Hatfield moved into the Douse family home with Mary and her parents, Richard and Ann Douse.

Six children were born to this marriage, four girls and two boys, but only three survived their childhood. Mary died at birth, Doris died at age three, and Margarita died as an infant. Charles J. Hatfield, Jr. was born May 27, 1915, in his maternal grandparents' house, Lot 10, Square 37, Beauregard Town, 522 Europe Street, Baton Rouge, Louisiana. His younger sister, Juanita, born January 11, 1921, married John Haydel of New Orleans, who, with his brother Whitney Haydel, owned and operated a cosmetics business on Rampart Street. Whitney was a chemist and the Haydel brothers sold their own brand of cosmetic, Mecos, mixed by Whitney. Hatfield's younger brother, Raymond, born two years later, rose to the rank of Chief Petty Officer before he retired from the Navy after thirty years of service and moved to Philadelphia with his wife, Elsie, and four daughters.

Charles Hatfield, Jr. was born with two club feet and wore braces as a child. Although his left foot straightened out beautifully, his right foot never properly turned. His feet became a problem for him when he worked for the United States Postal Service as a letter carrier and again while he was in the U.S. Army Infantry. Charles was baptized at St. Joseph's Catholic Church on June 20, 1915. Soon thereafter, his family moved to New Orleans where his father found work as a cook.

Hatfield was not yet two years old when his maternal grandmother, Ann Maria Purnell Douse, died. She was buried in the Catholic Cemetery in Baton Rouge, Louisiana, on January 19, 1917. Shortly thereafter, her husband, Richard Douse, moved to New Orleans to live with their daughter, Mary Douse Hatfield, and her family at 1919 Palmyra Street.[12]

Hatfield's grandfather showed him around New Orleans and reminisced about the Civil War days. Richard Douse had lived in New Orleans as a young man and had visited with his family there. He seemed to know everyone he met on the street and proudly introduced his young grandson to them all. Hatfield and his grandfather especially enjoyed the Mardi Gras, although Hatfield was frightened by the masks. He was not frightened when his grandfather took him to see the cadavers at the Tulane Medical School and talked to him about death.

Hatfield loved his grandfather. Though a stern taskmaster, Richard Douse loved his grandchild in return. Hatfield's grandfather was "so strict it was a pity!" In his company, children spoke only when spoken to, but his grandfather would spend time with Hatfield and teach him what he knew about plants, animals, and life. When Richard Douse felt that death was imminent, he asked that the family move back to the house on Europe Street in Baton Rouge. He wanted to die and be buried in Baton Rouge near his wife. In accord with his wishes, the Hatfields returned to Baton Rouge to reoccupy the house in Beauregard Town.

In Baton Rouge, Hatfield and his grandfather picked figs and peaches from the trees in their yard and stood together in the street to admire the Old State Capitol building, which they could see from their neighborhood. They went to the Mississippi River to catch river shrimp, skirting Catfish Town, a warehouse district near the Port of Baton Rouge where cheap liquor and loose women were readily available to visiting sailors.

Hatfield had fond memories of his grandfather, although he was only six years old when his grandfather died October 17, 1921, at the age of 88. Douse had been a 33 rd degree mason as well as a veteran so was buried in the National Cemetery in Baton Rouge with full military honors and complete masonic rites.[13] He was buried in a black casket and seven carriages carried family and friends to the funeral.[14] Hatfield's father was working at a country club in Memphis and his mother was pregnant with his younger brother, Raymond, at the time her father died.

After his grandfather's death, Hatfield's mother and her brother, John, divided the ownership of the house and property at 522 Europe Street one-half each.[15] Even though Mary and her family were living in the house at that time, John Douse sold his half ownership to William T. Byrd on January 23, 1923.[16] John resented watching his sister's family enjoy the fruit trees and the comfortable home while John owned half of the property, but enjoyed none of it. Mary was then forced to either buy

*Parents of Charles Hatfield, Jr.* c. 1930
(photos courtesy of the family)

***Parents of Charles Hatfield, Jr.*** *c. 1910*
(photos courtesy of the family)

John's interest from Byrd, or sell her interest and move out of the house. She was able to purchase John's one-half interest from William Byrd two weeks after Byrd's purchase.[17] Mary Douse Hatfield and her family lived in the house only four more years. In January 1927, she sold the house in which she and her children had been born.[18] Hatfield's family bought a two-family house at 2010 and 2012 Iberville Street, a few blocks away from the Palmyra Street house where they had lived in New Orleans before returning to Baton Rouge.

Hatfield worked with his father at the Southern Yacht Club and at the West End Club in New Orleans. Hatfield would again work in the West End Club while he was in college. Hatfield had just turned sixteen years old when his father died on June 12, 1931.[19] Hatfield believes that his father's excessive worries about the money and the property he had lost led to his early death. Hatfield's mother, 52 years old at the time, was unable to work. She tried to support her family during these depression years from the rents she received from tenants occupying the other side of her two-family home. Hatfield dropped out of school to help.

Mary Hatfield lost the house on Iberville in 1938 when she was unable to pay her real estate taxes. Hatfield then became the sole support for his mother and his younger brother and sister. He moved his family into the Lafitte housing project, 663 North Prieur Street, in New Orleans.[20]

Although Hatfield was not continually enrolled in school, he read voraciously. He especially sought out philosophy, history and political science. He read Jean-Jacques Rousseau and Francois-Marie Arouet, especially. Hatfield was intensely interested in what they wrote and was inspired by these philosophers in his pursuit of justice. Arouet, a writer and philosopher in France who used the pseudonym, Voltaire, is remembered as a man of independent thought and action who rejected conformity for individualism.

Rousseau was a political philosopher and writer in France known for his social contract theory that individuals unite to create "a form of association which defends and protects, with all the force of the community, the person and goods of each associate and by which each, in uniting himself with all would, however, obey only himself and remain as free as before."[21] Rousseau believed slavery to be an unnatural state, an idea that affirmed Hatfield's sense of right and wrong.

Hatfield managed to finish high school at Gilbert Academy on June 30, 1938. The William L. Gilbert Academy, located at 5318 St.

Charles Ave., was founded in 1865 in Baldwin, La., by the Methodist Church. An excellent college preparatory school, Gilbert moved to New Orleans in 1935, when New Orleans University merged with Straight College to form Dillard University. Gilbert was located on the site that New Orleans University had occupied beginning in 1873. Known for its strict rules, academic excellence, and staunch pride, Gilbert has graduated many illustrious alumni, including Andrew Young and Ellis Marsalis; many lawyers, including Louis Berry, who filed Hatfield's suit, and John Bowen III, whose mother was principal from 1935 to 1948; and many fine educators, including Charles Hatfield.[22]

Hatfield remembered how hard the teachers at Gilbert worked to ensure his success. "I can never forget how Mrs. Margaret D. Bowen, Principal of Gilbert Academy 1935 to 1948, was concerned about me graduating from high school. Mrs. Myrtle Banks gave me private instructions for courses leading to graduation. Mr. Crocker also helped me very much in this respect. . . . There were others whose names I cannot recall now, but I shall never forget."[23] Hatfield was almost 21 years old by the time he finished high school.

As soon as he turned 21, Hatfield registered to vote. His grandfather had registered voters in 1874 and Hatfield's study of Rousseau and Voltaire impressed upon him the importance of participating in the governing of his country. As Hatfield would write ten years later, "No other privilege traditionally belonging to citizens is of more ultimate importance than the exercise of the suffrage. The extent to and the conditions under which it is exercised determines to a large degree the democratic or undemocratic character of the government concerned."[24] Hatfield, who boldly presented himself before the registrar, was allowed to register to vote in 1936, despite Louisiana laws that generally impeded registration by Blacks.

Louisiana's Constitution of 1921, in effect in 1936, required a registrant to demonstrate his ability to read and write by correctly completing an application for registration in the presence of the registrar without assistance from any person or from notes; and to be able to read any clause of the Louisiana or United States Constitution. If unable to read and write, an applicant had to be a "person of good character and reputation, attached to the principles of the Constitution of the United States and of the State of Louisiana, and shall be able to understand and give a reasonable interpretation of any section of either Constitution when read to him by the registrar . . ."[25] The local registrars had full discretion to determine whether or not an applicant correctly interpreted any section of either constitution, although many registrars barely had a high school education themselves. Hatfield was not challenged when he sought to register, but many black applicants were turned away from the polls because they were black.

According to the 1940 Census of East Baton Rouge Parish, where the state capital and the state's largest historically black university are located, blacks constituted 38% of the local population, yet, voting rolls included only 144 blacks, 1.5% of the registered voters. While there were 34,000 registered white voters in Baton Rouge in 1946, only 540 registered voters were black.[26]

Louisiana based its 1921 interpretation requirement on a similar requirement in Mississippi's Constitution of 1890 which read, "On and after the first day of January, A.D. 1892, every elector shall, in addition to the foregoing qualifications, be able to read any section of the constitution of this state; or he shall be able to understand the same when read to him, or give a reasonable interpretation thereof." [27] Just prior to Mississippi's 1890 Constitutional Convention, Mississippi had 190,000 black voters and 69,000 white voters. The Convention, which had only one black member, included Mississippi's interpretation clause in its 1890 Constitution then adopted the Constitution without submitting it to the voters for ratification. The state then purged the voter's rolls and immediately held an election in which most blacks in Mississippi could not vote. By 1899, Mississippi had only 18,000 black registered voters, but had 122,000 white voters registered.[28]

In 1896, Henry Williams challenged the Mississippi provision, arguing that it gave each local registrar absolute authority, without review, to act as sole judge in determining who qualified to register to vote and who did not. Williams argued that, "This officer can reject whomsoever he chooses, and register whomsoever he chooses, for he is vested by the constitution with that power."[29] The United States Supreme Court did not disagree, but determined that this provision did not, on its face, discriminate between the races as it did not establish one rule for blacks and a different rule for whites. The registrar was equally free to reject whites as well as blacks at his discretion. In addition, according to the Court, Williams had not shown that the actual administration of the provisions was evil, "only that evil was possible under them."[30] The Court was content that the rule did not violate the Fourteenth Amendment to the United States Constitution.

When the Louisiana interpretation requirement was challenged in court, Antoine M. Trudeau, who sought to register to vote in New Orleans, met with the same result. Trudeau completed the registration application and, at the registrar's request, read and began an explanation of a portion of the Louisiana Constitution. The registrar stopped him and declared that Trudeau had not perfectly understood and explained the meaning of that constitutional provision.[31] Perhaps the registrar would have been satisfied with the response Moms Mabley, an entertainer and recording artist, offered on her recorded album, *Now Hear This*. In Moms Mabley's story, the registration applicant, faced with a challenging registrar like the one confronting Trudeau, is asked to recite the Constitution backwards, which he does. He is asked to recite the Old and New Testaments forward and backwards, which he does. The registrar of voters then hands him a Chinese newspaper and demands, "Let me hear you read that paper." The applicant looks at the registrar who asks, "What's it say? What's it say?" The applicant then slowly begins, "It says, 'Makes no difference what I do, you ain't gonna let me vote nohow.'"[32]

In Trudeau's case, the Fifth Circuit Court of Appeals determined that Louisiana's interpretation requirement did not abridge the equal protection of the laws because it applied to all voters alike. "It lays down but one test, that of intelligence, which applies uniformly and without discrimination to voters of every race and color."[33] In the court's opinion, the provision adopted by Louisiana, did not violate requirements for due process because it gave an applicant who was denied the opportunity to vote a right to apply to a state trial court for relief. This right to judicial review, the court argued, would discourage registrars from arbitrarily denying an applicant the right to register to vote. The appellate court, apparently, was blind to the reality that the rejected applicants who sought to protest the decision of the local registrar would appear before all white juries composed of the same voters who had elected that registrar to office. Black applicants could not expect these jurors to overrule their local registrar's decision. The appellate court provided no relief in Trudeau's case, and the Supreme Court of the United States refused to hear it.

Twenty years later, the courts continued to approve of the use of interpretation tests to determine who could and who could not vote. In Rapides Parish, a federal district court found that the registrar had correctly applied the interpretation test to deny registration to 300 whites and to 800 blacks. The court acknowledged that there might have been instances where whites and blacks did not receive identical treatment, but it determined that isolated cases of disparate treatment do not prove discrimination under the Federal Constitution. "[A]dministration of the laws by the defendant [did not] penalize Negroes any more than it did other citizens."[34]

Judge John Minor Wisdom finally disagreed. In 1963, Judge Wisdom labeled Louisiana's interpretation requirement "the highest, best-guarded, most effective barrier to Negro voting in Louisiana." He noted that it "enabled a registrar to flunk eight Negro school teachers while passing eight illiterate white persons." He quoted a December 14, 1960, report by the Louisiana Sovereignty Committee to the effect that between 1956 and 1960, "81,214 colored people became of voting age, when the registration figures of colored people actually declined 2,377. . . . 114,529 white people . . . became of voting age and . . . the white registration increased 96,620." Wisdom called the interpretation test a "scheme to disenfranchise Negroes."[35]

In his published opinion, Judge Wisdom reviewed Louisiana's incessant efforts to disenfranchise its black citizens. Article 98 of Louisiana's Constitution of 1868 extended the right to vote to all males aged twenty-one and over, allowing nonwhites to vote for the first time in the state's history.[36] This right to vote was protected in the 1879 Constitution by Article 188 which reads, "No qualification of any kind for suffrage or office, nor any restraint upon the same on account of race, color, or previous condition shall be made by law."[37]

The voting rights of Louisiana's black citizenry, given to them only thirty years earlier, were greatly circumscribed in 1898. Louisiana's 1898 Constitution required voting registrants to either own property assessed at $300 or more or to demonstrate that they are able to read and write. The article included a "grandfather" clause which exempted from either requirement any man whose father or grandfather was eligible to vote before January 1, 1867, when only white males could vote, or who was of foreign birth and naturalized prior to January 1, 1898.[38]

Louisiana's literacy and property requirements effectively eliminated black voters, while its "grandfather clause" gave the right to vote to illiterate whites who owned no property. In January 1897, Louisiana had 130,344 black voters. In March 1900, it had only 5,320 black voters. By 1910, only 730 blacks were registered.[39]

Louisiana's disenfranchisement of its black population was not accidental. A December 15, 1895, editorial in the *Shreveport Evening Judge*, a newspaper supporting the Democratic Party in Louisiana, declared, "It is the religious duty of Democrats to rob Populists and Republicans of their votes whenever and wherever the opportunity presents itself. . . . The Populists and Republicans are our legitimate political prey. Rob them!"[40] In their efforts to dominate the government in Louisiana, Democrats eliminated both black and poor white voters. Black voter registration dropped from 130,344 to 5,320 then to 1,342 in 1904. White registration dropped from 164,088 on January 1, 1897, to 125,437 in 1900, then to approximately 92,000 in 1904. Having finally regained control of the state, Louisiana Democrats limited access to the ballot box where their control might be lost.

Stripped of their political power, Louisiana's blacks entered an age of oppression and segregation reminiscent of slavery. The greater part of the political, education and economic gains of the post-Civil War era had been lost.

In 1915, in an Oklahoma case, the United States Supreme Court declared the grandfather clause unconstitutional, explaining that it violated the Fifteenth Amendment to the United States Constitution which prohibits states from denying the right to vote to any citizen based upon that person's skin color.[41] The Court noted that an exemption from property ownership and literacy requirements was available only to white males. Louisiana was forced to abandon its grandfather clause, which was identical to the unconstitutional Oklahoma clause. It adopted the Mississippi interpretation requirement in its place.

In addition, Louisiana authorized its political parties to restrict access to party primaries and conventions by permitting political parties to impose additional qualifications on voters seeking to be registered as members of that party.[42] The Louisiana Democratic State Central Committee chose to forbid participation by blacks. Its primary rule stated that, "no one shall be permitted to vote at said primary except electors of the white race."[43] As a consequence, any blacks who were permitted to register were registered as Republicans. The Democratic Party's dominance was so complete in Louisiana that the candidate elected during the party's primary election inevitably took office. Blacks, who could not vote in the Democratic party primary, had no input into the selection of their federal representatives or their state officials.

In 1944, the U.S. Supreme Court declared these whites-only primaries unconstitutional.[44] The Louisiana Democratic Party repealed its white primary rule[45] and black voter registration increased in Louisiana from 957 in 1942, to 161,410 by 1956. To reverse the increasing black enfranchisement, Louisiana actively employed the interpretation test adopted in 1921. Although in the 1940s and 1950s many more blacks were literate than in 1921, the Registrars of voters in Louisiana successfully manipulated Louisiana's interpretation test to disenfranchise even highly educated blacks.

In 1954, the State of Louisiana distributed to each parish registrar of voters a manual entitled, "Voter Qualification Laws in Louisiana – The Key to Victory in the Segregation Struggle." Its authors, William M. Shaw and William M. Rainach, both of Claiborne Parish, were chairman and counsel, respectively, of a "Joint Legislative Committee to provide ways and means whereby our existing social order shall be preserved and our institutions and ways of life . . . maintained."[46] Parish registrars were instructed to purge their voter's rolls and to strictly enforce the registration criteria, especially the requirement that each person attempting to register interpret the United States or the Louisiana Constitution. Although the manual did not expressly direct registrars to deny to blacks their right to register to vote, the title of the manual makes that intent clear.

Judge Wisdom recognized this discriminatory intent and declared that the registrar's "raw power" to grant or withhold registration was in violation of both the due process and equal protection clauses of the Fourteenth Amendment.[47] Judge Wisdom agreed with Henry Williams' argument in Mississippi that local registrars had too much discretion to determine who could and who could not vote. The interpretation barrier was lifted in 1963 and large numbers of blacks could now successfully register. As noted earlier, in 1936, Hatfield was one of a very small number of blacks in Louisiana with a voter's registration card.

In 1940, Hatfield enrolled in Xavier University in New Orleans, the only institution of higher learning in the United States that is both historically black and Catholic. Xavier was founded in 1915 by Sr. Katherine Drexel and her religious order, Sisters of the Blessed Sacrament, as a coeducational secondary school for blacks. Drexel, a wealthy white heiress from Philadelphia, dedicated her entire fortune to the education of blacks and Native Americans. In 1891, she founded a religious order, the Sisters of the Blessed Sacrament for Indians and Colored People, and, by 1915, her order was staffing schools for Native Americans in New Mexico, Arizona, Nebraska, South Dakota, Oklahoma and Pennsylvania and schools for American blacks in Virginia, Texas, Tennessee, Georgia, Alabama, Mississippi, Pennsylvania, and Louisiana.

Xavier benefitted from her largesse and, in 1917, Xavier became more than a secondary school when the order added a Normal School in which to train teachers. Then in 1925, it established the College of Liberal Arts and Sciences and Xavier became a University. Xavier is highly regarded for its ability to prepare students for medical fields and related sciences; a high percentage of its graduates are successfully placed in medical schools.

Hatfield attended Xavier, but he wasn't interested in medical school or in a medicine-related profession. Hatfield had plans to study law. He worked hard to maintain high grades so that he would be eligible and well prepared to attend the Louisiana State University Law School. Hatfield felt confident that he would be admitted. The *Gaines* case, decided in 1938, required that a state admit its qualified black applicants to its public white schools if the state did not otherwise offer the same training at a state's public black schools within the state. Louisiana did not offer law school training anywhere except at LSU and Hatfield was planning to be there.

Notes

1.*Provision of Adequate Educational Facilities for Negroes*, paper read at the Annual Meeting of the Southern Regional Unit of the National Catholic Education Asso. (Mar. 12, 1945).

2.1880 Census of East Baton Rouge Par., La. 5, supr. dist. 1, enum. dist. 103, but see death certificate which shows both parents to be natives of Louisiana. Reel # OD 25, Orleans Deaths, Vital Records (1931).

3.Charles Hatfield, "Brief autobiographical summary" (unpublished Dec. 1998).

4.1880 Census of East Baton Rouge Par., La. 5, supr. dist. 1, enum. dist. 103.

5.Interview with Hatfield (Oct. 29, 1998).

6.*Lee v. N.O. Great Northern R. Co.*, 125 La. 236, 239, 51 So. 182, 183 (1910). 1970 La. Acts 46 (Jun. 18, 1970), repealed 1983 La. Acts 441 (Jul. 2, 1983), defined as white only those with one thirty-second or less of Negro blood. La. R.S. 42:267 (1970). Louisiana law currently permits the parents of a child to determine and report their respective races on their child's birth certificate without statutory guidance or a numeric formula. La. R.S. 40:34 (2000).

7.VIRGINIA R. DOMINGUEZ, WHITE BY DEFINITION; SOCIAL CLASSIFICATION IN CREOLE LOUISIANA 161 (Rutgers Univ. Press 1986).

8.Interview with Hatfield (Dec. 11, 1998).

9.Vol. 18, Page 64, Property Records, East Baton Rouge Parish (Nov. 10, 1894).

10.CIVIL BIRTH AND DEATH REGISTERS FOR THE CITY OF BATON ROUGE 1874-1918 Part II, Page 6 (Judy Riflel, et al, *La Comite' des Archives de la Louisiane* Baton Rouge 2001).

11.Vol. 37, Page 597, Property Records, East Baton Rouge Parish (Feb. 9, 1907).

12.Petition, para IV, *Succession of Richard Douse and Ann M. Douse*, Probate No 3,364 (22nd JDC, Par. of East Baton Rouge, La., Jul. 29, 1922).

13.Application for Reimbursement (Jan. 20, 1922), Richard Douse Pension files, National Archives.

14.Bill from the Progressive Joint Stock Co., Undertakers and Funeral Directors, 1151 Convention Street, Baton Rouge, La. (Jan. 20, 1922) in Application for Reimbursement (Jan. 20, 1922), Richard Douse Pension files, National Archives.

15.Judgment, *Succession of Richard Douse and Ann M. Douse*, Probate No. 3,364, (22nd JDC, Par. of East Baton Rouge, La. Jul. 29, 1922)..

16.Book 114, Entry 125, Orig 1, Bundle 391, Property Records, East Baton Rouge Parish (Jan. 23, 1923).

17.Book 115, Entry 36-38, Orig 40-42, Bundle 393, Property Records of East Baton Rouge Parish (Feb. 7, 1923).

18.Book 185, Entry 152, Orig 70, Bundle 617, Property Records of East Baton Rouge Parish(Jan. 22, 1927).In a strange quirk of fate, this property is now used as a law office.

19.Orleans Deaths - Vital Records, Reel # OD 25, p. 1244, Louisiana State Archives, Baton Rouge.

20.The Federal Public Housing Authority provided low rent housing units for persons meeting certain income categories. In July 31, 1945, 769,000 low income housing units were available; 145,584 were designated for or occupied by blacks. NEGRO YEAR BOOK 1947 340 (Jessie Parkhurst Guzman, ed.) Dept. of Records and Research, Tuskegee Institute (1947). Of the seven Permanent Public Housing Projects in Louisiana in 1945 that could be occupied by black tenants, four were in New Orleans: Magnolia Street, Lafitte Avenue, Calliope Street and St. Bernard Avenue. NEGRO YEAR BOOK 1947 346. Louisiana law required separate black and white housing communities. 1924 La. Acts 118.

21.FREDERICK CHARLES GREEN, JEAN-JACQUES ROUSSEAU; A CRITICAL STUDY OF HIS LIFE AND WRITINGS 287-288(Cambridge Univ. Press 1955).

22.Times-Picayune, Jul. 17, 1993, 3rd ed., B1.

23.Letter from Hatfield to author 5 (Dec. 16, 1998).

24.Charles J. Hatfield, *On Citizenship and the Suffrage*, unpublished paper (1946).

25.LA. CONST. of 1921, art. VIII, s. 1(c-d).

26.*State v. Perkins*, 211 La. 993, 1005-06 (1947).

27.Ms. CONST. of 1890, s. 244.

28.U.S. v. Mississippi, 229 F. Supp. 925, 932 (S.D. Miss. 1964).

29.*Williams v. Mississippi*, 170 U.S. 213, 221 (1898).

30.*Williams v. Mississippi*, 170 U.S. at 225.

31.*Trudeau v. Barnes*, 1 F.Supp. 453 (E.D. La. 1932).

32.MOMS MABLEY AND EDDIE PARTON, NOW HEAR THIS! - PART I (Mercury Records).

33.*Trudeau v. Barnes*, 65 F.2d.563, 564 (5th Cir.), *writ den.* 290 U.S. 659 (1933).

34.*Williams v. McCulley*, 128 F. Supp. 897, 899 (W.D. La. Alex. Div. 1955).

35.*U.S. v. La.*, 225 F. Supp. 353, 355, 386, 385, 356(E.D. La., B.R. Div. 1963).

36.LA. CONST. of 1868, art. 98.

37.LA. CONST. of 1879, art. 188.

38.LA. CONST. of 1898, art. 197, s.3-5.

39.*U.S. v. La.*, 225 F. Supp. 353, 374.

40.JOE GRAY TAYLOR, LOUISIANA 142 (W.W. Norton & Co. 1976).

41.*Frank Guinn v. U.S.*, 238 U.S. 347, 365 (1915).

42. "No person shall vote at any primary election or in any convention or other political assembly held for the purpose of nominating any candidate for public office unless such person is at the time a registered voter, with such additional qualifications as may be prescribed by the party for which candidates for public office are to be nominated, ..." LA. CONST. of 1921, art. 200 (1920).

43.Mimeographed *Resolution* of the Democratic State Central Committee of Louisiana, adopted October 1, 1935, sent to O. Douglas Weeks by Mr. A.W. Newlin, Secretary to the Committee, in O. Douglas Weeks, *The White Primary*, 8-2 MISSISSIPPI L. J. 135, 140 (Dec. 1935).

44.*Smith v. Allwright*, 321 U.S. 649 (1944).

45.O. Douglas Weeks, *The White Primary: 1944-1948*, 42 Amer. Pol. Sci. Rev. 500, 503 (1948).

46.House Concurrent Resolution No. 27 (1954).

47.*U.S. v. La.*, 225 F. Supp. 353, 391.

# Chapter 6.

## The Gaines Case

*This case means nothing in 1937, but in 2000 A.D.
somebody will look back on the record and wonder why
the South spent so much money in keeping rights away
from Negroes rather than granting them.*

Charles Hamilton Houston[1]


In 1938, when the United States Supreme Court decided *Missouri
ex rel. Gaines v. Canada*,[2] Hatfield was astounded by the decision. He
thought the Court's decision was ridiculous and corrupt. It was clear to
Hatfield that separate could not be equal.

Lloyd Gaines had sought admission to the University of Missouri
School of Law. Although he was qualified, the University refused to
admit him for the sole reason that he was not white. The attorneys for
Gaines argued that the University's refusal violated his right to equal
protection guaranteed by the Fourteenth Amendment of the United States
Constitution. Hatfield agreed. In Hatfield's opinion, discrimination based
on skin color had lasted too long in the United States and needed to come
to an end.

The United States Supreme Court also agreed with Gaines'
attorneys. Missouri was in violation of the Fourteenth Amendment
because Missouri did not provide instruction in law for blacks within the
borders of the state while Missouri did provide instruction in law, within
its borders, for whites. Missouri excluded blacks from attending the only
law school it had established, the University of Missouri School of Law.
"[T]his discrimination," the Court declared, "if not relieved by the

provisions we shall presently discuss, would constitute a denial of equal protection."[3] The provisions discussed by the *Gaines* Court left Hatfield irate.

The *Gaines* Court required that Missouri provide for its black citizens, within the State of Missouri, the same educational opportunities as it provided for its white citizens within its borders, but permitted the state to establish separate facilities for blacks and whites so long as those segregated facilities were equal. It did not require that existing schools admit blacks. Hatfield was disgusted with the Court. He knew that without the complete desegregation of all educational facilities, educational opportunities for blacks would never be equal to opportunities available to whites. He was disappointed that the Court could not see the inequality inevitable with separation, but, instead, continued to permit segregation by skin color. He knew that equal treatment and equal facilities were not the intent of the segregating states.

In the *Gaines* case, attorneys for Missouri had argued that its laws had created Lincoln University and that Lincoln University was the proper institution to provide higher education opportunities for its black citizens. For any courses or any subjects offered at the State University of Missouri but not offered at Lincoln University, Missouri's laws allowed the Board of Curators in Missouri to arrange for its black residents to attend a university in any adjacent state, and to pay their reasonable tuition fees.[4] Missouri authorized and required Lincoln University to "afford to the negro [sic] people of the state opportunity for training up to the standard furnished at the University of Missouri whenever necessary and practicable . . . "[5] Missouri argued that through this authorization the state had created equal opportunities for its black citizens to pursue any course of study offered to its white citizens.

The Court applauded Missouri, noting that it had at least attempted to fulfill its obligation "to provide Negroes with advantages for higher education substantially equal to the advantages afforded to white students."[6] Missouri was known to be a pioneer in providing higher educational opportunities for blacks. It became the first state to offer post high school training to blacks when, in 1870, it opened a normal school to train black teachers. Although motivated by a desire to replace teachers from northern states, who were then present in large numbers in Missouri, Missouri was "the only State in the Union which . . . [at least by statute] . . . established a separate university for negroes [sic] on the same basis as the state university for white students."[7]

The Court decided, nonetheless, that the state's practice of providing scholarships for blacks to attend school outside of the state did not satisfy the equal protection requirement of the Fourteenth Amendment. It determined that the payment of tuition fees for school attendance in another state "does not remove the discrimination" of offering law school training within the state to whites, while not offering law school training within the state to blacks. The Court stated that, "By the operation of the laws of Missouri a privilege has been created for white law students which is denied to Negroes by reason of their race . . . This is a denial of the equality of legal right to the enjoyment of the privilege which the State has set up . . . "[8]

Equal provision of educational opportunities must be made within the state for blacks seeking an education or the state could no longer offer these educational opportunities to whites. The Court held that Gaines "was entitled to be admitted to the law school of the State University in the absence of other and proper provision for his legal training within the State."[9] Missouri provided no other law school within the state, so Lloyd Gaines traveled to Chicago, where he had attended graduate school, to retrieve his belongings in preparation for attending the law school at the University of Missouri.

Lloyd Gaines did not return to Missouri. Lucile H. Bluford, then managing editor of the *Kansas City Call*, and, later, an applicant to the University of Missouri, reported that Gaines spoke at the Centennial Methodist Church in Kansas City on April 27, 1939. Bluford then accompanied Gaines "to the Union Station the night he left Kansas City and saw him board the train for Chicago. He never returned to St. Louis as far as his family and his lawyers know."[10] Lloyd Gaines was last seen leaving his dormitory carrying his belongings. Although the national press cooperated in trying to locate him, carrying his picture in newspapers across the country, he was never found. The law school at the University of Missouri remained segregated.

In response to the *Gaines* decision, Missouri and North Carolina organized law schools at their historically black institutions. The Supreme Court had required that blacks be admitted to white schools only in the absence of some other provision for legal training within the state. To avoid desegregating their historically white state law schools, and still comply with the *Gaines* decision, each state could establish a separate law school for its black students so long as a "substantially equal" opportunity for a legal education was provided by the state within the state's borders.

In reaching this decision, the Court followed a landmark 1896 Louisiana case, *Plessy v. Ferguson*. On June 9, 1892, Homer Plessy purchased a first-class passage on the East Louisiana Railway to travel from New Orleans to Covington, Louisiana. He took a seat in a coach reserved for "passengers of the white race" and was asked by the conductor to move to the coach "assigned by said company (the railroad) for persons not of the white race."[11] When he refused, he was arrested and fined $25.00. Curiously, neither the restaurant at the train station nor the waiting room where Plessy purchased his ticket was segregated by law until 1894.

Plessy entered the railroad car reserved for whites to challenge the constitutionality of a July 10, 1890, act of the Louisiana Legislature requiring separate railroad cars for whites and blacks.[12] Plessy was a member of the politically active Citizens' Committee for the Annulment of Act 111, commonly known as the Separate Car Act. The Citizens' Committee had organized to overturn the segregation legislation newly appearing in post-Reconstruction Louisiana, especially the Separate Car Act.

The battle to integrate street cars in New Orleans was not new. Before the Civil War began, public transportation was segregated. Blacks were relegated to traveling only in those cars which carried a large black star and were called "star cars." During the war, black soldiers objected to this discrimination. They had to wait for overcrowded "star cars" while watching half-empty cars without stars roll past them. After protests and unpleasant confrontations during which black soldiers abused those conductors who asked them to exit the streetcars not displaying the stars, black officers were allowed to ride in the cars reserved for whites.

In 1867, the stars were removed from the streetcars. By 1869, state law prohibited "discrimination on account of race or color" against travelers on common carriers within the state.[13] Anyone discriminated against in seating or service while riding the streetcars could sue the railroad to recover damages. Twenty-three years later, the 1890 Separate Car Act re-instituted segregation on street cars in New Orleans.

Louis Andre' Martinet, an 1876 graduate of the Straight University law department in New Orleans, mobilized the black New Orleans community by denouncing the Separate Car law in the newspaper he founded in 1889, the *Daily Crusader*. He organized the Citizens' Committee for the Annulment of Act 111 to focus the protest. Martinet had formulated the strategy of bringing test cases before the courts, and Plessy had agreed to test the Separate Car Act.

In an earlier challenge to the statute, also prompted by the Citizens' Committee, Daniel Desdunes had been arrested by the Louisiana secret police for riding from one state to another in a car reserved by state law for whites. He was tried and acquitted by a Louisiana state court. The court determined that the Louisiana law requiring segregation of railroad passengers by skin color was unconstitutional because it sought to regulate interstate travel.[14] The state of Louisiana could not tell a railroad engaged in interstate commerce what it could or could not do. The Citizens' Committee had won its first test case. In its second case, Homer Plessy would ride a train that traveled only within the state; one not engaged in interstate travel.

Plessy argued, as had Desdunes, that the Louisiana statute violated his rights under both the Thirteenth Amendment to the United States Constitution, which abolished involuntary servitude except as punishment for crimes, and the Fourteenth Amendment, which prohibits states from enacting discriminatory legislation. After losing in the state courts, Plessy pursued his case to the United States Supreme Court. Albion Tourgee' filed his brief on behalf of Plessy seeking an end to segregation just one month after Booker T. Washington gave his Accommodation Speech at the Cotton States Exposition in Atlanta in 1895 stating:

> In all things that are purely social, we can be as separate as the fingers, yet one as the hand in all things essential to mutual progress. . . . The wisest among my race understand that the agitation of questions of social equality is the extremest folly . . . The opportunity to earn a dollar in a factory just now is worth infinitely more than the opportunity to spend a dollar in an opera house.[15]

The Supreme Court rejected Plessy's Thirteenth Amendment argument stating that, "A statute which implies merely a legal distinction between the white and colored races . . . has no tendency to destroy the legal equality of the two races, or reestablish a state of involuntary servitude."[16] According to the Court, the law separating the races in streetcars did not reestablish slavery.

Examining the Fourteenth Amendment claim, the Court determined that the Fourteenth Amendment did not intend "to abolish distinctions based upon color, or to enforce social, as distinguished from political, equality . . ."[17] It rejected Plessy's argument that the forced separation of the races "stamps the colored race with a badge of inferiority." The court concluded that, if the colored race is stamped with such a badge, that badge of inferiority exists "solely because the colored race chooses to put that construction upon it."[18] It reasoned that whites and blacks were treated equally by the law as whites were separated just as completely from blacks as blacks were separated from whites.

The Court stated that social segregation was not the target of the Fourteenth Amendment. Rather, the separation by skin color of persons using public facilities was a generally accepted phenomenon. To support its position, the Court noted that the public schools of Washington, D.C., under the supervision of the same Republican Congress that had sent the Fourteenth Amendment to the states for ratification, remained segregated.[19] The Court reasoned that the authors of the Fourteenth Amendment could not have intended that amendment to end social segregation in the states while they allowed social segregation to continue in the nation's capital.

The Court also cited the case of *Roberts v. City of Boston.* Prior to the Civil War, the state of Massachusetts had been a hotbed for anti-slavery activism, yet the Supreme Court of that state permitted Boston to maintain segregated elementary schools. The U.S. Supreme Court sought to show, by citing *Roberts*, that even in that anti-slavery environment social segregation was acceptable.

In *Roberts v. City of Boston,* five-year-old Sarah C. Roberts objected to walking past five primary schools in Boston to attend one of the two primary schools established for the exclusive use of black children. She wanted to attend a school closer to her home. Sarah Roberts' attorneys argued that, "maintenance of separate schools tends to deepen and perpetuate the odious distinction of caste, founded in a deep-rooted prejudice in public opinion."[20] The Massachusetts Supreme Court responded that this deep-rooted prejudice was "not created by law, and probably cannot be changed by law."[21]

The court explained that a citizen's rights could be regulated by law and that, once those rights are determined, they are entitled to the protection of the law. The court examined the law and determined that a school committee annually elected by the inhabitants of Boston was authorized to organize the schools in the city and assign students to those schools. Absent prohibiting legislation, the Boston school committee was free to maintain separate schools if it thought them best. The court found the schools for black children "as well conducted in all respects, and as well fitted, in point of capacity and qualification of the instructors," as the white schools.[22] It allowed Boston to continue to educate its black and white students in separate schools.

The *Plessy* Court examined the language of the Louisiana act and found no support for Plessy's belief that the state legislature intended to impose a badge of inferiority on blacks. According to the Court, Plessy's argument "assumes that social prejudices may be overcome by legislation, and that equal rights cannot be secured to the Negro except by an enforced commingling of the two races. We cannot accept this proposition to be true . . . Legislation is powerless to eradicate racial instincts, or to abolish distinctions based upon physical differences. . . "[23]

The *Plessy* Court failed to report that in 1855, only five and one-half years after *Roberts v. Boston*, and well before the Fourteenth Amendment was ratified, the Massachusetts Legislature prohibited distinctions "on account of the race, color or religious opinions" in the selection of scholars into its public schools.[24] The Massachusetts act allowed any child who was denied admission to a school on account of race, color or religious opinions to claim damages from the jurisdiction supporting that school. At the time the United States Supreme Court cited *Roberts v. Boston* in support of segregation, the contemporaneous law in Massachusetts prohibited segregated schools, in contrast to the result reached by the Court in *Plessy*.

The Citizens' Committee was sorely disappointed with the outcome of the *Plessy* decision. Its members had seen social prejudices falter when segregation was no longer supported by the law. They had borne arms, attended schools, and sat in the legislature with men of both races. They had witnessed their social status change to their detriment in the reactionary period following the Republican's loss of power in the state. They knew that the equal rights promised to blacks by the recent amendments to the United States Constitution could not be secured in the south unless the federal government would lend its support. They looked to the Supreme Court for relief and found it had turned its back on their freedom. That Court would not recognize that segregated facilities were inherently unequal until 1954.

The *Plessy* decision was decided by an application of the Thirteenth and Fourteenth Amendments. The *Desdunes* decision, with its contrary result, rested on the Interstate Commerce clause of the

Constitution, U.S.CONST. art. I, s.8, cl.3, "The Congress shall have Power To regulate commerce with foreign Nations, and among the several States, and with the Indian Tribes." It was consistent with an earlier Supreme Court decision concerning segregation aboard common carriers in ruling that a state could not regulate interstate commerce.

In July 1872, Mrs. Josephine DeCuir, a person of color, boarded a packet vessel in New Orleans to travel to her plantation in Pointe Coupee Parish further up the Mississippi River but within the State of Louisiana. She purchased passage to a landing called the Hermitage and requested a place in the ladies' upper cabin. She was denied that opportunity because that cabin was reserved for whites. The steamboat captain informed DeCuir of the boat's regulation that, "colored persons are not placed in the same cabin as white persons, or allowed to eat at the same table with them . . ."[25] and offered DeCuir passage in the lower cabin. DeCuir refused those accommodations and spent the night in a chair in a recess behind the ladies' cabin.

Not long after that ride, DeCuir brought an action for damages under a Louisiana statute that regulated "all persons engaged within this state in the business of common carriers of passengers."[26] That statute prohibited "discrimination on account of race or color." DeCuir, traveling on a packet vessel from one point in Louisiana to another, believed that Louisiana's anti-discrimination law entitled her to ride in the upper cabin.

The Louisiana courts agreed with DeCuir, but the U. S. Supreme Court did not. The river boat on which DeCuir traveled was engaged in interstate travel. It carried passengers from New Orleans to Vicksburg, Mississippi; it did not travel only within the State of Louisiana. The Court noted that the Constitution gave to Congress the sole power to regulate interstate commerce. State legislation which interfered with the freedom of interstate commerce encroached upon the exclusive power of Congress to regulate that commerce. The State of Louisiana could not tell a packet engaged in interstate commerce what it could or could not do. It could not tell the packet to refrain from discrimination in the *Hall* case, just as it could not require a railroad to provide segregated facilities as in the *Desdunes* case. State legislation regulating interstate commerce is unconstitutional no matter its effect.

In a 1905 Maryland case, the Court of Appeals of Maryland declared its state statute, requiring the segregation of passengers in railroad cars, invalid as to interstate passengers.[27] William Henry Harrison Hart was an interstate passenger, traveling from New York City

94

to Washington, D.C., through the State of Maryland. When the train entered Maryland, he refused to move from the car in which he was riding to the car reserved for blacks. The state court held, in accord with the *Hall* and *Desdunes* cases, that no state had the power to require segregation in interstate commerce. The *Hart* case suggests that, had more attorneys been available to handle the volume of litigation, the precedent established by *Desdunes* may have ended segregation in all interstate travel much earlier in our national history.

For common carriers traveling only within a state's borders, Congress did not have exclusive authority and a state could decide whether or not passengers would be segregated. Plessy's train traveled only within the state and Louisiana, not Congress, had power over the state's intrastate commerce. Louisiana could regulate its intrastate commerce so long as it did not violate some other provision of the Constitution. The Court found no Constitutional violation.

By permitting state-mandated segregation, the Court's decision in *Plessy* endorsed the oppression of blacks, essentially restoring many blacks to their pre-Civil War status as slaves to plantation owners. It ushered in an era of legal, social and economic repression that continues to permeate individual and collective decision making in the United States. The Court's *Plessy* decision, as had its *Dred Scott* decision of 1857, instructed that blacks had "no rights which the white man was bound to respect."[28]

In 1938, when the *Gaines* case was decided, the Court was not ready to overturn *Plessy*. The Court glibly accepted the claim that facilities, although separate, could be equal despite the pervasive and pronounced inequality of public facilities throughout the South. The logic of the *Gaines* decision eluded Hatfield and encouraged him to study law.

By any objective standards, Gaines had earned the right to enter Missouri's law school. Were it not for his skin color, Gaines would have been admitted into Missouri's law school without protest. No new law school established to segregate Gaines would match the quality of the law school already available to whites in Missouri. The new school would be separate, but it would not be equal. Hatfield planned to move the Court to alter its holdings in *Plessy* and *Gaines*. Hatfield wanted the Court to say that segregation, at its core, was a violation of the Fourteenth Amendment and contrary to natural law. He planned to fight his way into LSU, but first he had to finish at Xavier.

# Notes

1.Buffalo Courier Express, Mar. 23, 1937, Papers of Charles Houston, Moreland-Springarn Research Center, Howard Univ. in JUAN WILLIAMS, THURGOOD MARSHALL 96 (Random House 1998).

2.305 U.S. 337 (1938).

3.*Gaines*, 305 U.S. at 345.

4.Mo. St. Ann. s. 9622, p.7328 quoted in *Gaines*, 305 U.S. at 342-43; Mo. Appropriations 86-87 (Apr. 15, 1921).

5.Mo. Appropriations 86-87, Sec. 3 (Apr. 15, 1921); Mo. R.S. 1939, s. 10774.

6.*Gaines*, 305 U.S. at 344.

7.*Gaines*, 305 U.S. at 345.

8.*Gaines*, 305 U.S. at 349-50.

9.*Gaines*, 305 U.S. at 352.

10.Lucile H. Bluford, *The Lloyd Gaines Story*, 32 J. OF ED. SOC. 242, 246 (Feb. 1958).

11.*Plessy*, 163 U.S. 537, 538 (1896).

12.1890 La. Acts 111, s. 1 (amended by 1894 La. Acts 177 (Jul. 12, 1894), repealed 1972 La. Acts 262, s.1 (Jul. 5, 1972)).

13.1869 La. Acts 38, s. 1 (Feb. 23, 1869).

14.RODOLPHE LUCIEN DESDUNES, OUR PEOPLE AND OUR HISTORY 143-144 (1911, 1973 translation by Sister Dorothy Olga McCants, Louisiana State Univ. Press); *Accord, State ex rel W.C. Abbott v. W.O. Hicks, Judge,* 44 La. An. 770, 11 So. 74 (1892).

15.LANGSTON HUGHES, MILTON MELTZER & C. ERIC LINCOLN, A PICTORIAL HISTORY OF BLACK AMERICANS 244 (5th ed., Crown Publishers, Inc. 1983.) Booker T. Washington, 1856-1915, was founder and President of Tuskegee Institute in Alabama and was a celebrated proponent of and spokesperson for industrial education for blacks. As a black economic nationalist, Washington established the National Negro Business League in 1900 and counseled blacks to seek economic self-sufficiency and to soft-pedal civil rights and social equality.

16.*Plessy*, 163 U.S. at 543.

17.*Plessy*, 163 U.S. at 544.

18.*Plessy*, 163 U.S. at 551.

19.*Plessy*, 163 U.S. at 545. Public schools in Washington, D.C. remained segregated until after the decision in *Bolling v. Sharpe*, 347 U.S. 497 (1954), consolidated with *Brown v. Bd. of Ed of Topeka, Kan..*, 347 U.S. 483 (1954).

20.*Roberts v. City of Boston*, 59 Mass. (5 Cush.) 198, 209 (1849).

21.*Roberts v. Boston*, 59 Mass. at 209.

22.*Roberts v. Boston*, 59 Mass. at 205-206.

23.*Plessy*, 163 U.S. at 551.

24.1855 Mass. Acts 256 (April 28, 1855).

25.*DeCuir v. Benson*, 27 La. Ann. 1 (1875), *rev'd sub nom. Hall v. DeCuir*, 95 U.S. 485 (1877).

26.1869 La. Acts 38, s.1 (Feb. 23, 1869).

27.*Hart v. Maryland*, 100 Md. 595, 60 Atl. 457, 463 (1905).

28.*Dred Scott v. John F. A. Sandford*, 60 U.S. 393, 407 (1857).

# Chapter 7.

## The Army

*Once let the black man get upon his person the brass letters U.S.; let him get an eagle on his button, and a musket on his shoulder and bullets in his pocket, and there is no power on earth or under the earth which can deny that he has earned the right of citizenship in the United States.*

Frederick Douglass 1863[1]

While attending college at Xavier, Hatfield found employment with the United States Post Office at the Mid-City Station on Canal Street. He worked as a letter carrier, climbing steps to deliver mail to boxes affixed next to the front doors of raised houses in New Orleans. Hatfield's feet ached constantly. After a year, the stair climbing became too painful and he asked to be transferred to a position within the postal service that did not require the walking and climbing that hurt so much. He was not hired as a postal clerk, or in any other position which would allow him to work inside a Post Office building, because of the color of his skin.

Hatfield left the postal service and found employment where he could. He worked at the New Orleans Country Club waiting tables part-time. He worked as a second cook at the Southern Yacht Club, and at the West End Club where he and his father had worked before. He worked at other clubs and at hotels as a waiter; he worked as a butler for families; he sold insurance. He worked for the Works Project Administration building a seawall in New Orleans and worked with pipe fitters on various jobs.

Pipefitting appealed to a friend of Hatfield's who enrolled in the Delgado Community College to study plumbing. Begun in 1921 as the Isaac Delgado Central Trades School, Delgado Community College offered occupational and technical training programs. Hatfield's friend encouraged Hatfield to go to Delgado with him. Plumbing offered the promise of steady employment as a skilled laborer and the possibility of self-employment as a plumbing contractor, but Hatfield declined. He had plans to become a lawyer. He was determined to finish his studies at Xavier, and, by pushing the Fourteenth Amendment beyond the *Gaines* case, to attend the law school at the Louisiana State University.

While in college, Hatfield managed to woo and win Beulah Gertrude Ozenne. Beulah was a Creole originally from Jeannerette, Louisiana. She had come to Algiers, near New Orleans, when her father moved there to look for work. Beulah's cousin, Doris, visiting from Jeannerette, met Virgil Burthe at a dance. When Virgil came to visit Doris, he brought his best friend, Charles Hatfield, with him. Beulah fell in love. Beulah's mother said of Hatfield, "Oh, but that's a pretty man!" When Charles asked Beulah to go to the movies with him, Beulah agreed. Beulah's sister, Blanche, and Charles' sister, Juanita, both attended St. Mary's Academy on Orleans Street, the same school Hatfield's mother had attended in 1898. Blanche and Juanita, encouraged the couple, although very little encouragement was needed.

Beulah and Charles were married July 29, 1942. Beulah had been trained as a seamstress in high school and was working in a sewing factory when she met Hatfield. She learned tailoring there and sewed beautifully. She wanted to continue to work at the factory after her marriage but didn't. She did continue to sew. She made shirts, suits, dresses and skirts for her family and curtains for her home. Beulah remembers, "I left my parent's house on Broad Street, not a big house, but a very nice house, to move into the Lafitte housing project with Hatfield and his mother. I have no regrets. I loved my mother-in-law. She was a wonderful woman."[2]

World War II brought the U.S. Army into Hatfield's life. Shortly after the United States entered the war, a professor at Xavier University convinced Hatfield and other senior students there to join the Enlisted Officers Reserve Corps, 8th Command U.S.A., in preparation for Army service. The Army had promised these advanced students that they would be allowed to finish school at Xavier while in the Reserve Corps and then could enter Officers Training School as college graduates. Hatfield would not have been drafted into military service. He was classified 3-A, exempt from the military draft, because he was the sole support for both his birth family and his family by marriage.[3] Nonetheless, Hatfield signed up for the Enlisted Officers Reserve Corps in January 1942 and enrolled in a military tactics course at Xavier.

On his wedding day, Hatfield received notice of his enlistment in the Enlisted Reserve Corps effective August 8, 1942.[4] Hatfield had become a member of the U.S. Army Reserve Corps and he looked forward to serving his country. He continued his studies at Xavier during the 1942-43 school year, but never got to Officers Training School. He was called to active duty before he finished school and reported to Camp Beauregard, Louisiana, on May 10, 1943, as a private. He, and most of the other black college students who had hoped to be trained as officers, ended up in the infantry.

Camp Beauregard, five miles northeast of Alexandria, Louisiana, had been constructed in 1917 as a training camp for World War I soldiers. A total of 44,712 troops trained there in 1917 and 1918. After the war, the fifteen square miles of land were used as a summer camp for the Louisiana National Guard and as headquarters for District E of the Civilian Conservation Corps in the 1930s.[5] The Louisiana National Guard still uses the site for summer training exercises.

Hatfield arrived at the Camp Beauregard Reception Center and stood in the rain along with black college students from other Louisiana schools who had joined the Enlisted Officers Reserve Corps. The white soldiers waited inside dry buildings. It occurred to Hatfield that the Army didn't care too much about its black recruits.

Hatfield could have resigned his military commission even after arriving at Camp Beauregard. Under a joint resolution of Congress:

> Any member of any reserve component of the Army of the United States below the rank of captain who is ordered into the active military service of the United States pursuant to this joint resolution, who has any person or persons dependent solely upon him for support, and who has no other means of support except the wages, salary or other compensation for personal services that he earns, may resign or shall be discharged upon his own request made within twenty days of the date of his entry into such active military service.[6]

Hatfield was the sole support for his wife and mother, but was willing to serve his country in a fight for freedom as had his grandfather before him.

Hatfield's March 12, 1943, medical examination at Camp Livingston disclosed the deformity of his congenital club foot. Captain James W. Chambers of the Army Medical Corps recommended that he be assigned to limited duty only.[7] Hatfield was accepted for service on May 10, 1943, and, notwithstanding his foot, was assigned to the infantry. Hatfield's opportunity to attend Enlisted Officers Reserve Corps training failed to materialize.

Soon after he began his military training, Hatfield was injured while digging a bivouac in the middle of the night. He fell into the six by six hole and was hospitalized for twenty-eight days. As a result of his injuries, Hatfield was sent to the Army Hospital at Camp Claiborne, Louisiana, southwest of Alexandria. Hatfield was luckier than others. Many of his fellow soldiers died in training from heart attacks, from exhaustion or by accident or intent.

Camp Claiborne was a tent camp that operated from 1940 to 1945. It was used to train infantry, airborne, engineering, and service forces and to house prisoners of war. Nearly 500,000 troops trained there. The hospital doctors - Hatfield was surprised to find "colored" doctors there - recommended that Hatfield either be discharged or be put on limited duty. The doctors noted his college courses in economics and his uncorrected club foot, which had been aggravated by his infantry duties. They suggested that Hatfield be assigned to limited duty in finance or in personnel to accommodate his disability and better utilize his college training. The Army chose to discharge Hatfield instead. Hatfield left the service in October 1943. Despite his short term of service, Hatfield was a veteran of the United States Armed Services, and entitled to all of the benefits accruing to that status. He had shown himself willing to serve. Hatfield returned to New Orleans to finish college.

### Notes

1. BENJAMIN QUARLES, THE NEGRO IN THE CIVIL WAR 184 (DaCapo Press, Inc. 1989).

2.Interview with Beulah Hatfield (Oct. 29, 1998).

3.Selective Training and Service Act of 1940, ch. 720, 54 Stat. 885, s. 5.(e) (1940).

4.Letter from G.S. Higginbotham, 1st Lieutenant, A.G.D., Assistant Adjutant General, Office of the Corps Area Commander, Headquarters Eighth Corps Area to District Recruiting and Induction Officer, U.S. Army, New Orleans, La. (Jul. 25, 1942).

5.POWELL A. CASEY, ENCYCLOPEDIA OF FORTS, POSTS, NAMED CAMPS, AND OTHER MILITARY INSTALLATIONS IN LOUISIANA, 1700-1981, 21-23 (Claitor's Publ. Div. 1983).

6.54 Stat., Ch 68, s.3(e) (Aug. 27, 1940).

7.Record at Time of Reporting for Active Duty of Members of Reserve Components for Charles Joseph Hatfield (Mar. 12, 1943) St. Louis Army Archives.

Part 2.

Spawning

a

Law School

# Chapter 8.

## *Challenging an Institution*

*The whole history of the progress of human liberty
shows that all concessions yet made to her August
claims, have been born of earnest struggle. . . . If there
is no struggle there is no progress. Those who profess
to favor freedom and yet deprecate agitation, are men
who want crops without plowing up the ground, they
want rain without thunder and lightning. They want the
ocean without the awful roar of its many waters. . . .
power concedes nothing without a demand.*

*Frederick Douglass*[1]

Hatfield continued his studies at Xavier University during the summer sessions of 1944 and 1945 and the fall semester of 1945. He finished at the end of spring semester 1946, receiving a Bachelor of Philosophy degree from the College of Liberal Arts. He had earned 138 semester hours and majored in History, Spanish and English, with a minor in Economics and Political Science. Hatfield had initially enrolled in Xavier in the fall semester 1940 with an entrance deficiency in foreign languages.[2] After completing two semesters of high school Spanish to remove his deficiency he continued to study Spanish and eventually majored in and taught high school Spanish in New Orleans. Before he retired, he served as head of the Department of Languages at Carver Senior High School.

As a former employee, Hatfield readily found employment again with the Postal Service in New Orleans, this time sorting mail and in other capacities inside the Main Post Office at 600 Camp Street. He continued to work at the Post Office until 1963, except while he was in graduate school in Atlanta, Georgia, in 1947 and 1948.

A few of his coworkers at the Post Office shared Hatfield's interest in law and politics; others were not as hospitable. Hatfield spent long hours in discussions about current events and civil rights with coworkers John Rousseau and Frank Sypos. Rousseau was a feature writer and editorialist for the *New Orleans Sentinel*, the Louisiana edition of the *Pittsburgh Courier*, the Shreveport *Herald*, and the New Orleans *Louisiana Weekly* newspapers. Sypos was a white New Yorker who had moved to Louisiana and become friends with Hatfield and Rousseau. Their discussions often continued beyond the confines of the Post Office and sometimes included Alexander P. Tureaud, Hatfield's friend and attorney.

Hatfield and his coworkers applauded President Franklin D. Roosevelt's administration. Hatfield considered Roosevelt's New Deal the "most socially constructive legislation in the history of the country."[3] He considered Roosevelt the greatest president in the country's history. Roosevelt sought to reverse the impact of the Depression by instituting an aggressive program of government intervention. He planned to increase the purchasing power of individuals, especially farmers and wage-earners, to enable them to consume more of the output of the capitalists. Roosevelt expected that as the demand for goods increased, America's industrial capacity would grow and provide greater employment opportunities for workers. The demand for workers would then increase their wages and consequent purchasing power. President Roosevelt determined to "bring about a wiser, more equitable distribution of the national income"[4] in an effort to end the country's economic depression.

Roosevelt recognized that the social and economic problems facing the country were not local in scope, but national, and that their solution would have to come from the federal, and not the local, government. Roosevelt believed that the United States Constitution could be interpreted to support national solutions to these national problems so he proposed national legislation. Between January 1935 and June 1936, the United States Supreme Court struck down major components of Roosevelt's New Deal legislation declaring them unconstitutional.[5] The Court generally opposed the expansion of federal governmental power and narrowly interpreted the Interstate Commerce clause. The Court was reluctant to give Congress authority to regulate activities Congress had never before regulated.

On February 5, 1937, Roosevelt submitted to Congress a plan to reorganize the Judicial branch of government, particularly targeting the Supreme Court. Under this plan, a Supreme Court Justice could retire at age 70 and receive his full salary. Whether a Justice who had reached age 70 retired or continued to sit on the bench, the President could appoint a new, younger Justice to the Court, up to a total of fifteen sitting Justices. When Roosevelt proposed his reorganization, six of the nine Justices on the Court were over age 70. If his proposal was accepted, Roosevelt could appoint six new Justices and provide a more receptive Court for his proposed legislation.

President Roosevelt was not the originator of this court-packing scheme. The House of Representatives had approved a similar plan in 1869 and Justice James McReynolds had promoted this proposal in 1914 when he was the nation's Attorney General. In 1937, when Roosevelt proffered the plan, Justice McReynolds was sitting on the Court at age 72 and routinely voted against Roosevelt's New Deal legislation.[6]

The plan, though not new, was neither ushered in like an old friend nor welcomed with open arms. From the time of its initial presentation, Roosevelt's court-packing scheme met a blizzard of criticism from Congress, the Press and the Court itself. Many believed that the plan would allow the Executive branch of government to circumvent the checks and balances inherent in the Constitution. In our Constitutional design, they argued, the Court's role was to provide oversight to curb excesses of the legislative and executive branches. It needed to be independent of the other two branches of government.

Although Roosevelt's plan was soundly defeated, the Supreme Court soon began to lower the Commerce Clause barriers to centralized planning and upheld federal and state legislation designed to bring the nation out of its economic depression. On March 29, 1937, the Court upheld a minimum wage law enacted by the State of Washington.[7] The Court upheld the Social Security Act, the National Labor Relations Act, the Firearms Act, and the Fair Labor Standards Act.[8] Moderate Justice Owen J. Roberts, who had earlier voted in opposition to New Deal legislation, had begun to support Roosevelt's economic initiatives. Roberts' transformation from opponent to supporter has been called the "Switch in time that saved Nine," but it is widely believed that his decision to support Roosevelt's program was made prior to the announcement of Roosevelt's plan.[9]

When conservative Justice Willis Van Devanter retired on May 18, 1937, Roosevelt was given his first opportunity to nominate to the bench a supporter of his program of government intervention. Additional opportunities to appoint new Justices came about through a combination of retirements and deaths and, during his four terms in office, Roosevelt appointed eight Justices and one Chief Justice to the Supreme Court. [10] From 1937 to 1947, the New Deal Court, with a more expansive interpretation of the Constitution, overturned thirty pre-1937 decisions.[11] In Hatfield's opinion, the social legislation enacted during Roosevelt's administrations marked the first time in American history that the masses were given priority in government spending.

Hatfield and his coworkers were encouraged by the changes on the Court and believed that the New Deal Court would be willing to overturn *Plessy*. Hatfield determined to present to it that opportunity. He knew that his effort would be dangerous, but he was willing "to accept nothing less" than equal treatment in the country of his birth.[12] Hatfield was thirty years old at the time and was married with two children.

On January 10, 1946, during his last semester before graduating from Xavier, Hatfield wrote the following letter to the registrar at the Louisiana State University and Agricultural and Mechanical College in Baton Rouge to request an application for admission to the law school there:

Dear Sir:

I am interested in matriculating in the school of law in the State University this summer and I understand that the only Law school provided by the state of Louisiana is located at LSU There fore [sic] I am writing or would like to make application for admission beginning with the summer session.

I am expecting to receive my Bachelor's Degree at the end of the next semester which ends in May. I am expecting to graduate from Xavier University of New Orleans.

I shall be expecting to hear from you within the very near

110

future. Thank you in advance for your kindness.[13]

The stated admission requirements for the law school at LSU presented no obstacle for Hatfield. The law school accepted, as an entering student, anyone who held a Bachelor of Arts, Bachelor of Science, or equivalent degree. Hatfield would receive his Bachelor's degree in May 1946. In addition, the LSU law school accepted anyone who had completed three academic years of the work required for a Bachelor degree in an approved college or university with an average not lower than C. Hatfield was in the final semester of his fourth year at Xavier University, a college accredited by the Southern Association of Colleges and Secondary Schools. He had already completed 118 of the 128 hours needed for graduation. His grade-point average of B+ was well above the C required by LSU. Hatfield was more than qualified to enter LSU's law school.

Hatfield waited two weeks then, impatiently, sent a second letter on January 25, 1946, stating that he had not yet received a response from his earlier letter. To have proof of mailing, Hatfield sent his letters by registered mail, return receipt requested. Hatfield did not expect the officials at LSU to let him just waltz through the door. The administrators and alumni of that institution had been consistent in their support of segregation. Hatfield anticipated that he would have to bring suit against LSU to enforce his right to enter its law school. He was preparing carefully for that litigation. Hatfield collected the return receipts from his letters and kept them, along with copies of his letters, in a simple folder.

Hatfield's letter to the LSU Registrar was forwarded to Paul M. Hebert, then Dean of the law school. Hebert did not send an application form, but, instead, advised Hatfield, "As you know, the State of Louisiana maintains separate schools for its white and colored students. Louisiana State University does not admit colored students."[14] No law required or even permitted colleges or universities in Louisiana to discriminate in their admissions policies. Hatfield could not attend the state's only state supported law school simply because decision makers at LSU did not want black students there.

Dean Hebert had not seen Hatfield, nor had he asked about his skin color. Hebert could easily conclude that Hatfield was a person of color because Hatfield was enrolled at Xavier University, a historically black college. In 1946, Louisiana's tradition of segregated education meant that any student attending Xavier was black. Had Hebert seen

111

Hatfield, Hebert might have mistaken him for a white person. Looks alone, however, did not resolve the question of race in 1946. That question of fact was decided by "evidence of reputation, of social reception, and of the exercise of the privileges of a white man."[15] Hatfield had not exercised the privileges of a white man; he had attended a school established for blacks.

Dean Hebert further advised Hatfield, in his letter, that Southern University "is the principal Louisiana university for negroes. [sic] . . ." and noted that "the State of Louisiana has authorized that University to establish and maintain a department of law."[16] Hebert and Hatfield both knew that the State of Louisiana provided no law school for its African-American citizens at Southern University or anywhere else.

Southern University, "the principal Louisiana university for negroes [sic]," was chartered in January 1880 as a state-supported post secondary institution for the education of persons of color. [17] It had a Primary Department for children as young as age 10 until 1893. It offered a preparatory or high school, Normal training to prepare school teachers, an Industrial Department and a College Department. Seven students were graduated from its Normal or Higher English Department in 1887, but, by as late as 1898, only ten students were taking college-level courses.

Southern University's existence is credited to P.B.S. Pinchback, T.T. Allain, and T.B. Stamps, Reconstruction politicians. P.B.S. Pinchback offered the resolution to establish the school during the Constitutional Convention of 1879. T.T. Allain, a member of the Louisiana House of Representatives 1872 to 1874, and T.B. Stamps, State Senator 1872 to 1876, supported and lobbied for the resolution in their former legislative bodies. Establishing Southern University created an important educational opportunity for blacks, as no other school supported by the state of Louisiana offered post secondary education to blacks. It also cast in stone a system of segregated higher education in Louisiana that has yet to be completely dismantled. Historically black schools in Louisiana continue to have a predominantly black enrollment while historically white schools continue to have a predominantly white enrollment.[18]

Louisiana's Constitution of 1868 (superceded 1879) provided that, "There shall be no separate schools or institutions of learning established exclusively for any race by the State of Louisiana."[19] The plan to create a separate segregated university embroiled the black community in a dispute that echoed the debate over segregated elementary and

112

secondary schools immediately after the close of the Civil War. In 1868, black taxpayers complained of the cost of a dual school system, but complained more vehemently because they believed segregation was degrading and would perpetuate discrimination based on skin color. Indeed, whites resisted the integration of their schools because it would admit to their equality with blacks. For whites, segregated schools served as public recognition of their intellectual superiority.

Black delegates to Louisiana's Constitutional Convention of 1868, working with sympathetic whites, were able to include in that Constitution the language of article 135 prohibiting discrimination in public education. Only a few days after ratification of article 135, in April 1868, New Orleans blacks began to desegregate the public schools. Twenty-eight girls enrolled in the Bayou Road School. The principal of the school later asserted that the twenty-eight girls were so light-skinned that she was unaware that they were black. The New Orleans School Board, controlled by Democrats who opposed school desegregation, required the girls to transfer back to black schools. In 1870, State Superintendent of Schools, Thomas W. Conway, a Republican, gained control of the New Orleans schools and began to desegregate them.

As many as a thousand black children attended no fewer than nineteen integrated schools. Throughout New Orleans, approximately one-third of the schools was all black, one-third was all white, and one-third was integrated. In response, many white parents withdrew their children from the public schools and enrolled them in private schools, some of which offered little more than the guarantee that all of their classmates would be white. White students did not stay away long. George Washington Cable, a writer for the newspaper, the *Picayune*, wrote, "I saw . . . children and youth of both races standing in the same classes and giving each other peaceable, friendly, effective competition."[20] Relative calm characterized the public school system from 1871 to 1874.

This successful coexistence was ended by segregationists who organized themselves into a paramilitary group known as the White League. Willing to use violence to support their cause, and encouraged by white newspapers which stridently opposed desegregation, members of the White League, and those they inspired, forcibly ejected blacks from their classrooms in December 1874. The white vigilantes met black resistance and the two groups fought with stones, clubs and bottles. White high school boys broke more than 350 windows and killed an elderly black man and a child during their rampage, prompting even hard-core White Leaguers to call a halt to the violence. Schools were closed a week ahead of schedule for the Christmas break and attendance at integrated schools was low in January and February 1875. By March, attendance returned to normal. Eventually all of the high schools in New Orleans accepted black students.

In September 1875, P.B.S. Pinchback used his position as School Director of New Orleans to appoint E.J. Edmunds, a native of New Orleans, to teach mathematics at the elite Boys Central High School. Pinchback was appointed School Director by the State Board of Education and served in that position from March 1871 until 1877. Edmunds had graduated fifth in his class of 200 at the *Ecole Polytechnique* in Paris. Whites who protested his appointment called him incompetent. In their minds, no credentials existed that would qualify a black man to teach white boys in New Orleans. Edmund challenged any white mathematician to meet him at any blackboard and silenced his detractors.

Outside of New Orleans, opposition to mixed schools was fairly universal. In some northern parishes, DeSoto and Bienville, for example, blacks did not have access to even segregated public facilities. In Rapides Parish, in contrast, nearly all of the public school students were black. White parents were willing to "pay for the privilege of indulging their prejudices,"[21] and enrolled their children in private schools rather than allow them to sit next to black children. Apparently, "White Louisianians valued their racial supremacy far more than economic self-interest, political tranquility, or even education itself."[22]

As minimal as it was, public school desegregation was not destined to last. After the withdrawal of the Federal troops in 1877, whites in Louisiana quickly gained control of parish and local government, ousting blacks and northerners out of their positions of authority. Bourbon leaders, who did not support public education either before or after the Civil War, re-segregated the public schools and then shepherded their decline. By 1898, public elementary and high schools were segregated by express law.[23]

By the time the creation of Southern University was proposed in 1879, Louisiana State University had successfully withstood all efforts to force it to admit black students. Many blacks accepted that their only possibility for a state-financed post high school education lay in a school designated "for the education of persons of color..."[24] While Louisiana's

114

1868 Constitution stated that children were to be admitted to free public schools "without distinction of race, color, or previous condition," Louisiana's 1879 Constitution did not contain that language.[25] Blacks no longer had a right under the state constitution to demand admission to the state's public schools.

Henry Demas, a black delegate to the 1879 Constitutional Convention from St. John the Baptist Parish, presented a petition to the convention protesting against the creation of a segregated university. He believed that creating a school solely for one race established a legal distinction between citizens of the same state based on skin color. He feared that students henceforth would be assigned to schools according to racial classifications. In his opinion, the segregated college was a disservice to Louisiana's Black and Creole communities.

The editor of the New Orleans *Weekly Louisianian*, a newspaper principally under the control of P.B.S. Pinchback, challenged Demas to enter his children in the white university if he could. Pinchback's newspaper supported the creation of Southern University as a "special concession to the educational welfare" of Louisiana's black citizens. In the opinion of the *Weekly Louisianian*, a segregated university was better than no university at all.

Rodolphe Desdunes, the son of a Cuban mother and Haitian father, wrote in 1911 that accepting this separate school contradicted efforts to obliterate racial discrimination under the law:

> The black people whose weakness led them to sanction the principle of segregation of the races . . . should not have attended it [the 1879 Constitutional Convention] if they were not able to stand up for their rights. Certainly, giving the appearance of consenting to their own debasement was not a role that suited the representatives of the oppressed. . . . The vote of the representatives helped to create a system they knew would deprive the black children of the advantages of education available to other children of our state. These men knew that this line of demarcation, once established, chiefly by their consent, would serve as the basis and the pretext for other measures contrary to the interests and rights of our citizens. They knew that this action on their part was a move of regression, that they were sacrificing all the

progress that the past had consecrated and that they themselves had worked to obtain.[26]

The practice of racial segregation in higher educational facilities was endorsed by the Second Morrill Act, a federal statute providing funds for agricultural and mechanical education at the college level.[27] Under the First Morrill Act, each state was offered a grant of federal land on which a college could be located or which could be sold to create a permanent endowment to use to fund a college. The college funded by the Morrill Act would emphasize agricultural and mechanical arts, in addition to the classical, scientific and military subjects typically taught at colleges.[28] Only three Southern states shared their largesse with historically black institutions. Mississippi took control of Alcorn University, which had been a private institution, and gave three-fourths of its land grant income to it beginning in 1871. From 1872 to 1920, Virginia gave one-half of its income to Hampton Normal and Agricultural Institute, a private college. From 1879 until 1896, South Carolina sent one-half of its proceeds to Claflin University, also private.[29]

To ensure that blacks in the south would benefit from this generous federal program, the Second Morrill Act, while substantially augmenting the funding available, required states accepting the land-grant monies to either open their agricultural and mechanical colleges without distinction of race or color or to establish separate land grant colleges for black students.[30] The legislatures of the states providing separate institutions were instructed to equitably divide the funds made available by this program between the white and black institutions. Congress advanced the cause of higher education for blacks by insisting that some monies be spent for their education, but it gave a federal blessing to the practice of segregation in state institutions of higher learning.

Although no Southern state had any constitutional or statutory provision that excluded blacks from their state colleges and universities,[31] by 1900, all of the southern states except Virginia and Tennessee established separate land-grant colleges for blacks. Virginia continued to contribute land-grant funds to Hampton Institute; Tennessee established its land-grant college for blacks in 1912. Most of these public colleges for blacks were colleges in name only. In 1928, 62.5 per cent of students enrolled in land-grant colleges for blacks were in the elementary and secondary grades.

Louisiana established Southern University in 1880 as the separate

116

land-grant college for "colored students,"[32] in keeping with the requirements of the Second Morrill Act. The state legislature had authorized a department of law at Southern as early as 1888,[33] but the legislature had not funded it. Until November 1918, Louisiana's state constitution limited Southern's appropriation for maintenance and support to a total of ten thousand dollars per year.[34] Federal land-grant funds supplemented this amount. In 1946, the appropriation for Southern University was $503,000.00 while the appropriation for Louisiana State University was $5,198,041.00.[35] Nevertheless, Hatfield wrote to Dr. Felton Grandison Clark, President of Southern University, as Dean Hebert had instructed.

Dr. Clark had inherited the presidency of Southern University from his father, Joseph Samuel Clark, who was president from 1914 to 1938. His mother, Octavia Head Clark, was a registrar and music teacher at the University. Dr. Clark's intense love for Southern manifested itself in territoriality and despotism. He protected the school from its detractors, inside and out, and worked strategically to guarantee its continued funding. Smooth and articulate, Clark was a racial diplomat who ensured the survival and controlled the future of his school.

Hatfield told Dr. Clark of his interest in studying law in the State of Louisiana, and of his desire for admission to the Department of Law at Southern University. Using the language of Dean Hebert's letter, Hatfield wrote, "I understand that the State Department has authorized the establishment and maintenance of a Law School at this institution."[36] Anxious to establish his record of communications, Hatfield wrote to Dr. Clark again on February 14, 1946, repeating the contents of his earlier letter. To hasten a reply, he added a second "very" to his closing paragraph: "I thank you very much in advance for your kindness and anticipate a reply from your institution in the (very) near future."[37]

F.G. Clark wrote to Hatfield on February 15, 1946, telling him that, "Southern University does not have a Law School." President Clark's letter continued:

> For your information, I might state that at the last session of the Legislature, a Bill was introduced under the sponsorship of the State Board of Education, designed to provide funds for scholarship subsidies to Negro citizens which would enable them to obtain out-of-state graduate and professional education based upon in-state facilities

for white citizens. It happens that the Bill was vetoed because it was felt that state funds were not available to finance it.

Much interest is being given this whole matter of providing for the professional education of Negroes in the State at the present time. Becuase [sic] of this, my feeling is that very probably Louisiana might soon provide out-of-state tuition subsidies as several of the other progressive southern states are now doing and have been doing for several years.[38]

Hatfield knew that the legislation Dr. Clark anticipated would only establish a subsidy program which the *Gaines* Court had eight years earlier declared inadequate and unconstitutional. Louisiana could not support a law school within the state and require its black citizens to attend a law school elsewhere. Hatfield wanted much more than what Clark had to offer. Hatfield wanted to attend LSU.

Dr. Clark sent copies of his letter to Governor Jimmie H. Davis, to State Superintendent of Public Education John E. Coxe, to George T. Madison, Chairman, Legal Committee, State Board of Education, and to Joseph E. Gibson, Director of Higher Education, State Board of Education. Hatfield placed his letter from Clark in his folder.

Hatfield told no one except his family about his correspondence. He knew that he had put his life in jeopardy. Lloyd Gaines, the plaintiff in the *Missouri ex rel. Gaines v. Canada* case, had disappeared after the United States Supreme Court ordered that he be admitted into the University of Missouri Law School. Hatfield's mother and wife were terrified, but Hatfield gave no sign of fear.

Hatfield surprised John Rousseau, the newspaper reporter who was his friend and co-worker at the Post Office, with his collection of letters. Hatfield's folder contained his correspondence with the administrators at LSU and Southern University, his return receipts, and a brief he had drafted in support of his right to attend LSU's law school. As he showed Rousseau the folder, he asked Rousseau if he thought A.P. Tureaud might like a civil rights case.

Alexander Pierre Tureaud, born February 26, 1899, in New Orleans, graduated from the Howard University Law School in 1925. He was admitted to the bar in Louisiana on January 13, 1927. His law copy

Louisiana State University

Law School

Baton Rouge, Louisiana

24 January 1946

Charles J. Harfield, III,
663 N. Prieur Street,
New Orleans, Louisiana

Dear Sir:

Your letter of January 10, 1946, wherein you expressed
an interest in making application for admission to the Law
School of Louisiana State University this summer, has been
referred to this office for reply.

As you know, the State of Louisiana maintains
separate schools for its white and colored students. Louisiana
State University does not admit colored students. Southern
University, located at Scotlandville in East Baton Rouge Parish,
Louisiana, is the principal Louisiana university for negroes.
That University is governed by its own Board of Trustees and
is under the supervision of the State Department of Education;
and, the State of Louisiana has authorized that University to
establish and maintain a department of law.

Very truly yours,

Paul M. Hebert
Dean

PMH:fma

*Dean Paul M. Hebert's letter to Charles Hatfield, Jr.*

qopy

Southern University

F. G. Clark, President

Scotlandville, Louisiana

February 15, 1946

Mr. Charles J. Hatfield
863 N. Prieur Street
New Orleans, Louisiana

Dear Mr. Hatfield:

I am acknowledging your letter of January 26, in which you apply to Southern University "for admission to the Department of Law."

Southern University does not have a Law School. For your information, I might state that at the last session of the Legislature, a Bill was introduced, under the sponsorship of the State Board of Education, designed to provide funds for scholarship subsidies to Negro citizens which would enable them to obtain out-of-state graduate and professional education based upon in-state facilities for white citizens. It happens that that the Bill was vetoed because it was felt that state funds were not available to finance it.

Much interest is being given this whole matter of providing for the professional education of Negroes in the State at the present time. Because of this, my feeling is that very probably Louisiana might soon provide out-of-state tuition subsidies as several of the other progressive southern states are now doing and have been doing for several years.

Sincerely yours,

F. G. Clark,
President.

cc: Governor Jimmie H. Davis
    Superintendent John E. Coxe
    Honorable George T. Madison
    Mr. Joseph E. Gibson

**President Felton G. Clark's letter to Charles Hatfield, Jr.**

partner, Joseph Antonio Thornton, born November 3, 1887, in West Baton Rouge Parish, Louisiana, had graduated from the Howard University Law School in 1913. Thornton was admitted to the bar of the District of Columbia in October 1913, and admitted to the bar of Louisiana on June 8, 1914. Thornton and Turead practiced together at 612 Iberville Street in New Orleans until Thornton's death late in 1946.

Thornton and Tureaud were the only African-American attorneys practicing law in New Orleans in 1946, and Tureaud was Hatfield's friend. Both were active members of the Catholic fraternal order, the Knights of Peter Claver, and Hatfield had begun to study law under Tureaud's tutelage. Louisiana allowed its citizens to "read" law and then sit for the state bar examination without first obtaining a diploma from an approved law school. Applicants for admission to the Bar who had no formal law school training were required to "prove a course of study under the supervision of a reputable, Louisiana lawyer for a period of not less than three years."[39] "Reading" law provided an alternative to attending law school but Hatfield wanted to attend LSU.

Rousseau told Hatfield that Federal District Court Chief Judge Herbert W. Christenberry had encouraged Tureaud to file more civil rights law suits and that Tureaud would be happy to get Hatfield's suit. Judge Christenberry, a native of Louisiana and a graduate of Loyola Law School in New Orleans, consistently stood firm against segregationists. He, along with Judge J. Skelly Wright, also on the District Court, and Chief Judge Richard T. Rives of the Circuit Court of Appeals, all appointed by President Harry Truman, would later expressly repudiate the doctrine of interposition, an argument proffered by the state that a citizen could refuse to obey federal law and the federal courts if the state interposed itself between the citizen and the federal government.

Conceived in response to the 1955 *Brown v. Board of Education* decision, the doctrine of interposition was explicitly stated in a Louisiana statute: "The decisions of the federal district courts in the State of Louisiana, prohibiting the maintenance of separate schools for whites and blacks and ordering such schools to be racially integrated . . . are null, void and of no effect as to the State of Louisiana."[40] The three judge court of Christenberry, Wright and Rives labeled the doctrine "unconstitutional and null and void."[41]

Tureaud was surprised and glad to see what his friend had done. On his own, Hatfield had documented Louisiana's violation of the Fourteenth Amendment. Louisiana offered law school training to whites, but did not offer it to blacks. After reading the contents of Hatfield's folder, Tureaud told Hatfield, "You've got some nerve!"[42] He warned Hatfield of the danger he faced and called him the bravest of men. He asked Hatfield if he really wanted to go forward with the litigation. Hatfield responded, "If you are willing, so am I."[43]

On February 20, 1946, Hatfield engaged the services of Joseph A. Thornton and A.P. Tureaud, for the sum of five hundred dollars, payable upon final determination or in installment payments, as his attorneys in his litigation against LSU.[44] Tureaud agreed to take the case but advised Hatfield to do nothing more until he was safely out of undergraduate school. Tureaud was concerned that Hatfield's efforts to attend LSU's law school might result in someone pressuring Xavier to deny Hatfield his undergraduate degree.

## Notes

1. *West India Emancipation,* speech delivered at Canandaigua, New York, Aug. 4, 1857, in PHILIP S. FONER, II THE LIFE AND WRITINGS OF FREDERICK DOUGLASS 437 (International Publ. Co., Inc. 1950, this printing 1975).

2. Unofficial transcript of Charles Joseph Hatfield, Xavier Univ., New Orleans.

3. Interview with Hatfield (Oct. 15, 1999).

4. THOMAS H. GREER, WHAT ROOSEVELT THOUGHT: THE SOCIAL AND POLITICAL IDEAS OF FRANKLIN D. ROOSEVELT 50-51 (Michigan State Univ. Press 1958).

5. *See, for ex.,* Railroad Retirement Act, 48 Stat. 1283 (Jun. 27, 1934) in *R.R. Retirement Bd. v. Alton R. Co.,* 295 U.S. 330 (1935); Agricultural Adjustment Act, 48 Stat. 31 (May 12, 1933) in *U.S. v. Butler,* 297 U.S. 1 (1936); Bituminous Coal Conservation Act, 49 Stat. 991 (Aug. 30, 1935) in *Carter v. Carter Coal Co.,* 298 U.S. 238 (1936).

6. *See, for ex., R.R. Retirement Bd. v. Alton R. Co.,* 295 U.S. 330 (1935); *A.L.A. Schechter Poultry Corp. v. U.S.,* 295 U.S. 495 (1935); *U.S. v. Butler,* 297 U.S. 1 (1936); *Carter v. Carter Coal Co.,* 298 U.S. 238 (1936).

7. "Minimum Wages for Women," 1913 Wash. Laws 174 (Mar. 24, 1913) in *W. Coast Hotel Co. v. Parrish,* 300 U.S. 379 (1937).

8. The Social Security Act, 49 Stat. 620 (Aug. 14, 1935) in *Chas. C. Steward Mach Co. v. Davis,* 301 U.S. 548 (1937), and *Helvering v. Davis,* 301 U.S. 619 (1937), the National Labor Relations Act, 49 Stat. 449 (Jul. 5, 1935) in *NLRB v. Jones & Laughlin Steel Corp.,* 301 U.S. 1 (1937), the Firearms Act, 48 Stat. 1237 (Jun. 26, 1934) in *U.S. v. Miller,* 307 U.S. 174 (1939), and the Fair Labor Standards Act. 52 Stat. 1060 (Jun. 25, 1938) in *U.S. v. Darby,* 312 U.S. 100 (1941).

9. KELLY W. HARBISON, THE AMERICAN CONSTITUTION: ITS ORIGINS AND DEVELOPMENT 764 (4th ed. 1970).

10. THE SUPREME COURT JUSTICES, ILLUSTRATED BIOGRAPHIES, 1789-1995, 2nd ed., 541-543 Clare Cushman, ed. (Cong. Q. Inc. 1995). Chief Justice Stone, and Justices Black, Reed, Frankfurter, Douglas, Murphy, Byrnes, Jackson, and Rutledge were appointed by Roosevelt.

11.Neal Devins, *Government Lawyers and the New Deal,* 96 COLUM. L. REV. 237, 249 (Jan. 1996).

12.Letter from Hatfield to Glenn Labbe (Mar. 19, 1993) in possession of Glenn Labbe.

13.*See* Letter from Hatfield to The Registrar, Louisiana State University (Jan. 25, 1946, dated 1945 in error) which notes and quotes from Hatfield's January 10, 1946, letter to the Registrar. (Hatfield Papers, Amistad Research Center, Tulane University, New Orleans, La.)

14.Letter from Paul M. Hebert to Charles J. Hatfield, III, (Jan. 24, 1946) (Tureaud Papers, Box 66, Folder 22, Amistad Research Center, Tulane University); *Hatfield v. Bd. of Supv.,* No. 25,520, petition, para X, (19th JDC, Par. of East Baton Rouge, La. Oct. 10, 1946).

15.*Lee v. N. Orleans Great Northern Rail Co.,* 125 La. 236 (1910).

16.Letter from Paul M. Hebert to Charles J. Hatfield, III, (Jan. 24, 1946) (Tureaud Papers, Box 66, Folder 22, Amistad Research Center, Tulane University); *Hatfield v. Bd. of Supv.,* No. 25,520, petition, para X, (19th JDC, Par. of East Baton Rouge, La. Oct. 10, 1946).

17.1880 La. Acts 87 (Apr. 10, 1880).

18.The United States, through the U.S. Attorney General, began litigation on March 14, 1974, to dismantle the prior de jure system of segregated education in Louisiana's public colleges and universities based on race. *U.S. v. Louisiana,* 543 F. 2d 1125 (5th Cir. 1976). As recently as 1993, unnecessary program duplication at Louisiana's proximate state institutions continued to raise issues of intentional segregation. *U.S. v. Louisiana,* 9 F. 3d 1159, 1166 (5th Cir. 1993). The parties to this litigation have since entered into a Settlement Agreement intended to more equitably distribute the state's resources among the historically white and historically black state institutions and to mollify their racial identities. *U.S. v. La.,* No. 80-3300, Settlement Agreement (adopted by the four governing boards of public institutions of higher education in Louisiana Nov. 4, 1994). While the Louisiana State University will remain the "flagship institution and its only comprehensive research institution ... [with] the greatest number of graduate and research programs and selective admissions criteria, Southern University, and other historically black institutions, will receive funds to enhance their infrastructure and to offer a larger array of graduate programs."*U.S. v. La.,* No. 80-3300, Settlement Agreement 4-6.

19.LA. CONST. of 1868, art. 135. ("The general assembly shall establish at least one free public school in every parish throughout the State, and shall provide for its support by taxation or otherwise. All children of this State between the years of six and twenty-one shall be admitted to the public schools or other institutions of learning sustained or established by the State in common, without distinction of race, color, or previous condition. There shall be no separate schools or institutions of learning established exclusively for any race by the State of Louisiana.")

20.DEVORE AND LOGSDON, CRESCENT CITY SCHOOLS: PUBLIC EDUCATION IN NEW ORLEANS 1841-1991 73 (Center for La. Studies, Univ. of Southwestern La.1991).

21.JOHN W. BLASSINGAME, BLACK NEW ORLEANS 1860-1880 115 (Univ. of Chicago Press 1973).

22.ROGER A. FISCHER, THE SEGREGATION STRUGGLE IN LOUISIANA 1862-77 109 (Univ. of Ill. Press 1974).

23.LA. CONST. of 1898, art. 248. ("There shall be free public schools for the white and colored races, separately established by the General Assembly, throughout the State, for the education of all the children of the State between the ages of six and eighteen years...")

24.LA. CONST. of 1879, art. 231.

25.Compare LA. CONST. of 1868, art. 135, and LA. CONST. of 1879, art. 224, ("There shall be free public schools established by the General Assembly throughout the State for the education of all children of the State between the ages of six and eighteen years;...")

26.RODOLPHE LUCIEN DESDUNES, OUR PEOPLE AND OUR HISTORY 137-138 (1911, 1973 translation by Sister Dorothy Olga McCants, Louisiana State Univ. Press).

27.26 Stat. 417 (Aug. 30, 1890).

28.12 Stat. 503 (Jul. 2, 1862).

29.U.S. COMM. ON CIVIL RIGHTS, EQUAL PROTECTION OF THE LAWS IN PUBLIC HIGHER EDUCATION 1960 7 (Greenwood Press 1968.)

30.26 Stat. 417, s.1. ("no money shall be paid out under this act to any State or Territory for the support or maintenance of a college where a distinction of race or color is made in the admission of students, but the establishment and maintenance of such colleges separately for white and colored students shall be held to be a compliance with the provisions of this act if the funds received in such State or Territory be equitably divided...")

31.Tennessee, in 1901, became the first state to statutorily require segregation at all colleges in the state. Tenn. Laws 1901, ch. 7, p. 9; 1960 CIV. RIGHTS COMM. RPT. 11.

32.1880 La. Acts 87, s. 1 (Apr. 10, 1880). ("That there shall be established in the city of New Orleans a university for the education of persons of color, to be named and entitled the "Southern University.")

33.1888 La. Acts 90 (Jul. 12, 1888). ("There may be also established by said board of trustees a department of law and of medicine. The department of law shall consist of three (3) or more learned professors, learned and skilled in the practice of law in this State, who shall be required to give a full course of lectures on international, constitutional, commercial and municipal or civil law and instruction in the practice thereof.")

34. LA. CONST. of 1879, art. 231; LA. CONST. of 1913, art. 257, amend. 1918 La. Acts 48.

35.1946 La. Acts 66 (Jul. 12, 1946).

36. Letter from Hatfield to Dr. Felton Clark (Jan. 26, 1946) (Tureaud Papers, Box 66, Folder 22, Amistad Research Center).

37.Letter from Hatfield to Dr. Felton Clark (Feb. 14, 1946) (Tureaud Papers, Box 66, Folder 22, Amistad Research Center).

38.Letter from Dr. Clark to Hatfield (Feb. 15, 1946) (Tureaud Papers, Box 66, Folder 22, Amistad Research Center).

39.1924 La. Acts 113, s. 1.

40.1960 La. Acts, 1st Ex. Sess, No. 2, "An Act to interpose the sovereignty of the State of Louisiana against the unlawful encroachments by the judicial and executive branches of the Federal Government in the operation of public schools of the State of Louisiana..."

41.*Bush v. Orleans Parish School Board, 188 F. Supp. 916, aff'd.* 364 U.S. 500 (1960).

42.Interview with Hatfield (Dec. 11, 1998).

43.Letter from Hatfield to Glenn Labbe (Mar. 19, 1993).

44.Agreement between Hatfield and Thornton and Tureaud (Feb. 20, 1946) (Tureaud Papers, Box 66, Folder 22, Amistad Research Center).

# Chapter 9.

## *Litigating in Louisiana*

*As I stood there in the dark that night,*
*A thousand doors I could see,*
*Meant that this would be a fight*
*Should I persist that they open to me.*
*But why should I live in fear and hate,*
*When eternity to everyone comes sooner or later.*

*Charles J. Hatfield[1]*

Welcoming Hatfield's case, Tureaud asked Thurgood Marshall, then Special Counsel for the NAACP Legal Defense and Education Fund, Inc., and Louis Berry, a Louisiana native and a law professor at Howard University in Washington, D.C., to act as co-counsel for Hatfield. Marshall's employer, the NAACP Legal Defense and Education Fund, Inc., had been organized as the legal action arm of the National Association for the Advancement of Colored People, Incorporated and was separated from the NAACP on March 20, 1940. Its primary objective in 1946 was to destroy racial segregation through litigation. Marshall traveled throughout the United States litigating civil rights cases with local counsel. He was working with A.P. Tureaud on a voter's registration case in Shreveport, Louisiana, *Hall v. Nagel,*[2] while Hatfield was writing letters to LSU.

Louis Berry, born October 9, 1915, in Shreveport, Louisiana, was a Howard University Law School graduate. Admitted to the Louisiana State Bar on August 1, 1945, he became the first black admitted to the practice of law in Louisiana since Tureaud was admitted eighteen years earlier. In 1946, Berry was a Professor of Law at Howard's law school. He left his teaching duties at Howard and returned to Louisiana in 1947, where he practiced law in association with John Perkins, licensed to practice law in Mississippi but not in Louisiana, at 407 South Thirteenth Street, Baton Rouge.

Dr. Clark, President of Southern University, was chairperson of a Baton Rouge group organized in 1943 by J.K. Haynes to demand that the state provide graduate educational opportunities for blacks in Louisiana. Haynes was a Louisiana educator and an active voice in support of equal rights for blacks. He moved to Baton Rouge after his life was threatened in northern Louisiana for his outspokenness.

W.W. Stewart, Dean of the College of Education at Southern University, was a member of the Haynes/Clark group and wanted to file suit to force the integration of graduate school programs at LSU. Clark was concerned that Southern's funding might be cut in retaliation should a group of educators affiliated with Southern University demand that black students have access to LSU. Clark suggested that the group seek tuition support for out-of-state graduate training. In 1944, a bill to finance out-of-state tuition passed both houses of the legislature but was vetoed by Governor Jimmie Davis. As anticipated by Dr. Clark in his February 15, 1946, letter to Hatfield, similar legislation was passed at the state's next legislative session two years later and signed into law.[3]

The Louisiana State Legislature appropriated $50,000 to the State Department of Education to enable the department to provide scholarship subsidies for the education of black students, "in schools and colleges located outside the State of Louisiana . . . "[4] It ignored the very clear holding in *Gaines*. Louisiana had an obligation to make graduate and professional training available to blacks inside Louisiana. LSU had to admit Hatfield into the law school at LSU unless the State provided Hatfield with an opportunity to study law in a manner equal to that provided for whites. The Legislature could not fulfill Louisiana's duty to provide equal educational opportunities to its black students by sending them away.

In addition, the out-of-state scholarship program was woefully underfunded. In its first year, 71 qualified applicants were disappointed because funds were not available. During the 1947-48 academic year, 46 applicants received scholarships for the first and second semesters and 56 received funds for summer school. In 1948-49, 400 applications were filed. The State Board of Education estimated that it needed $330,000 annually to continue the program. Only $50,000 was made available.

This limited funding would assist some students to attend graduate or professional school outside of Louisiana, but it was wholly inadequate to fulfill the constitutional duty that the state owed to its black citizens as recognized by the United States Supreme Court in both *Plessy* and *Gaines*. Hatfield was entitled to equal treatment from the state. Louisiana "was bound to furnish within its borders facilities for legal education substantially equal to those which the State there afforded for persons of the white race . . ."[5] Hatfield had a right to attend LSU, unless the State of Louisiana made "other and proper provision for his legal training within the State."[6]

On August 2, 1946, Hatfield wrote his final letter seeking admission to the LSU law school for the fall term of 1946. Addressing the LSU Board of Supervisors, he explained that Dean Hebert had directed him to apply to Southern University and that Dr. Clark, at Southern, had written that Southern had no law school. He remonstrated that, "There is no law school in Louisiana available to members of the Negro Race . . ." and ended, "Please advise whether or not I may be admitted to the Law School of Louisiana State University in the fall term of 1946."[7]

Hatfield"s attorneys considered filing his suit in federal court. He traveled to Shreveport in August 1946 to discuss his case with a federal judge. He left New Orleans with A.P. Tureaud, Alvin Jones, a professor of economics at Xavier, John Rousseau, his friend and coworker, and Louis Berry. Hatfield had never before been in a courtroom. The judge in Shreveport advised Hatfield and his attorneys to exhaust all their state remedies before filing suit in federal court. While Hatfield was in Shreveport, his wife, Beulah, and his mother, Mary, sat in the kitchen of their third floor apartment praying for his safe return, each holding a child on her lap. Beulah remembers that Hatfield never worried. She and Mary did all the worrying at his house. The comfort of her mother-in-law's presence helped Beulah immensely.

On August 12, 1946, representatives of LSU and the State Board of Education met at the State Capitol and admitted the inadequacy of the out-of-state scholarship program. To their credit, representatives of LSU noted that the scholarship system failed to satisfy the requirements of *Gaines*:

> While the recent legislative action is appreciated by responsible negro [sic] leaders in the state and will serve

to postpone a number of pressing demands for professional or graduate work not now offered for negroes [sic] at Southern University, there are no means of controlling the individual action of any negro [sic] who prefers to assert his rights under the Gaines case.[6]

In addition, they acknowledged that the civil law system prevalent in Louisiana, "presents a situation which makes the requirement of legal education within the state peculiarly applicable to Louisiana . . . "[7] Many of Louisiana's legal principles follow the tradition of the Roman Civil Law rather than that of the English Common Law which dominates in the other forty-nine states of the United States. Lawyers able to study the civil law in Louisiana are exposed to a civilian methodology and gain insight into civilian principles invaluable for practice in Louisiana. Representatives of the State Board of Education suggested, nonetheless, that they should first meet with Dr. Clark of Southern University to explore the possibility that Hatfield would accept an out-of-state scholarship instead of pursuing admission to LSU.

After an afternoon meeting with Dr. Clark, George T. Madison, Chairman, Legal Committee of the Board of Education, Honorable John E. Coxe, Superintendent of Education, J.E. Williams, Supervisor of Negro Education, and Mrs. Eleanor H. Meade, member of the State Board of Education, reported their disappointment. "There appears to be little doubt in the mind of Dr. Clark that this is a bona fide case to be sponsored as a test case against the University; the chances, therefore, of a withdrawal of the application by Hatfield are not good."[8]

Dr. Clark was correct. Hatfield, too, recognized the uniqueness of Louisiana's law and wanted to benefit from this special body of knowledge. He wanted to be able to observe Louisiana courts while he was in law school, and to share in the prestige afforded by the citizens of Louisiana to its publically supported law school.[9] He wanted to study Louisiana law at LSU, his own state's university, which his taxes and those of his family and friends helped to support. As a citizen of Louisiana, soon to have a bachelor's degree from an accredited undergraduate school, he felt entitled to do so.

On August 22, 1946, A.P. Tureaud wrote Dean Hebert inquiring whether there had been a change in the policy at LSU since the Dean had last advised Hatfield that he could not enter LSU's law school because of his race.[10] B.B. Taylor responded to Tureaud, without answering his

126

question, by explaining that Tureaud's letter was referred to Taylor "as attorney for the University on account of the absence of Dr. Hebert from the state and his illness since his return. Mr. McLemore, Chairman of the Board of Supervisors of the University, was also absent from the state at this time."[11] Mary Hebert reports that Hebert and McLemore were intentionally absent from the state. She quoted an August 12, 1946, letter from Taylor to McLemore, "We might get a little time from these colored students by telling them that you are out of the state and will not return for some weeks."[12] The State of Louisiana was not inclined to allow Hatfield to attend LSU.

The state made "other provision" for Hatfield's legal education within the State of Louisiana. On September 5, 1946, representatives of the Louisiana State University, the Louisiana State Board of Education, and the Louisiana State Department of Education met as a special committee. The State Department of Education was responsible for primary and secondary schools and was headed by an elected Superintendent of Education. The State Board of Education consisted of eleven members elected to provide policy supervision to the Department of Education. The special committee members agreed to recommend to their respective boards that "a law school for qualified Negro students" be established in connection with Southern University:

> The special committee, composed of representatives from the Board of Supervisors of Louisiana State University, the Louisiana State Board of Education, and the Louisiana State Department of Education, met in the Board Room on the Sixteenth floor of the State Capitol at eleven o'clock on Thursday morning, September 5, 1946, for the purpose of discussing plans for the graduate and professional education of Negroes in Louisiana. The following members were present: Mr. James McLemore, Mr. E. Monnet Lanier, Mr. Thomas W. Leigh, and Mr. Jerome A. Broussard, Members of the Board of Supervisors of Louisiana State University; Dr. W.B. Hatcher, President of Louisiana State University; Dr. Paul M. Hebert, Dean of the Law School of the University; Dr. Fred C. Frey, Dean of the University; Mr. Lawrence Brooks, representing Mr. B.B. Taylor, the University's attorney; Mr. George T. Madison, Mr. Morgain W.

Walker, and Mrs. Eleanore H. Meade, members of the State Board of Education; Mr. J.E. Williams, Supervisor of Negro Education in the State Department of Education; and Mr. John E. Coxe, State Superintendent of Education.

The meeting was called to order by Mr. Madison. Dean Hegert [Hebert] presented a summary of the problem confronting the committee which has arisen as the result of the application by a Negro for admission to the Law School of Louisiana State University. After considerable discussion of the various aspects of the situation, the following action was taken:

On the Motion of Mr. Lanier, seconded by Mr. McLemore, the joint committee of the Louisiana State Board of Education and the Board of Supervisors of the Louisiana State University unanimously voted to recommend to their respective boards that, in view of the decision in the Gaines case and the demand that has been made by a Negro applicant who is otherwise apparently qualified for admission to the Law School of Louisiana State University, steps be initiated immediately by the Louisiana State Board of Education for the establishment of a law school for qualified Negro students in connection with Southern University and that the staff and faculty of the Law School of Louisiana State University be requested to cooperate in the establishment of this chool [sic]; that the plan be projected upon the basis of operation for the 1947-48 academic session; and that the committee continue its tudies [sic] of the problems related to higher education for Negroes in Louisiana.[13]

No one in attendance at the meeting represented Southern University, the school with which the new law school for qualified Negro students would be connected, and no one disputed the fact that Hatfield was "otherwise apparently qualified" to attend the Law School at LSU. Only his racial designation kept him out.

Lawrence W. Brooks, an attorney with Taylor, Porter, Brooks & Fuller, the law firm representing LSU, attended the meeting and reported the substance of the meeting to Tureaud in a September 11, 1946, meeting with Tureaud and again by letter dated September 17, 1946. Brooks included in his letter a copy of the minutes of the September 5th meeting, and reminded Tureaud of his recommendation that Hatfield, "attend a law school outside the State of Louisiana . . . availing himself of a scholarship as provided by the 1946 session of the Legislature, . . ."[16]

Tureaud's answer to Brooks' September 17th letter was short and to the point. He wrote, "[I]t is our opinion that there is no commitment made which satisfies the desire of our client, Charles J. Hatfield."[17] Hatfield did not intend to leave Louisiana to obtain a legal education. Hatfield wanted to exercise his right as a citizen of Louisiana to attend Louisiana's existing public law school.

Hatfield went forward with his litigation. On October 10, 1946, Louis Berry filed Hatfield's suit against the Board of Supervisors of LSU, W.B. Hatcher, LSU President, and Paul M. Hebert, Dean of the Law School.[18] Hatfield asked the court to issue a mandamus directing these administrators to admit Hatfield into LSU's law school. The suit described Hatfield's qualifications for the study of law and related the substance of his correspondence with Dr. Clark and Dean Hebert. It claimed that the policy, custom and usage of representatives of LSU, in denying Hatfield the right to attend law school there because of his color, "amounts to a systematic denial of the equal protection of the laws and is, therefore, in violation of relator's right under the Fourteenth Amendment of the federal constitution."[19]

Two weeks earlier, Tureaud, Berry and Marshall had filed suit on behalf of Viola M. Johnson who wanted to attend medical school at LSU.[20] Ms. Johnson, a native of New Iberia, Louisiana, had completed her first year of medical school at Meharry College of Medicine in Nashville, Tennessee, and applied to complete her second and third years closer to home. She sought to transfer from Meharry College to the LSU Medical School in New Orleans, but was denied admission. Her suit against the LSU Board of Supervisors, W.B. Hatcher, its President, Vernon W. Lippard, Dean of the Medical School, and Vivian Johnson, Registrar, was filed on September 23, 1946. Hatfield's suit against the LSU officials was the second filed that fall by a person raced black seeking admission to one of LSU's professional schools. Newspapers and radio newscasts made much ado about this litigation.[21] Hatfield learned of it while listening to a radio newscast.

As a result of his lawsuit, Hatfield received threatening phone calls late at night warning him to forget about enrolling in law school and calling him vicious names. Hatfield was cursed and threatened on his job. He watched his back and was mindful to stay close to a friend while at work. According to Hatfield, "That Post Office where I worked was a hotbed for racism. The white people who worked there hated to see a black person in a position inside the Post Office other than pushing a mop and broom."[20] There was constant abuse, and Hatfield's lawsuit only incited more abuse.

Ada Fisher, a black applicant for admission to the segregated law school at the University of Oklahoma, experienced a similar response after she filed suit in Oklahoma. "I had begun to receive many letters . . . . Some used abusive language to tell me that I should learn to stay in my place. . . . A few threatened physical violence. . . . One letter was addressed simply to 'Ada Lois Sipuel, nigger, Oklahoma.' It came directly to my home."[21]

Bricks were thrown into windows of the NAACP offices at Orleans and Claiborne Streets in New Orleans. Hatfield was accused of wanting to shut LSU down. That Hatfield's apartment was fairly inaccessible, in the middle of a housing project, may have saved his life.

Not too long after his suit was filed, Hatfield received an unsigned letter asking him to meet with someone on the 13th floor of the Pythian Temple to discuss his suit. The letter indicated that its author was somehow connected with the state program which provided tuition subsidies to black students to study at schools outside of Louisiana. It suggested that additional money would be made available to Hatfield if he would withdraw his litigation against LSU. Hatfield was curious to meet the person with the nerve to make him such an offer. He wanted to tell the writer of this letter that the *Gaines* decision had given notice that out-of-state tuition subsidies were insufficient to satisfy the Fourteenth Amendment. He wanted to say that the *Gaines* decision requiring that states treat blacks the same as whites was eight years old. Louisiana had an overdue obligation. He wanted to tell whoever he met there that he intended to attend LSU's law school.

The Pythian Temple, a twenty-story building on Common Street, near Gravier and Simon Bolivar, was owned by the Knights of Pythias, a black social organization. Once teeming with activity, the building was only partially occupied in 1946. Hatfield entered the iron-gated elevator of the building with trepidation, not knowing who or what to expect. He was propelled by anger and a feeling of righteousness, and ignored the caution of common sense. When the elevator doors opened onto the thirteenth floor, the reality of his situation struck him. He had been invited to meet an unknown person on an empty floor of a nearly vacant building. The only available light on the thirteenth floor came from the natural sunlight shining in, as best it could, through dirty windows.

The meeting was short. The man Hatfield met there held out some money and promised more would come if Hatfield would agree to drop his lawsuit and attend a law school outside of Louisiana. Hatfield flatly refused, and the man with the money disappeared into the shadows. Hatfield never knew who he was and could not describe what the man looked like or even whether he was black or white. Hatfield turned to leave and noticed in the dim light that, although the iron gate to the elevator shaft was open, the elevator was gone. Had he not hesitated, Hatfield might have fallen to his death in the open elevator shaft. Hatfield quickly found the stairs and ran down them and out of the building.

## Notes

1.Speech at 50th Anniversary Celebration of Southern Univ. Law Center (Oct. 18, 1997).

2.154 F. 2d 931 (5th Cir. 1946).

3.1946 La Acts 142 (Jul. 15, 1946).

4.1946 La. Acts 142, s. 1 (Jul. 15, 1946). ("Be it enacted by the Legislature of Louisiana, That there is hereby appropriated from the General Fund of the State of Louisiana to the State Department of Education the sum of Fifty Thousand Dollars ($50,000.00) for the fiscal year beginning July 1, 1946, and ending June 30, 1947 or so much thereof as may be necessary, and the sum of Fifty Thousand Dollars ($50,000.00) for the fiscal year beginning July 1, 1947, and ending June 30, 1948, or so much thereof as may be necessary, for the purpose of providing, in schools and colleges located outside the State of Louisiana, educational opportunities for the specialized, professional, or graduate education of Negro Physicians, dentists, veterinarians, public health workers, nurses, agriculturists, home economists, teachers, and others requiring specialized or advanced education.")

5.Missouri ex rel. Gaines v. Canada, 305 U.S. 337, 351-352 (1938).

6.Gaines, 305 U.S. at 352.

7.Letter Hatfield to LSU Board of Supervisors (Aug. 2, 1946) (Tureaud Papers, Box 66, Folder 22, Amistad Research Center).

8.Report of a Meeting of Representatives of LSU and A.&M. College and Representatives of the State Board of Education held at the Louisiana State Capitol on Aug. 12, 1946, p. 4, (emphasis in original) (LSU Bd. of Supv. Records, Record Group A0003, Folder 310, Negro Education, 1946, LSU Archives, LSU Libraries, Louisiana State Univ.)

9.Report of a Meeting of Representatives of LSU and A.&M. College and Representatives of the State Board of Education held at the Louisiana State Capitol on Aug. 12, 1946, p. 3, (emphasis in original) (LSU Bd. of Supv. Records, Record Group A0003, Folder 310, Negro Education, 1946, LSU Archives, LSU Libraries, Louisiana State Univ.)

10.Report of a Meeting of Representatives of LSU and A.&M. College and Representatives of the State Board of Education held at the Louisiana State Capitol on Aug. 12, 1946, p. 5 (LSU Bd. of Supv. Records, Record Group A0003, Folder 310, Negro Education, 1946, LSU Archives).

11.*Gaines v. Canada*, 305 U.S. 337, 348-349 (1938); *Sweatt v. Painter*, 339 U.S. 629, 634 (1950). The U.S. Supreme Court used these criteria: observing local courts and sharing prestige, in *Gaines* and *Sweatt* respectively, to explain why a program of out-of-state scholarships or a hastily assembled in-state segregated facility did not satisfy the Fourteenth Amendment requirement for equal treatment.

12.Letter from Tureaud to Hebert (Aug. 22, 1946) (Tureaud Papers, Box 66, Folder 22, Amistad Research Center).

13.Letter from B.B. Taylor to A. P. Tureaud (Aug. 27, 1946) (LSU Bd. of Supv. Records, Record Group A0003, Box 7, Folder 313, Negro Education, 1946, LSU Archives).

14.MARY JACQUELINE HEBERT, BEYOND BLACK AND WHITE: THE CIVIL RIGHTS MOVEMENT IN BATON ROUGE, LOUISIANA, 1945-1972 63 (Doctoral Dissertation, Louisiana State Univ. 1999).

15."Minutes of Meeting of Special Committee on Higher Education for Negroes in Louisiana, Sept. 5, 1946." Enclosed with letter from Taylor, Porter, Brooks & Fuller by L.W. Brooks to A.P. Tureaud (Sept. 17, 1946) (Tureaud Papers, Box 66, Folder 22, Amistad Research Center).

16.Letter from L.W. Brooks to A.P. Tureaud (Sept. 17, 1946) p. 1 (Tureaud Papers Box 66, Folder 22, Amistad Research Center).

17.Letter from Tureaud to Brooks (Sept. 27, 1946) (Tureaud Papers Box 66, Folder 22, Amistad Research Center). In a mandamus action, the plaintiff claims a clear right to the performance of a particular act and asks the court to order the defendant to perform that act. Hatfield believed that *Gaines* had given him a clear right to attend the law school at LSU.

18.Letter from Berry to Tureaud (undated) (Tureaud Papers Box 66, Folder 22, Amistad Research Center).

19.*Hatfield v. Bd. of Supv.*, No. 25,520, petition para. XII, (19th JDC, Par. of East Baton Rouge, La. Oct. 10, 1946).

20.*La. ex rel Viola M. Johnson v. Bd. of Supv., LSU, W.B. Hatcher, Pres., Vernon W. Lippard, Dean of Medical School and Vivian Johnson, Registrar*, No. 25414 (19th JDC, Par. of East Baton Rouge, La. Sept. 23,1946).

21.*Times-Picayune*, New Orleans, La., p. 12, col. 2-3 (Oct. 11, 1946).

22.Interview with Hatfield (Oct. 29, 1998).

23.ADA FISHER, A MATTER OF BLACK AND WHITE 114 (Univ. of Oklahoma Press 1996).

# Chapter 10.

# The Louisiana State University and Agricultural and Mechanical College

*Let it become what it was intended to be — an instrument to elevate the standard of scholarship in the State in every branch of academic learning.*

*W.B. Egan[1]*

The target of Hatfield's suit, the Louisiana State University and Agricultural and Mechanical College, was Louisiana's premier higher education facility. A bronze plaque in front of the Memorial Tower to World War I veterans on the Baton Rouge campus, flanked by foundation stones from the school's first home at Pineville, Louisiana, contains the following brief history of the University:

> Louisiana State University and Agricultural and Mechanical College began as the Louisiana State Seminary of Learning and Military Academy. Opening its doors for the first session on January 2, 1860 at Pineville, La.
>
> William Tecumseh Sherman was the first

President. He resigned before the start of the second session to take command in the Union Army at the outbreak of the Civil War. The student body joined the Confederate forces.

The seminary was closed during the war and was reopened in 1865 under the leadership of David French Boyd, a member of the original five-man faculty.

A four year period of postwar hardships was climaxed in 1869 by a fire which destroyed the seminary building. Classwork was resumed two weeks later in a building housing the State School for the Deaf in Baton Rouge.

In 1870 the Seminary was designated as the Louisiana State University and seven years later the University and the Agricultural and Mechanical College, which previously had been located in New Orleans, were merged.

In 1886 the University was moved to the Pentagon Barracks, Historic Military Post situated on the grounds of the present state capitol.

Steady growth of its student body and expansion of its research and extension services led to the building of this "greater university," envisioned by President Thomas Duckett Boyd and made a reality by Governor John M. Parker, during whose administration construction of this campus was begun in 1922. The site was formally dedicated on April 30, 1926. The transition from the old campus to the present one was completed in 1932.[2]

In 1946, when Hatfield sought admission, LSU described itself as "the culmination of the state public school system . . . attempting to serve the educational interests of the state in the broadest and most thorough manner possible."[3] It boasted seventeen divisions[4] and offered advanced degrees in 32 subject areas.[5] It bragged of its well-equipped laboratories, efficient teaching staff, and opportunities for advanced work and scientific research. Its libraries contained 416,108 volumes, 69,224 of which were in the Law School library. From 1860 to 1946, LSU had awarded approximately 12,000 degrees. LSU had never knowingly admitted a black student; it was closed to blacks in 1946.

An opportunity to desegregate LSU nearly a century earlier had been cruelly frustrated. In August 1867, the *New Orleans Republican* described the Louisiana Seminary of Learning and Military Academy as a stronghold of rebel spite and resistance. It noted that the faculty consisted of rebel officers and that most of its students had been Confederate soldiers or were sons of rebel planters. It decried the school as an obstacle to Reconstruction and an enclave of the Confederacy.

Louisiana's post-Civil War Constitution of 1868 provided that:

> All children of this State between the years of six and twenty-one shall be admitted to the public schools or other institutions of learning sustained or established by the State in common, without distinction of race, color, or previous condition. There shall be no separate schools or institutions of learning established exclusively for any race by the State of Louisiana.[6]

It continues: "No appropriation shall be made by the General Assembly for the support of any private school or any private institution of learning whatever."[7] The drafters of this constitution envisioned that all state-supported education would be available to all of the state's citizens on a non-segregated basis.

Contradictive to this goal of free, universal, and integrated education, Republican Governor Henry Clay Warmoth, in office from 1868 to 1872, shielded the seminary from desegregation during his administration. On June 25, 1868, Congress recognized Louisiana's State Constitution and Louisiana was readmitted into the Union. Oscar J. Dunn was Lieutenant Governor. David French Boyd, a member of the Seminary's first faculty, was appointed President of the Seminary after he returned from fighting on behalf of the Confederacy in the Civil War.

Boyd met with Louisiana's newly elected Governor shortly after Louisiana was readmitted into the Union. Governor Warmoth assured Boyd that he "would do nothing toward forcing the admission of negroes [sic]."[8] Although Warmoth received a great deal of criticism from fellow

Republicans for his refusal to support the desegregation of Louisiana's public schools, he was unmoved. Nothing was done to integrate LSU while Warmoth was Governor.

Although he was a Republican, Warmoth was not a beacon of hope for either the newly freed former slaves, or for the sons and daughters of blacks who had been free for generations. Warmoth was considered almost as much a white supremacist as any member of the Knights of the White Camellia would be. Organized in May 1867, the Knights of the White Camellia proclaimed that its objective was to maintain the supremacy of the white race. Warmoth vetoed Louisiana's first civil rights act and only reluctantly signed the second. The first act would have made race discrimination in places of public accommodation a crime punishable by a fine up to a $500 and a year in jail.[9] Warmoth explained in his veto message that the bill failed to distinguish between intrastate travel, which the state could regulate, and interstate travel, which it could not regulate. He added that the act attempted to criminalize behavior that arises out of private contracts negotiated between individuals.

A subsequent civil rights bill, more precise in particularizing what behavior was acceptable and what was not, required that all licenses issued by the state be issued on condition that the licensee make no distinction on account of race or color in providing the service permitted by the license.[10] Yielding to pressure, Warmoth signed this bill on February 23, 1869.

The greatest threat to the all-white nature of the Louisiana State Seminary came from Louisiana's beneficiary program. As early as 1821, the Louisiana legislature required its public schools to accept students from indigent families. These beneficiary students could attend school at no cost and were furnished with books, quills, and paper.[11] In 1866, Louisiana appropriated $15,600 to the Seminary for the maintenance and education of fifty-two beneficiary cadets, at the rate of $300 per year per cadet.[12] The cadets were selected by the Police Juries of each parish, the local governing body, except in New Orleans where the Board of Directors of each of the public school districts selected the beneficiary cadets.[13] Eligible cadets were in need of financial assistance and were required to teach within the state for two years immediately after graduation.[14]

Throughout Louisiana blacks and sympathetic whites had been elected to the parish police juries. A very real possibility existed that one or more of the police juries would find a suitable candidate who happened to be black to send to the Seminary as a beneficiary student. Segregationists prominent in Seminary affairs repeatedly expressed concern that Reconstructionists would open the school to black cadets. The 1868 Constitutional provision declaring that all public schools would be open without distinction added urgency to segregationist efforts to preserve the school for the use and benefit of young white men only.

Governor Warmoth, working with Boyd and State Senator J. C. Egan from the 20th Senatorial District, Bienville, Claiborne and Bossier Parishes, thwarted efforts to integrate the Seminary by convincing the legislature to extend the beneficiary program to allow the scholarship to be used at Straight University, a private black college in New Orleans, ignoring the state constitutional prohibition against using state funds to support a private institution.[15] The sum of $35,000 was appropriated to the Medical Department at Straight University in 1870 on condition that its faculty receive one indigent student from each parish for a period of ten years.[16]

Any black candidates for the beneficiary program nominated by Police Juries could take advantage of the state-supported education available through the program, but would not attend LSU. Walter Fleming, who has written a history of LSU, reports that, "After Straight University was designated as the state college for Negroes there was little danger of Negroes being appointed to the Seminary until the close of Warmoth's administration."[17]

Straight University was new. It was established by the American Missionary Association on June 25, 1869, "for the education and training of young men and women, irrespective of color or race,"[18] and named for Seymour Straight, a produce merchant in New Orleans and Ohio, who donated the land for the school and was its chief benefactor during its early years. Located on the corner of Esplanade and Burgundy Streets in New Orleans, Straight University primarily intended to educate the newly freed slaves. It offered Normal School training and college, law, medical, and theology training. In April 1871, 965 students were enrolled at Straight, although most were in primary and secondary classes. Its instructional staff of twenty-six was exceptional for Louisiana during its Reconstruction. Eighteen of its faculty members held degrees higher than a bachelor's degree.

Its medical department was headed by a member of the Louisiana Board of Health and had seven professors, including a second member of the Louisiana Board of Health. Students could practice at the New Orleans Charity Hospital. Straight's law school was organized by Louis A. Bell, a graduate of Howard Law School. Its faculty included a former judge and a former Attorney General of Louisiana. It was later headed by Rufus Maples, a professor of Admiralty, Maritime and International Law and an author of books on these topics. Law students who graduated from Straight were automatically admitted to the practice of law in Louisiana.

The 1870 legislature instructed Straight University to accept one beneficiary student from each parish in exchange for the appropriation to its medical school. That legislature changed the name of the Louisiana State Seminary to Louisiana State University and appropriated $350 for each beneficiary student enrolled.[19] Two beneficiary students from each parish could attend the LSU, while New Orleans could send twenty.

By 1874, Straight had greatly reduced the number of students enrolled in primary and secondary grades and maintained its enrollment at around 200. Two hundred three students were enrolled in that year including: 10 in Medicine, 15 in Law, 23 in Theology, 6 in College, 20 in Normal School, 18 in College Preparatory and 30 in Academic Training; its faculty numbered twelve. In 1875, four women graduated from the Normal School. In 1876, two women graduated from college and eight men earned law degrees.

Straight University had much more to offer to students and to the state than did the Louisiana State University. LSU had very few students or faculty in 1876 and conferred no bachelor degrees between 1874 and 1882. It had no law school until 1906 and had no medical school until 1931. LSU had little more than David Boyd with his vision to create a great school and his determination to keep blacks out of it.

William Pitt Kellogg, a Radical Republican from Connecticut, was elected governor in 1872 replacing Warmoth. Kellogg, who held office from 1873 to 1877, supported efforts to integrate the state's public schools. In 1873, the state legislature withdrew all support from the Louisiana State University because Superintendent Boyd refused to admit black students. Boyd discharged all of the beneficiary students and complained that, "Now the legislature won't support us, because we have no Negroes here; and the whites are afraid to send us their sons, because the negro [sic] may come here."[20] Only thirty-one students attended LSU in 1875, compared to a high enrollment of 173 in the 1866-67 session. That number would dwindle to five before the semester ended.[21]

In early 1874, Boyd was patient. He stated, "[T]he negro [sic] may

138

have the upper hand in Louisiana for a few years, but it can't last. This is bound to be a white man's country and the negro [sic] must take his rightful position, an inferior place."[22] A report on the student body at the school stated, unabashedly, that:

> Most of the older cadets were, from 1866 to 1869, members of an organization later known as the "Knights of the White Camellia." This order was a part of the general uprising in the South known as the "Ku Klux" movement. The seminary students joined the local order in Alexandria. The members were pledged to maintain at all hazards the supremacy of the white race, to enforce the separation of the races, to keep the Negroes out of office, to protect the whites from the radical and negro [sic] encroachment, and in general to restrain the "African race to that condition of social and political inferiority for which God has destined it."[23]

In an address given in 1904, an 1871 graduate of LSU, Judge A.A. Gunby, described Boyd's response to article 135 of Louisiana's 1868 Constitution which prohibited racial segregation in Louisiana's public schools:

> Article 135 was the most malicious clause in that constitution, and it meant the complete ostracism of the Southern whites from the public schools of Louisiana. . . Boyd was the chief factor in avoiding the terrible alternative between mixed schools and no schools at all. . . . By Act 81 of the regular session of 1870 $35,000 was appropriated to Straight University, which was exclusively for the negro [sic] students, and provision was made for the education of one indigent pupil from each parish. By such means, Egan and Boyd obtained munificent appropriations for the white Seminary at Alexandria and Baton Rouge.[24]

After the 1876 legislative election in Louisiana, both Democrat and Republican candidates claimed to have won, and each party convened its respective legislature. At the national level, Samuel Tilden, the

Democratic candidate for President, had won the popular vote but was short one electoral vote. The Compromise of 1877 resolved both the state and the federal election disputes. The Democrats in Louisiana agreed to cast their electoral votes in favor of the Republican, Rutherford B. Hayes, in exchange for federal recognition of the Democratic state government in Louisiana and for the removal of federal troops from the state. The Compromise of 1877 gave the Presidency to Hayes and gave the State of Louisiana to Democratic Redeemers antagonistic to the political or economic progress of former slaves. Federal troops were removed from the state and Radical Reconstruction ended in Louisiana in April 1877. As Boyd had predicted, the "Negro's upper hand" in Louisiana did not last.

In 1862, Congress passed the Morrill Act, which donated public lands to the states to use for colleges or to sell to generate a fund to support colleges which would instruct in agriculture and the mechanical arts.[25] Louisiana accepted the federal land grant in 1869,[26] but Louisiana's Agricultural and Mechanical College did not open until the summer session of 1874. William G. Brown, who served as Louisiana's State Superintendent of Education from 1873 to 1877, set up the school shortly after he took office. The Louisiana A&M College provided military drill, and its enrollment ranged as high as one hundred fifty students during the four years it operated in Chalmette, east of New Orleans.

Unlike, LSU, the A&M College abided by the mandate of the 1868 Constitution to admit students irrespective of race or color. The *New Orleans Bulletin* complained that the College began its operations with fifty students ranging in age from twelve to fifteen and ranging in color from pure white to absolute African.[27] It enjoyed an integrated student body until it was merged with the Louisiana State University in 1877 and moved to Baton Rouge.[28] The combined institutions opened on October 5, 1877, as the Louisiana State University and Agricultural and Mechanical College. Funding to LSU was fully restored. With the Democrats in control of the state government and federal troops gone, the new school could expect uninterrupted federal and state funding and would exclude blacks. David Boyd was President and Professor of Engineering.

The Reconstruction Era threat to desegregate LSU was over. Louisiana's Constitution of 1898 specifically provided for separately established public schools for "the white and colored races" for children aged six to eighteen and specified that Southern University was established for the education of persons of color. Louisiana still had no express constitutional or statutory provision requiring that blacks be separated from whites at the college or higher level. Nonetheless, everyone understood, especially after the creation of Southern University, that LSU would remain all white. Hatfield's and Johnson's suits challenged that understanding.

## Notes

1. Former member of the Seminary Board of Supervisors in a letter to President Boyd objecting to the growing militarism of the LSU seminary circa January 1861 in WALTER FLEMING, LOUISIANA STATE UNIVERSITY 97 (Louisiana State Univ. Press 1936).

2. V.L. BEDSOLE AND OSCAR RICHARD, EDS., LOUISIANA STATE UNIVERSITY; A PICTORIAL RECORD OF THE FIRST HUNDRED YEARS 10 (Louisiana State Univ. Press 1959).

3. 39 N.S.-3 University Bulletin Louisiana State Univ. Catalogue Issue 1946-1947 65 (Apr. 10, 1947).

4. Junior Division, John McNeese Junior College at Lake Charles, Northeast Junior College at Monroe, College of Agriculture, College of Arts and Sciences, College of Chemistry and Physics, College of Commerce, College of Education, College of Engineering, Law School, Library School, School of Medicine in New Orleans, School of Music, School of Social Welfare, Graduate School, Summer Term and General Extension Division for nonresident students. *Id.*

5. Master of Arts, Master of Arts in Journalism, Master of Business Administration, Education, Forestry, Music, and Music Education, Master of Science, Master of Science in Agricultural Engineering, Chemical Engineering, Chemistry, Civil Engineering, Electrical Engineering, Game Management, Library Science, Mechanical Engineering, Petroleum Engineering, Physical Education, Physics, Sanitary Engineering, and Sugar Engineering, Doctor of Philosophy, Bachelor of Laws, Master of Laws, Master of Civil Law, Bachelor of Science in Library Science, Doctor of Medicine and Certificate of Social Welfare. *Id.* at 66.

6. LA. CONST. of 1868, art. 135.

7. LA. CONST. of 1868, art. 140.

8. FLEMING, LOUISIANA STATE UNIVERSITY 153.

9. JOURNAL OF THE HOUSE 1868 26, in ROGER A FISCHER, THE SEGREGATION STRUGGLE IN LOUISIANA 1862-77 64 (Univ. of Ill. Press 1974).

10. 1869 La. Acts 38, s. 3 (Feb. 23, 1869). ("That all licenses hereafter granted by this State, and by all parishes and municipalities therein, to persons engaged in business or keeping places of public resort shall contain the express condition that the place of business or public resort shall be open to the accommodation and patronage of all persons without distinction or discrimination on account of race or color, and any person who shall violate the condition of such license, shall, on conviction thereof, be punished by forfeiture of his license, and his place of business or of public resort shall be closed and, moreover, shall be liable at the suit of the person aggrieved to such damages as he shall sustain thereby before any court of competent jurisdiction.")

11.1821 La. Acts "An Act to extend and improve the system of Public Education in the State of Louisiana" s. 5 (Feb. 16, 1821) ("The trustees shall admit in the school or schools of their respective parishes, eight day scholars, taken from those families who are indigent, which day scholars ... shall receive instruction gratis, and be moreover furnished with classical books, quills and paper, at the cost of said school or schools.")

12.1866 La. Acts 63 s. 1. ("Also, the further sum of fifteen thousand six hundred dollars for the maintenance and education of fifty-two State or beneficiary cadets, or so much thereof as may be necessary to support such cadets at the rate of three hundred dollars per year; ...")

13.1860 La. Acts 98 s. 10. ("That the said Seminary shall educate and maintain free of charge, for four years, one beneficiary Cadet from each parish in this State; the selection of such Cadets to be made by the Police Jury of the parish; and the Board of Directors of the four Public School Districts of New Orleans shall each select one; ...")

14.1866 La. Acts 63 s. 1. ("*provided,* that the cadets to be chosen ... shall be chosen in the manner now provided by law, from among those who have not themselves, or whose parents have not the means of paying their expenses, ... that the beneficiaries whose education is thus provided for, shall be required, at the close of their term at said institution to pursue the occupation of teaching school, within the State, for two years thereafter, ... ")

15.LA. CONST. of 1868, art. 140. ("No appropriation shall be made by the general assembly for the support of any private school or any private institution of learning whatever.")

16.1870 La. Acts 81 s.7. ("*Be it further enacted, etc.,* That the sum of thirty-five thousand dollars be and the same is hereby appropriated to the 'Straight University,' for the use of the medical department, to construct suitable buildings, and secure illustrations of medical science; and that the said sum be paid to the order of the Board of Trustees on the warrant of the Auditor of Public Accounts, from the treasury of the State, provided State aid be rendered this department the faculty shall receive one indigent student from each parish free from charge of tuition, which obligation shall continue for ten years; said students to be nominated by the trustees of the university.")

17.FLEMING, LOUISIANA STATE UNIVERSITY 158.

18.1870 La. Acts 81 s.1.

19.1870 La. Acts 47 s.1 - 2.

20.Letter Boyd to Sanford (Apr. 1, 1874) in FISCHER, THE SEGREGATION STRUGGLE IN LOUISIANA 108.

21.MARCUS M. WILKERSON, THOMAS DUCKETT BOYD 38 (LSU Press 1935); FLEMING, LOUISIANA STATE UNIVERSITY 160.

22.FLEMING, LOUISIANA STATE UNIVERSITY 269.

23.FLEMING, LOUISIANA STATE UNIVERSITY 180.

24.FLEMING, LOUISIANA STATE UNIVERSITY 154-156 .

25.Morrill Act, Pub. L. No. 37-130 (1862).

26.1869 La. Acts 62 (May 5, 1869).

27. FLEMING, LOUISIANA STATE UNIVERSITY 288.

28.1876 La. Acts 145 (May 19, 1877).

# Chapter 11.

## *Louisiana's "Gaines" School*

*[E]stablish separate schools, and you by that very act declare the white children the superior of the colored, you teach them to look upon colored children as inferiors, and without enumerating the many disadvantages the colored children would labor under, in the way of poor teachers, bad school houses, etc., you prolong if not perpetuate that despicable prejudice that has such deep roots in the whites of America . . .*

*P.B.S. Pinchback[1]*

*If you build it, they will come.*

*Attributed to Benjamin "Bugsy" Siegel[2]*

On October 22, 1946, the Louisiana State Board of Education held an emergency meeting in Lafayette, Louisiana, and accepted the recommendation from the "special joint committee of the Board of Supervisors of Louisiana State University and the State Board relative to the establishment of a law school at Southern University."[3] The State Board agreed to open the school beginning with the 1947-48 academic session. The defendants in Hatfield's suit could now argue that the state would soon satisfy the *Gaines* requirement for equal facilities within the state.

On December 16, 1946, the defendants filed an exception of no right or cause of action along with their answer to Hatfield's petition. The defendants admitted that Louisiana maintained no school where Hatfield could study law, but argued that LSU had no duty to provide Hatfield with an opportunity to study law. They told the court that Hatfield should insist that Southern University, the "school for Negroes," offer law training for him there. "If a mandamus be an appropriate remedy," they argued, "he should seek a mandamus against Southern University and not against respondents, because respondents are under no duty or obligation to him whatsoever."[4]

The defendants noted that:

> The Louisiana State Board of Education had taken positive steps to establish a Law School for Negroes at Southern University, the said law school to be in operation for the 1947-1948 session, and to furnish Negro citizens of Louisiana with legal schooling substantially equal to that furnished at Louisiana State University and Agricultural & Mechanical College Law School.... With the establishment of a law school at Southern University, the issues raised by relator herein will become moot.[5]

In their further defense, the defendants noted in their answer that the law school at LSU had begun its fall session in September. It was now December, too late for Hatfield to begin the 1946-47 session. The defendants explained that the LSU law school enrolled first year students only in September and had no ability to absorb new students at the beginning of the second semester. B.B. Taylor, representing LSU, told the court that, "The mingling of the two races in the past has always resulted in friction and trouble."[6]

Louisiana's creation of a separate law school exclusively for "Negro" citizens would satisfy the requirements of the Fourteenth Amendment as stated by the United States Supreme Court in *Gaines v. Canada*,[7] if the separate school was equal in quality to the existing school, but it would not satisfy Hatfield. The *Gaines* case did not prohibit segregated educational facilities; it required that Missouri offer the same opportunities for legal training within the state to black students as it offered within the state to white students. The Supreme Court had not yet indicated how equal this equality needed to be. So long as Louisiana's *Gaines* school made proper provision for Hatfield's legal training within

144

the State, Louisiana could expect that the Court would find no Fourteenth Amendment violation of Hatfield's right to equal treatment by the State. Hatfield had no state-supported law school that he could attend now, but Louisiana's *Gaines* school would be in session by the next fall.

Six years earlier, a federal district court in Missouri ruled that states could wait to provide equal facilities for blacks until after they received a request for the facilities and that, after receiving such a request, states would be allowed a reasonable time in which to make the equal facilities available.[8] Plans for the law school were approved by the State Board of Education at its January 10, 1947, meeting. The local state court would not consider a few months an unreasonable period for Hatfield to wait.

Civic leaders in New Orleans denounced the new law school and noted that no provision had been made for Viola Johnson to attend medical school. Clarence A. Laws, executive secretary of the New Orleans Urban League, declared the plan "less than half a measure." Dr. C. Charles Taylor, president of the Louisiana Freedman Missionary Baptist General Association, called it "socially detestable, educationally inadequate and a serious threat to better racial understanding." In evident sarcasm, Dr. J.M. Carr, pastor of Greater Tulane Baptist Church, said, "It appears that the proposed law school at Southern University is to be established along the lines that Negroes are so mentally keen that they can become finished lawyers with only a part-time faculty of four members."[9] The court, however, accepted that Louisiana would soon provide a substantially equal law school for its black citizens to attend.

Judge S. Caldwell Herget dismissed Hatfield's case on April 9, 1947. To explain the dismissal, Judge Herget referred the readers of the *Hatfield* opinion to the reasons he gave in his written opinion in Viola Johnson's suit for admission to LSU's Medical School.[10] Judge Herget had ruled against Ms. Johnson on April 1, 1947. Herget accepted the defendants' argument that the mandamus should issue against Southern University and not against LSU. He stated that LSU had no duty to provide either law or medical training to black citizens of Louisiana. The judge noted that the legislative act creating Southern University permitted Southern to create both law and medical departments,[11] and was convinced that the act imposed a mandatory duty on the Board of Southern University to establish a law school and a medical school. Southern University had not been made a party to the litigation so no mandamus against it could be issued. The judge admonished Ms. Johnson to "make demand upon Southern University for the establishment of a School of Medicine . . . "[12]

Hatfield's attorneys appealed Herget's opinions in both cases to the Louisiana State Supreme Court, but the cases were not scheduled to be heard by that court until October 1947, after its summer recess. By then, the *Gaines* school at Southern University would be in operation and the 1947-1948 session of the LSU Law School would have begun. Marshall turned his attention to parallel litigation in South Carolina, Texas and Oklahoma where the appeals to lower court decisions would be heard more promptly. The appeals in both Hatfield's case and in Johnson's case were considered abandoned and dismissed by the Louisiana State Supreme Court on June 11, 1953. By 1953, a federal court had ordered the LSU law school to enroll a black student, Johnson had returned to Meharry to finish medical school and Hatfield was teaching high school in New Orleans.

On June 14, 1947, the Board of Liquidation of State Debt appropriated $40,000 for the operation of a law school at Southern University.[13] In response to the *Gaines* suit eight years earlier, Missouri had appropriated $200,000 to establish a law school for its black citizens.[14]

Despite its meager funding, the Law School at Southern University opened in September 1947 with four full-time professors and thirteen students. Housed in the University Library, the law school offered a three-year program for college graduates and a six-year program in combination with the College of Arts and Sciences leading to two degrees, the Bachelor of Arts and Science and the Bachelor of Law degrees. Tuition was free for Louisiana residents.

The nascent faculty of the law school included Aguinaldo A. Lenoir, Acting Dean, A.B., Xavier University, LL.B., Lincoln University; Thomas S. E. Brown, A.B., Lincoln University, LL.B., Harvard University; Vanue B. Lacour, A.B., Xavier University, LL.B., Howard University; Edward L. Patterson, Jr., B.S., Tuskegee Institute, LL.B., Lincoln University, M.A., The University of Chicago. C. Vernette Grimes, A.B., Fisk University, B.S., Tennessee State College, LL.B., Kent College of Law (Chicago) served as Librarian. Louis Berry, one of Hatfield's attorneys, taught part-time. Berry, Lenoir and Lacour were from Louisiana.

The law school occupied two offices on the first floor of the university library for its Dean and its faculty offices, a seminar room on the second floor and a portion of the attic where a law library was located. The school's library benefitted from a gift from the Russell Sage Foundation of New York, and during the 1949-1950 school year, the attic library contained 11,652 volumes.

The law school recognized its need to instruct in Louisiana's civil law and devoted a large portion of its curriculum to civilian courses. Unfortunately, none of Southern's faculty had been trained in Louisiana. No black had graduated from a law school within the State of Louisiana since 1886 when Straight University closed its law school. The Louisiana Civil Code and Civil Procedure courses offered at Southern were initially taught by professors from the Louisiana State University Law School including Harriet Spiller Daggett, Louisiana State Normal School, B.A., M.A., LL.B., L.S.U.; Joseph Dainow, B.A., B.C.L., McGill Univ. Doctorate in Law, Univ. of Dijon, S.J.D., Northwestern Univ.; Robert A. Pascal, B.A., J.D., Loyola Univ. New Orleans, M.C.L., L.S.U., LL.M., Univ. of Michigan; John Denson Smith, LL.B., L.S.U., J.S.D., Yale, and local lawyers trained in Louisiana's laws. According to LSU folklore, Professor J. Denson Smith invited his class to meet with him at LSU so he could avoid the ten-mile trip to Southern's campus. When the black students and professors were discovered on LSU's campus, Smith was chastised and forbidden to repeat his invitation. Southern professors audited these courses and, by 1949, were teaching Civil Law courses.

The Southern University Law School awarded its first Bachelor of Laws degrees to six students in June 1950. All of these graduates were veterans of World War II and all were admitted to the practice of law by motion. Louisiana's rules for admission allowed law school graduates who had served in the armed forces of the United States during World War II prior to August 15, 1945, and who matriculated before October 1, 1950, to become attorneys without taking the state bar exam.

Veterans of World War II who attended an ABA accredited law school outside of Louisiana could be admitted to practice law in Louisiana without taking the state bar examination if they earned sixteen hours of course credit in Louisiana Code and Code of Practice courses, with a grade of at least "C" in each subject, and if they spent twenty-four weeks in residence at an approved law school located within Louisiana.[15] Black veterans with law degrees from schools in other states could attend classes at the newly created Southern University Law School and become members of the Louisiana bar without examination.

The six graduates of Southern's first law school class spread

147

across the state and the nation, a tradition that continues today. Ellyson Frederick Dyson opened a law practice in Franklinton, Louisiana. Saint Elmore Johnson opened a law practice in Monroe, Louisiana, and Alvin Basile Jones opened a law practice in New Orleans. Alex Louis Pitcher, from Baton Rouge, remained in Baton Rouge. Jesse N. Stone, Jr. practiced law in Shreveport, Louisiana, and returned to Southern University to serve as law school Dean, 1971-1972, as president of Southern University, 1974-1985, as a full-time faculty member of the law school, 1985-1991, and as a member of Southern University's Board of Supervisors, 1991-1997. Leroy White, from Lake Charles, enrolled in a University of Chicago graduate program in taxation and, after a distinguished career as an Estate Tax attorney, returned to teach part-time at Southern's law school and at the law school of the Louisiana State University.

Southern's law school moved out of the University Library and into its own building in 1953. In addition to increased classroom and office space, the 17,532 square foot building contained a practice court room, space for a law review staff, and an air-conditioned law library. The school was provisionally approved by the American Bar Association in August 1953 and was accredited by the American Bar Association at the end of the three-year probationary period. In 1985, the law school was designated a Law Center and became a separate campus within the Southern University System.

While many other *Gaines* schools were closed after the *Brown v. Board of Education* case overruled the *Plessy* doctrine of separate but equal, the law school at Southern University has continued to serve its state and the nation. By 2003, the Law Center could boast of having graduated more than 2,600 students. Approximately 6% of Louisiana's state legislators and 10% of the state's District Attorneys were graduates of the school. Southern's graduates have served in Louisiana's judiciary at all levels and have served in the legislatures and judiciaries of other states.

Southern University's law school was not the first law school within the state of Louisiana open to blacks. The state's very first law school was at the University of Louisiana, 1847-1861 and 1865-1884, and may have admitted blacks. Both blacks and whites attended the law school at Straight University which opened in 1874. Straight's law school graduated its first class in 1876. It enrolled a total of 115 law students and produced 81 graduates before its last class graduated in 1886.[16] It consistently graduated both black and white students. "Three of the first eight law graduates were white as were eight of the ten 1878 graduates."[17]

Among the first law school graduates of Straight University was Louis Andre' Martinet. Already a medical doctor, Martinet took and passed the Louisiana State Bar Exam at the end of his first year in law school. He taught French while in law school to help pay for his education and was a member of the Louisiana Bar when he graduated in 1876. Martinet practiced law in New Orleans, and, beginning in 1890 when the Louisiana legislature enacted a series of Jim Crow[18] laws, published a newspaper, the *Daily Crusader,* to galvanize the black community of New Orleans to fight political repression.

Martinet used his newspaper to denounce legalized segregation and to organize the Citizens Committee for the Annulment of Act No. 111, the Louisiana statute requiring segregated seating on its streetcars and railway trains. Supported by the Citizens Committee, Martinet laid the groundwork for the test cases that would challenge Act 111 in court. Martinet's efforts resulted in the successful *Desdunes* case and in the notorious *Plessy v. Ferguson* opinion. In 1898, Louis A. Martinet was appointed to the position of notary public in New Orleans. In keeping with Louisiana's civilian tradition, he was responsible for maintaining notarial records in the city, much as the parish Clerks of Court are custodians of notarial records now.

Another Straight student, Pinckney B.S. Pinchback, had been elected Lieutenant Governor of Louisiana by his fellow State Senators in 1871 to fill the position left vacant by Oscar Dunn's death and sat as Governor for forty-three days in 1872 during Governor Warmoth's impeachment hearings. He was a member of the Straight University Board of Trustees when he entered its law school in 1885 and passed the bar exam after one year of study. He eventually moved to Washington, D.C., where he practiced law until 1921.

A member of Straight's last graduating class of 1886, Rene' Carl Metoyer, was appointed notary public in New Orleans by Governor Ruffin Pleasant on June 27, 1917. Metoyer was the second black to have been so appointed. He practiced law in New Orleans for forty years.

When the law school at Straight University closed in 1886, law school training for blacks was no longer available in Louisiana. It would remain unavailable for the next 61 years. Of the three law schools operating in Louisiana in 1946, none admitted black students. Southern would offer law school training to black citizens in Louisiana beginning

149

fall semester 1947.

Hatfield was not satisfied that Louisiana was finally complying with the eight-year-old *Gaines* opinion by offering a segregated law school within the state. Hatfield wanted Louisiana to open the segregated LSU Law School to blacks.

Dean Hebert recognized that creating a law school at Southern University might not be enough to comply fully with the requirements of the *Gaines* decision. He worried that the favorable court decision denying Hatfield's mandamus to enter LSU might lull state officials and legislators into a false sense of security. Louisiana did not have the resources to replicate for black students all of the educational facilities made available by the state to white students. He noted particularly the "financial impossibility" of establishing a School of Medicine at Southern University and warned that, although placing a law school at Southern University would render Hatfield's suit moot, an appeal of Ms. Johnson's suit to the United States Supreme Court might "become the vehicle for the repudiation of the South's policy of racial segregation in educational institutions."[19] Hebert anticipated the logical outcome of Houston's strategy. Demanding equal educational opportunities for black students would force states to desegregate because they would not be willing to pay to duplicate all of their segregated institutions.

## Notes

1. Draft of speech, "On need for equality in education," ca. 1865-1866. P.B.S. Pinchback Papers, Moorland-Springarn Collection, Howard University in JAMES HASKINS, PINCKNEY BENTON STEWART PINCHBACK, THE FIRST BLACK GOVERNOR 117 (Africa World Press, Inc. 1973).

2. Reportedly a member of a New York crime organization, Siegel convinced investors to finance the first luxury hotel/casino in Las Vegas, Nevada.

3. 35 SOUTHERN UNIVERSITY BULLETIN - THE SCHOOL OF LAW 9 (August 1948).

4. *Hatfield v. Bd. of Supv.*, No. 25,520, answer para.16, record at 27 (19th JDC, Par. of East Baton Rouge, La. Dec. 16, 1946). The exception of no right of action argues that no law supports the plaintiff's claim to a judicial remedy or to judicial relief. The exception of no cause of action argues that no facts support the plaintiff's claim.

5. *Hatfield v. Bd. of Supv.*, answer para 22, record at 29.

6. The Reveille, Baton Rouge, La. (LSU's student newspaper) at 1, col.4 (Dec. 17, 1946).

7. *Missouri ex rel. Gaines v. Canada*, 305 U.S. 337 (1938).

8. *Bluford v. Canada*, 32 F. Supp. 707, 710 (W.D. Mo. 1940).

9. *Pittsburgh Courier, Louisiana Ed.* (Nov. 1946).

10.*Johnson v. Bd. of Supv.*, No. 25,414 (19th JDC, Par of E. Baton Rouge, La. Sept. 23,1946).

11.1880 La. Acts 87, amended by 1888 La. Acts 90 of 1888, 2459. ("DEPARTMENTS OF ARTS AND LETTERS, LAW AND MEDICINE. --- There shall be established by said board of trustees a faculty of arts and letters, which shall be competent to instruct in every branch of a liberal education, and under rules of and in concurrence with the board of trustees, to graduate students and grant degrees appertaining to letters, and arts known to universities and colleges in Europe and America, on persons competent and deserving the same.
There may be also established by said board of trustees a department of law and of medicine. The department of law shall consist of three (3) or more learned professors, learned and skilled in the practice of law in this State, who shall be required to give a full course of lectures on international, constitutional, commercial and municipal or civil law and instruction in the practice thereof. The medical department of the university shall consist of not less than three professors.") Act 87 of 1880, s.7, as amended by Act 190 of 1888, Dart's Stats. s. 2459 (1946).

12.*Johnson v. Bd. of Supv.*, No. 25414, slip op. at 14, record at 49 (19th JDC, Par. of East Baton Rouge, La. Sept. 23,1946).

13.Letter from John L. Madden, State Attorney General, to John E. Coxe, State Supt., Dept. of Ed. (Jun. 16, 1947). OPINIONS AND REPORTS OF THE ATTORNEY GENERAL OF THE STATE OF LOUISIANA APRIL 1, 1946 - APRIL 1, 1948. FRED S. LEBLANC, ATTORNEY GENERAL.

14.Lucile H. Bluford, *The Lloyd Gaines Story,* 32-6 J. OF ED. SOCIOLOGY 242-244 (Feb. 1958).

15.37 SOUTHERN UNIVERSITY BULLETIN - THE SCHOOL OF LAW 10 (Aug. 1950);Articles of Incorporation of the Louisiana State Bar Association Art. XII, s. 7-3. (Mar. 15, 1941, as amended to Dec. 1950), 4 DART'S ANNOTATIONS TO LOUISIANA REVISED STATUTES 1950 39 (Bobbs-Merrill Co., Inc. 1951).

16.Straight University continued to operate its other departments until it was merged with the New Orleans University, also a Methodist school, to form Dillard University in 1935.

17.Joe M. Richardson, *The American Missionary Association and Black Education in Louisiana, 1862-1878* 160 in ROBERT R. MACDONALD, LOUISIANA'S BLACK HERITAGE. (La. State Museum 1979)

18.Jim Crow was a character in a song and dance routine presented by Thomas D. Rice in the early nineteenth century. The act presented a stereotype of a Negro who sang and danced to an anonymous song called Jim Crow. The term has become an adjective used to describe the segregated facilities designated for use by blacks in the United States and the laws prohibiting intermingling of ethnic groups on equal terms in public places. Webster's Third New International Dictionary 1216 (G. & C. Merriam Co. 1971).

19.Letter from Paul M. Hebert to Acting President Fred C. Frey (Apr. 3, 1947), LSU Bd. of Supvs. Records, Record Group A0003, Box 8, Folder 47, *Suits Against University - Charles Hatfield*, LSU Archives, LSU Libraries.

# Chapter 12.

## *Part of a Larger Movement*

*The Negro knocks at America's door, and cries out:*
*"Let me come in and sit by the fire. I helped build the*
*house."*

George Vaughn[1]

Hatfield's was one of many suits filed across the south by the NAACP Legal Defense Fund, Inc. in an effort to dismantle legal segregation. In July 1935, Charles Hamilton Houston, an honor graduate of Amherst College and of Harvard Law School, accepted a position with the National Association for the Advancement of Colored People as Special Counsel, its first full-time paid staff attorney. Houston was hired to "carry out a planned legal campaign against discrimination in education and transportation."[2]

Charles Houston graduated Phi Beta Kappa from Amherst College in Massachusetts and was selected, by means of an oratorical contest, to be a commencement speaker for his Class of 1915. In his speech, Houston described the life and work of Paul Laurence Dunbar, 1872-1906, an African-American author and poet, who published his first collection of poems, OAK AND IVY, in 1893. Houston greatly admired Dunbar and wanted others to know about him.

After his graduation, Houston served in the United States Armed Services in France during World War I and suffered abuse and indignities as American whites spread their racism across Europe. Houston returned to the United States committed to effect change. He enrolled in the

Harvard Law School.

Houston was an outstanding law student and earned election to the editorial board of the *Harvard Law Review*. He graduated in the top 5 per cent of his class and won a Langdell scholarship, which supported graduate study in law at Harvard. Harvard awarded Houston a Doctorate Degree in Juridical Science in 1923. Houston again distinguished himself, and the faculty of Harvard awarded Houston the Sheldon Traveling Fellowship to study in the University of Madrid's civil law program in Spain. Houston received a Doctor of Civil Law degree there.

In 1924, Houston began to practice law with his father, William L. Houston, in Washington, D.C. That same year, Houston joined the faculty of the Howard University Law School, an evening school organized by John Mercer Langston in 1869. Houston's father had attended classes there after working as a high school principal during the day. Howard University is a private school significantly funded by the federal government. Its charter was approved by President Andrew Johnson on March 2, 1867, and it opened its law school, headed by Langston, in 1869.

John Mercer Langston was an Oberlin College graduate. Located in northern Ohio, Oberlin College was notorious before the Civil War for its opposition to slavery. Faculty and students at the school, along with the residents of the surrounding town, were active abolitionists. Many helped slaves escape to Canada. Some were jailed for rescuing an escaped slave from slave catchers in Wellington, Ohio. Some went to Harper's Ferry with John Brown.

The trustees of Oberlin began to admit male and female students regardless of race as early as 1835. Langston did not attend a law school, but was admitted to the bar in Ohio in 1854 after studying law with an experienced attorney. Langston was admitted to practice before the U.S. Supreme Court in 1867 and practiced law in Richmond, Virginia, before coming to Howard University. After leaving Howard, Langston served as Consul General to the government of Haiti and represented the State of Virginia in Congress.

Although a significant number of black Americans studied law at schools in Europe, many of the blacks who became lawyers in the United States in the 1800s did so by reading law with a seasoned attorney. The first black to graduate from an American law school, George Lewis Ruffin, did so in 1869 when he finished at the Harvard Law School.

Houston was hired by Howard to teach in Howard's evening

154

school, but Houston envisioned Howard as a full-time, fully accredited day school which would enroll larger numbers of students and train them to be advocates for the rights of black people throughout the nation. By June 1929, the Howard University trustees had selected Houston as Resident Vice-Dean in charge of the Law School's day program and of the law library, positioning him to transform the law school into a full-time day school. Houston successfully ushered Howard Law School through the application and inspection processes as it earned accreditation from both the American Bar Association and the American Association of Law Schools, in 1930 and 1931, respectively. Howard's law school was now fully accredited and ready to train "social engineers."

Houston told his students of his intent:

> to prepare a group of young scholars as attorneys who would not only be skilled in law but would also be familiar with methods of sociology, economics, history, and other liberal arts disciplines. They would not only be lawyers but also social engineers, using the law as an instrument for social justice.[3]

He wanted Howard University graduates to return to their African-American communities as interpreters of the law and advocates for social justice. Houston's students nicknamed him Iron Shoes because of the high standards he set for them and because he demanded that they perform at their best.

In 1935, Houston resigned his position as head of Howard's Law School to accept employment at the NAACP Legal Defense Fund but he did not sever his relationship with the law school. Houston used Howard's Law School as a laboratory where he would test his arguments and legal theories before presenting them to the courts. Law students would listen to his strategy and ask questions of him or offer comments. Houston, thus, became aware of any pitfalls in his argument or evidence and was enriched by the new ideas and viewpoints provided by the students.

The students experienced an opportunity to hear a master litigator and to play a part in creating new law on issues of social justice. Houston's continued presence in the law school inspired students to take up the fight for civil rights. As Houston traveled across the country litigating for the NAACP, he sought out his former students, recruiting them to join him in handling local cases. He continued to train them while spreading his workload and facilitating his access to local courts.[4] He set an example of service and excellence for his students, both as an academician and as a practicing attorney, and he challenged them to take responsibility for effecting change -- to become social engineers.

Thurgood Marshall, perhaps Houston's best known student, accepted employment with Houston as Assistant Special Counsel for the NAACP Legal Defense Fund in October 1936, three years after graduating from Howard at the top of his class. When Houston resigned from the NAACP in July 1938, Marshall replaced him as Special Counsel but frequently called upon him for advice and direction. Marshall continued the systematic dismantling of legal segregation begun by Houston and continued working with local counsel throughout the south. Marshall distinguished himself as a civil rights litigator and, in 1967, was appointed a Justice of the United States Supreme Court.

In the early 1930s, the NAACP hired Nathan Margold, a 1923 graduate of Harvard University and an expert on Constitutional Law, to develop a legal strategy to use to attack segregation in public schools. Margold cautioned against a direct attack on segregation and recommended that the NAACP begin by insisting on truly equal schools for blacks. Houston agreed with Margold, reasoning that, when forced by the courts to provide equal opportunities for blacks, the southern states would choose to admit blacks into their existing facilities rather than bear the cost of providing equal facilities. Houston focused first on the most costly and least available schools, graduate and professional schools.

In 1935, when Houston accepted employment at the Legal Defense Fund, opportunities for blacks to attend graduate or professional schools were extremely limited. Across the south -- seventeen states and the District of Columbia -- black and white students attended separate public schools. Although required by *Plessy* to provide equal facilities for blacks and whites, not one of these eighteen jurisdictions did so. Public support for higher education for blacks was limited. Support for their graduate and professional training was virtually nonexistent. While banning the admission of blacks into their historically white state-supported graduate and professional schools, no state offered graduate or professional training at their historically black schools and only a few states offered blacks any access to graduate or professional training at all.

Missouri, Maryland and Oklahoma offered financial support to black citizens who were willing to attend graduate and professional schools outside of their home state. A 1921 Missouri statute authorized the Board of Curators of Lincoln University, a historically black public school, to pay reasonable tuition fees for any black resident to study in an adjacent state any subject or course offered at the University of Missouri, which was closed to blacks, but not offered at Lincoln University.[5] Money for the out-of-state scholarships came from the budget for the state's historically black school. No new money was appropriated.

A 1933 Maryland statute authorized the Regents of the University of Maryland to establish a partial scholarship at Morgan College, a private liberal arts college in Baltimore, or at institutions outside of the state, to allow blacks to take professional courses or other work offered at the University of Maryland, but not offered at Princess Anne Academy, its historically black school.[6] No appropriation was made until 1935 when $10,000 per year was made available for scholarships in the amount of $200 per student.[7] In just eighteen days, from June 1, 1935, when the appropriations act went into effect, until June 18, 1935, 113 applications for the fifty available scholarships were filed.

In 1935, Oklahoma appropriated $5,000 to provide scholarship aid, up to the amount of $250 per academic year, plus three cents per mile for transportation for students to attend schools outside the State of Oklahoma.[8] After two years of college within Oklahoma, students could use the funds to leave the state to pursue a course of study available at the University of Oklahoma but not available at Langston University, Oklahoma's historically black school. Thirteen states -- Alabama, Arkansas, Delaware, Florida, Georgia, Kentucky, Louisiana, Mississippi, North Carolina, South Carolina, Tennessee, Texas, and Virginia -- made no provision whatsoever for the professional or graduate education of their black citizens.

Only the District of Columbia offered a meaningful range of publically supported opportunities for graduate and professional study within its jurisdiction. Howard University had offered professional training since shortly after the Civil War. Training in Medicine was first offered in 1868, Religion in 1868, Pharmacy in 1868, Law in 1869, Dentistry in 1882, and Dental Hygiene in 1935. Howard University housed the only publically funded law school in the south that was open to blacks.

West Virginia was unique in that West Virginia University admitted blacks to its extension classes in the mid-1920s.[9] In addition, a 1927 West Virginia statute authorized the state to pay a portion of the

157

tuition and fees of students attending schools outside of West Virginia when the course of study the student wanted to pursue was available at West Virginia University but not available at a state school the student could attend and, because of segregation laws, the student could not attend West Virginia University.[10] The statute was amended in 1929 limiting this scholarship to only those students with at least two years of college.[11] In 1938, complying with the U.S. Supreme Court's ruling in *Missouri v. Gaines,* West Virginia University opened all its graduate and professional schools to blacks.

Charles Houston sought to erode the principle of segregation by documenting that the southern states had not complied with the *Plessy* admonition to provide equal facilities for blacks and whites in their graduate and professional school offerings. He would then demonstrate that it was neither reasonable nor equitable for states to support separate educational facilities. Houston traveled throughout the South collecting and analyzing data contrasting the states' facilities and offerings for white and black students. He wrote articles for general circulation and thematic reports directed at educators and legislators to inform decision makers of the consequences of the doctrine of separate but equal. States across the south would have to spend hundreds of millions of dollars at their black institutions to comply with *Plessy.*

Houston firmly believed that southern states could not and would not appropriate the level of funding needed to provide even remotely equal separate graduate and professional facilities as required by *Plessy,* so would choose to open their existing schools to blacks. Once the states accepted the desegregation of their graduate schools, Houston premised, segregation would fall in all of its ugly ramifications. Houston did not anticipate the level of Southern resistance he and others would experience. Only after years of litigation, persistence and patience did the desegregation of even graduate educational facilities he targeted become the law of the land, if not its reality.

Houston began his assault on segregated education by demanding that those states which provided professional and graduate schools for their white citizens, but did not provide similar facilities or opportunities for their black citizens open the doors of their white facilities to the state's black citizens. Earlier litigation seeking admission into state financed schools had produced limited, but promising, responses from the states.

In April 1932, Thomas R. Hocutt brought suit to attend the

University of North Carolina School of Pharmacy. His application had been rejected because it was North Carolina's policy to separate the races in its schools and Hocutt was "colored." His subsequent lawsuit was decided against him. He abandoned his appeal because his undergraduate college, North Carolina College for Negroes at Durham, would not certify his scholastic record. Hocutt's application and suit prompted the Governor of North Carolina to appoint a commission to study the state's educational offerings to blacks. In 1939, North Carolina established the Departments of Law, Pharmacy, and Library Science at the North Carolina College for Negroes and appropriated scholarship funds to assist blacks to secure other graduate and professional training outside of the state.[12]

In 1935, Alice Carlotta Jackson applied to attend the University of Virginia Graduate School of Romance Languages. She had graduated from Virginia Union University then attended Smith College in Massachusetts where she completed about half of the work required for a master's degree in French. Her application to complete her master's degree was rejected by the University of Virginia, but spurred the state to redress the absence of state-supported opportunities for blacks to study in graduate or professional schools. Virginia authorized those state schools which refused to admit qualified black applicants to pay the costs to allow the rejected students to attend a private school within the state or to attend a school outside of the state.[13] The state school choosing to maintain segregation was charged to bear the cost of its decision. In that same year, the Virginia Department of Education resolved to offer graduate training to blacks within the state at its State College for Negroes at Ettrick. By November 1938, eighteen black graduate students were enrolled in Elementary Education, Home Economics, Secondary Education, English, History, Science, Mathematics, and Sociology.

Also, in 1935, Donald Murray applied to attend the University of Maryland's law school. His suit did not result in a separate, segregated institution. Murray, a 1934 graduate of Amherst College, Charles Hamilton Houston's alma mater, was denied admission to the University of Maryland's law school because of his race. Thurgood Marshall relished the opportunity to represent Murray in this litigation in his home state of Maryland. Marshall earlier had been denied admission to Maryland's law school and was pleased to "get even with Maryland for not letting me go to its school."[14]

The Maryland state court ruled that Maryland's program

providing scholarships for blacks to study outside of the state fell short of *Plessy*'s requirement that states provide facilities for blacks substantially equal to those provided by the state for whites.[15] The court noted that the state laws of Maryland did not allow it to order Maryland to establish a separate law school for blacks. Consequentially, the court's only remedy was to order that Murray be admitted to the already existing state-supported law school in the state.

When Murray entered the University of Maryland law school in October 1935, Maryland became the first of the segregating states to admit blacks to its historically white public law school since Reconstruction. Blacks had attended the law schools at the University of Maryland and the University of South Carolina in the 1880s, but none had attended more recently. Murray's litigation was the beginning of a series of lawsuits that would result in southern states providing access to graduate and professional training for its black citizens.

Murray's case motivated William B. Redmond to apply to attend the University of Tennessee School of Pharmacy in September 1936. When his application was rejected, he sued demanding either admission to the University or equivalent separate instruction. The court did not address the merits of his argument, but dismissed his case because he had failed to appeal his rejected application to the state Board of Education or to the legislature before seeking assistance from the courts. Hatfield was, similarly, told to exhaust his state administrative remedies before filing his lawsuit and, complying, sent an August 1946 letter to the LSU Board of Supervisors.

The Tennessee legislature responded to Redmond's suit in the same manner in which the Louisiana legislature responded to Hatfield's suit. It provided scholarships for black students to attend private schools within the state or to attend out of state schools for professional study not available to them at the state's public colleges.[16] The $2,500 allocated for these scholarships was to be taken from the regular appropriations for Tennessee's Agricultural and Industrial College for Negroes.

Murray's case prompted southern states to revisit their educational offerings. Some southern states funded out of state scholarship programs or established graduate and professional programs at their historically black schools, or both, frustrating Houston's plans to force the integration of already existing state schools. A 1936 Kentucky statute provided $5,000 for scholarships in the maximum amount of $175 per student, per academic year.[17] Texas appropriated $12,000 to establish a graduate department at its State College for Negroes at Prairie View in 1937.[18] Pursuant to a resolution from the Louisiana Department of Education, Louisiana established graduate courses in education in the summer of 1938 to be held at Southern University, but under the direction of the Dean of Graduate Study of the Louisiana State University. Only West Virginia, as noted above, opened its graduate and professional schools to blacks in 1938, accomplishing Houston's intent.

That same year, North Carolina commissioned a study that would result, in 1939, in the state offering tuition grants for professional study outside of the state and offering professional training at its historically black school. By 1938, Kentucky, Maryland, Missouri, Oklahoma, Tennessee and Virginia offered scholarships. Texas would begin its scholarship program in 1939.[19] Seven states – Alabama, Arkansas, Delaware, Florida, Georgia, Mississippi, and South Carolina -- made no provision at all to offer or support any graduate or professional education or training for their black populations.

Officials in Georgia responded to the demand for postgraduate training for blacks by studying the problem. A 1938 report prepared under the direction of Dean Walter D. Cocking of the University of Georgia College of Education recommended that the "rather superior facilities for graduate work . . . at Atlanta University, and at certain other Negro institutions located in the Southwestern region" be used by the state to respond to the increasing demand on the part of Negroes for graduate and professional education.[20] Cocking recognized the high cost of graduate work and the extensive facilities required. He realized that the southern states were neither able nor willing to finance equal educational opportunities for blacks.

Cocking recommended that "no facilities for graduate work be provided in the public Negro colleges in the near future." In his opinion, students should be sent to already existing private schools at state expense. He noted that, "It is fair and just that the State should provide higher educational advantages to all citizens alike," but was concerned about the cost. "Where the cost of separate graduate and professional schools for the races is prohibitive, the State should make available, through other means, similar opportunities."[21]

Georgia could hardly satisfy the equal treatment requirement of *Gaines* by providing funds to the private schools within its borders. The supply of private schools in Georgia offering graduate school training for blacks was insufficient in 1938 as elsewhere throughout the south.

Atlanta University offered graduate training in Social Work, Library Science and Business Administration. Theology and Religious Education were offered at Morehouse School of Religion, Gammon Theological Seminary, and Turner Theological Seminary, also located in Atlanta.

Howard University in Washington, D.C. offered Medicine, Dentistry, Law, Pharmacy, Religion, and Dental Hygiene. Meharry Medical College in Tennessee offered Medicine, Dentistry, Pharmacy and Nursing. Fisk University in Tennessee offered graduate instruction in Biology, Chemistry, Education, English, History, Mathematics, Music, Physics, Religion and Social Science. Xavier University in Louisiana offered Pharmacy and Social Service. Dillard University in Louisiana offered Nursing. Hampton Institute in Virginia offered Business, Library Science and Nursing. Theology was offered at Johnson C. Smith University in North Carolina, Payne Theological Seminary in Ohio, and Simmons University Bible College in Kentucky. Only these courses of study were available and few graduate students were enrolled in these schools during the academic year 1938-1939.[22]

*Gaines* required states to provide publically funded schools for all its citizens equally. Sending public money to private schools was not the same as providing a broad range of educational opportunities in public institutions. Funding private schools instead of desegregating existing public schools was impossible in those states with limited professional or graduate programs in their private schools. Southern states with "rather superior facilities for graduate work" at their historically black private schools were few and far between.

The *Gaines* case in 1938 reminded the states of their obligation to provide educational opportunities to blacks equal to those provided to whites, as promised by the *Plessy* Court's interpretation of the Fourteenth Amendment. The *Plessy* decision, left in place by the *Gaines* Court, allowed states to offer these equal opportunities in separate facilities. As a result of and immediately after the *Gaines* decision, Missouri opened a law school at Lincoln University, a college founded in 1866 by the officers of the 62nd U.S. Colored Infantry, U.S. Army, and transferred to the state in 1879. The law school at Lincoln operated until 1955.

In response to both *Gaines* and the state's study of higher education, North Carolina opened a law school at North Carolina Central University in 1939. That law school remains open and is one of only four historically black law schools currently accredited by the American Bar Association. The four schools include those at North Carolina Central,

162

Southern, Texas Southern, and Howard Universities.[23]

Other states reluctantly made graduate and professional study available within the state after blacks applied to or sued to enter historically white state schools. On October 18, 1939, in Tennessee, four students sought admission to the University of Tennessee Graduate School while two applied to be admitted to its College of Law. They were all denied admission, and they filed suit.

While their cases were pending, the state enacted legislation directing the State Board of Education to provide "educational training and instruction for negro [sic] citizens of Tennessee equivalent to that provided at the University of Tennessee by the State of Tennessee for white citizens of Tennessee," noting that, "members of the negro [sic] race and white race shall not attend the same institution . . . "[24] In its defense of the lawsuit filed by the rejected applicants, the state promised that the requested facilities, if not already available, would be made available soon.[25]

Lucile Bluford applied to attend the University of Missouri Graduate School of Journalism in September 1940. When officials there refused to admit her, she demanded damages from the school. The federal court which heard her suit said that *Plessy v. Ferguson* gave the state the right to maintain segregated schools and that the *Gaines* case did not deprive a state of a right to "notice and reasonable opportunity to furnish facilities not theretofore requested." The court told Bluford that she must allow the authorities at Lincoln University, the state school for black students, an opportunity to prepare facilities at Lincoln for her before demanding admission to the state school for white students. She could "not complain that defendant has deprived her of her constitutional rights until she has applied to the proper authorities for those rights and has been unlawfully refused."[26] The Circuit Court of Appeals dismissed her appeal, and Missouri opened a Graduate School of Journalism at Lincoln University in February 1942.

In 1943, Arkansas established a State Tuition Fund using $5,000 transferred from the Agricultural, Mechanical and Normal College (Negro) Fund to help pay tuition for qualified black students to attend school outside of Arkansas.[27] In January 1945, the Committee on Regional Education of the Southern Governors Conference declared, "The Supreme Court of the United States has ruled unequivocally that every state must maintain equal educational facilities within its borders, if demanded, to all citizens who are similarly qualified. The Negro's need and eligibility for higher education are steadily growing, . . . "[28]

In the summer of 1945, the Conference of Deans of Southern Graduate Schools acknowledged that no historically black institution offered a doctoral degree and that very few offered a master's degree. No more than six of the black institutions had a library that would support graduate training. The Conference, attended by both black and white educators, adopted resolutions acknowledging that "graduate programs for Negroes are far from adequate . . ." and recognizing that out-of-state scholarships are a temporary expedient. The Conference favored "strong regional graduate schools" to satisfy the academic needs of its black citizens.[29] Black educators at the Conference rejected that idea. It did not conform to the "within the state" requirement of *Gaines*, and would impose an unfair burden on black students. Some educators would settle for the separate but equal standard set by *Plessy* if only the separate facilities would be equal, while others wanted access to all public educational institutions and an end to segregation.

## Notes

1.Addressing the U.S. Supreme Court in *Shelley v. Kraemer*, 334 U.S.1 (May 3, 1948).

2.GENNA RAE MCNEIL, GROUNDWORK 133 (Univ. of Pennsylvania Press 1983).

3.ADA FISHER, A MATTER OF BLACK AND WHITE 88 (Univ. of Oklahoma Press 1996).

4.Attorneys licensed to practice in one state are allowed to litigate in other states where they are not licensed if they associate with a local attorney who will introduce the out-of-state attorney to the court and serve as the court's contact person for the case.

5.1921 Mo. Laws p. 86, s. 7 (Apr. 15, 1921).

6.1933 Md. Laws 234 (Apr. 21, 1933).

7.*Pearson,* 169 Md. at 485-486.

8.1935 Okla. Laws, ch. 34, p. 138 (May 2, 1935).

9. Lawrence V. Jordan, *Educational Integration in West Virginia - One Year Afterward*, 24-8 J. of Negro Education 371, 372 (1955).

10.1927 W. Va. Acts ch. 10, p. 13 (Apr. 27, 1927).

11.1929 W. Va. Acts ch, 34, p. 165 (Feb. 12, 1929).

12.1939 N.C. Laws ch. 65, p. 88 (Mar. 1, 1939).

13.1936 Va. Acts ch. 352, p. 561 (Mar. 27, 1936).

14.JUAN WILLIAMS, THURGOOD MARSHALL 76 (Random House 1998).

15.*Pearson v. Murray*, 169 Md. 478, 487, 182 A. 590, 593 (1936).

16.1937 Tenn. Acts, ch. 256, p. 1048 (May 21, 1937).

17.1936 Ky. Acts, ch. 43, p.110 (Feb. 25, 1936).

18. 1937 Texas Laws, ch. 444, s. 5, p. 979 (Jun. 8, 1937).

19. 1939 Texas Special Laws, ch. 8, p. 310, 359 (Jul. 10. 1939).

20. Report on the Study of Higher Education of Negroes in Georgia, Submitted to the Board of Regents of the University System of Georgia on October 15, 1938, quoted in FRED MCCUISTION, GRADUATE INSTRUCTION FOR NEGROES IN THE UNITED STATES 63 (George Peabody College for Teachers, Nashville, Tn. 1939).

21. MCCUISTION, GRADUATE INSTRUCTION FOR NEGROES 62-63.

22. MCCUISTION, GRADUATE INSTRUCTION FOR NEGROES 60. McCuistion counted 363 black graduate students in 1938-1939, but did not count students at Fisk or Dillard Universities

23. A fifth law school attached to an historically black university enrolled its first class in August 2002. (FAMU College of Law Admissions Requirements and Procedures http://www,famu.edu/acad/colleges/law/admissions/admissions.html visited Jan. 16, 2003.) The legislature of the State of Florida authorized Florida A & M University to open a law school to be located in Orlando, Florida. (Summary, www.it.famu.edu/it/famulaw/ visited May 22, 2001.)

Florida created a law division of the Florida Agricultural and Mechanical College for Negroes on December 21, 1949, in response to a law suit filed by Virgil D. Hawkins seeking admission to the College of Law of the University of Florida. (*Hawkins v. Board of Control of Florida*, 47 So.2d 608 (Fla. 1950).) Funds for the College of Law were provided in 1951 and the law school operated from that fall until it was closed in 1968. (Summary, www.it.famu.edu/it/famulaw) The College of Law admitted its first white student in September 1964, (FAMU College of Law Timeline, www.it.famu.edu/it/famulaw) and, in July 1965, the Florida legislature opened a law school at Florida State University, a historically white university just a few miles away. The law school at Florida A & M was closed when its 1965 entering class graduated. (*South Florida Sun-Sentinel*, Nov. 18, 2000, 1B, 2000 WL 28991294.)

24. 1941 Tenn. Pub. Acts, Chap. 43, s. 1. (Feb. 12, 1941).

25. *Michael v. Witham*, 165 S.W.2d 378, 381 (Tn. 1942).

26. *Lucile Bluford v. S. W. Canada*, 32 F. Supp. 707, 710-711 (W.D. Mo. 1940).

27. 1943 Ark. Acts 345 (Mar. 24, 1942).

28. JESSIE PARKHURST GUZMAN, ED., NEGRO YEAR BOOK 1941-1946 101 (Tuskegee Institute 1947).

29. GUZMAN, ED., NEGRO YEAR BOOK 1941-1946 100.

# Chapter 13.

# *Creating Opportunities*

My race needs no special defenses. For the past history of
them in this country proves them to be the equal of any
people anywhere. All they need is an equal chance in the
battle of life.

*Robert Smalls[1]*

In 1946, the same year in which Hatfield sued Louisiana State
University, Thurgood Marshall filed suits on behalf of black college
graduates demanding entry into their respective state-supported law
schools in South Carolina, Texas, and Oklahoma.[2] In response to these
suits, South Carolina and Texas, like Louisiana, promptly established law
schools at their state-supported historically black colleges to satisfy the
*Gaines* requirement that equal educational facilities be made available
within the state for all state citizens. Hastily created, low-budget law
schools were up and running by the fall semester of 1947. Irrespective of
the lawsuit filed in Oklahoma, officials there refused to establish a
*Gaines* school or admit Ada Sipuel to their white law school until the
United States Supreme Court explicitly directed them to do so.

*South Carolina*

John Howard Wrighten III sued for admission to the University
of South Carolina Law School. The State of South Carolina authorized

the Colored Normal, Industrial, Agricultural and Mechanical College of South Carolina to organize graduate Law and Medical Departments in 1945.[3] Established in 1896 in Orangeburg, S.C., this institution was renamed South Carolina State College in 1954. In 1946, South Carolina appropriated $25,000 to fund a graduate school for blacks and $5,000 to create a scholarship fund to support study at any medical college within or outside of the state.[4] In 1947, South Carolina appropriated $60,000 for both graduate and law school training and then authorized the use of the money to maintain and operate a law school.[5]

In Wrighten's litigation, state officials assured the court that, by the college's next session, beginning in September 1947, a law school for blacks would be "in active operation, equipped, fitted and staffed, and ready for the giving of instruction on a complete parity with the University [of South Carolina] Law School."[6] Relying on this assurance, the court deferred action on the case. It allowed the state to accomplish one of three alternatives. The state could allow Wrighten to attend the Law School of the University of South Carolina as he had requested; it could create another state law school on substantial parity with the University Law School, as it had promised; or, it could furnish no law school education to any person, white or black, within the state of South Carolina.

Had Wrighten been admitted to the Law School at the University of South Carolina, he would not have been the first black to attend school there. Unlike Louisiana, South Carolina had not fully protected its public university from its black citizens. T. McCants Stewart and Richard T. Greener graduated from the University of South Carolina Law School in 1875 and 1876, respectively. Greener had served as a professor there. Nevertheless, the state chose the second alternative, to create another state law school which Wrighten could attend.

The third option, to close the existing segregated school, was rejected by South Carolina and by most other jurisdictions but was popular in Virginia. In the wake of the Supreme Court's decision in *Brown v. Board of Education*, the State of Virginia closed public elementary and high schools in Front Royal, Charlottesville, and Norfolk in 1958 rather than submit to court-ordered integration.[7] White students in Virginia could attend private schools with the aid of state-funded tuition grants.

In Prince Edward County, Virginia, where the local school board closed its schools, public school education was unavailable for five years,

1959 to 1964. White children were carried in public school buses to and from the newly organized and partially state-funded Prince Edward Academy, while black children, and those white children whose families could not afford to pay the private school tuition, sat at home.

Prince Edward County, located seventy miles southwest of Richmond, Virginia, is a rural area with its county seat in Farmville. In 1939, two high schools were built. The white Farmville High School had a gymnasium, locker rooms, cafeteria, infirmary and auditorium with fixed seats. The black Moton High School had none of these facilities. Farmville High School offered courses in Physics, World History, Latin, Stenography, Industrial Arts and Drawing. Moton High School did not and its Science budget was only $300 per year. Moton High, built to serve 175 students, had more than 350 students enrolled in 1946. One class met in a school bus in the school's parking lot.

On April 23, 1951, students at Moton High marched out of their school and down the hill to the county courthouse where they confronted the superintendent of schools. They complained of their inadequate and overcrowded facilities and demanded the "equal" part of *Plessy's* "separate but equal" promise. During their strike, the students contacted Oliver W. Hill and Spottswood Robinson III, Howard Law School graduates, and these attorneys filed suit on their behalf directly attacking Virginia's school segregation laws.[8] The three judge panel found the two high schools grossly unequal in buildings, facilities, curricula and bus service, but refused to rule that the Virginia laws which required segregated schools were unconstitutional. The court concluded that, "the separation provision rests neither upon prejudice, nor caprice, . . . it declares one of the ways of life in Virginia."[9]

Two months after the black students marched to the office of the superintendent of schools, the Prince Edward County Board of Supervisors appropriated $850,000 to replace the Moton High School but their decision came too late to stop the students' momentum. A new segregated school would not satisfy them now, even if it could be made equal. The students wanted an end to segregation. The *Davis* litigants appealed their case to the U.S. Supreme Court which consolidated it with cases from Delaware, Kansas and South Carolina.[10]

The Supreme Court ruled in the consolidated cases that, "Separate educational facilities are inherently unequal. . . . such segregation is a denial of the equal protection of the laws."[11] When the Court ruled a year later that Davis and all the other plaintiffs should be admitted "to public

169

schools on a racially nondiscriminatory basis with all deliberate speed,"[12] Virginia enacted a series of laws eliminating compulsory attendance, providing tuition grants for students to attend private schools, and authorizing the closing of schools. Even after these laws were declared unconstitutional by both federal and state courts,[13] Prince Edward County established a private, publicly funded school for white children and the county's public schools were locked and chained for the next five years.

In Wrighten's case, the federal court accepted South Carolina's promise of a separate law school as "adequate provision" for its black citizens. It nonetheless warned that, "[W]here the State does not make preparations in advance to furnish facilities to which its citizens are entitled, it runs the risk of being forced to share the facilities furnished to members of one race with those of another race."[14] South Carolina officials were quick to establish a law school at the South Carolina State College so that John Howard Wrighten III and other blacks could study law within the state yet outside of the University of South Carolina. Fifty-one students received their legal degrees from the law school at South Carolina State College before it closed in 1966.

Of the four 1946 litigants, Wrighten was the only one to attend the *Gaines* school that resulted from his litigation. He enrolled in the school in 1949 and graduated in 1952. He practiced law in Charleston where he battled against discrimination and segregation and was an outstanding fighter in the cause of human rights in the south.

*Texas*

Heman Sweatt filed suit against Texas officials on May 16, 1946. By February 1947, Texas had a separate and segregated law school ready for him. Like Hatfield, Sweatt had been a postman and was a veteran of World War II when he applied to be admitted to the law school. Unlike Hatfield, Sweatt's father had been a charter member of the Houston branch of the National Association for the Advancement of Colored People and Sweatt had the support of both the local branch and the national organization from the very beginning of his efforts to attend the University of Texas Law School. Thurgood Marshall had asked NAACP branches in the south to identify plaintiffs who were interested in attending graduate or professional school and were willing to sue for admission into segregated state schools. When Lulu White, Director of NAACP branches in Texas, pleaded for someone to "stand up and challenge segregation," Sweatt stood and, like Hatfield, was willing.

Sweatt applied to the University of Texas Law School on February 26, 1946, and was denied admission solely on the basis of the color of his skin. Texas law at that time explicitly restricted admission to the University of Texas to white students.[15] The State of Texas provided no law school that Sweatt could attend although *Gaines* required that one be made available.

Sweatt's case was tried on June 17, 1946. The trial court allowed the state six months to establish for Sweatt "a course for legal instruction substantially equivalent to that offered at the University of Texas."[16] Texas officials committed to open a law school for Sweatt beginning February 1947.

The Texas legislature went straight to work. It created a new entity, the Texas State University for Negroes, to be located in Houston, and appropriated $2,000,000 for land, buildings and equipment, and $500,000 per annum for maintenance.[17] It instructed the Texas State University for Negroes to be in operation by September 1, 1947, and to offer courses in law and other professions, all of which were to be equivalent to those offered at the University of Texas. To provide legal instruction to blacks while the Houston school was under development, the legislature provided $100,000 to create a "separate school of law at Austin," to offer law courses until the Texas State University for Negroes in Houston began its operations. The writ of mandamus that would admit Sweatt into the University of Texas Law School was denied on December 17, 1946.

The School of Law of the Texas State University for Negroes in Austin had four University of Texas law professors assigned to teach classes there in addition to teaching their regular courses at the University of Texas Law School. The school had two classrooms. Its students had no library of their own, but were instructed to use the State Law Library in the Capitol Building. Heman Sweatt refused to attend.

The Texas state court decided that the state had satisfied the Fourteenth Amendment's requirement for equal protection under the law. It recognized the state's "sincere and earnest bona fide effort to afford every reasonable and adequate facility and opportunity guaranteed to Relator under the Fourteenth Amendment, within the State's settled policy (constitutional and statutory) of race segregation in its public schools," and determined that the state had provided "equal, if not better, opportunities for the study of law."[18] The court reasoned that, not only would the new school have the same curriculum and the same professors as the school for whites, it would have smaller classes and easier access to the Texas Supreme Court library.

The attorneys for Sweatt had argued against segregation, claiming that segregation was inconsistent with equality, but the Texas court was not interested. The court limited its "appropriate judicial inquiry" to determining whether or not the facilities furnished for the black law students were equivalent or substantially equivalent to what was offered at the University of Texas Law School. The Texas court determined that they were and that Heman Sweatt, who now had a Texas law school he could attend, had no right to attend the University of Texas Law School.

The United States Supreme Court disagreed. The Supreme Court could see the great disparity between the two schools offered by the State. The University of Texas Law School had sixteen full-time and three part-time professors on its faculty. It had 65,000 volumes in its library and had moot court facilities, scholarship funds and a law review. It had a nationally recognized faculty and distinguished, well-connected graduates. The temporary law school for blacks in Austin had no independent faculty or library; no moot court facilities or law review. The law school for blacks in Houston had five full-time professors and a library of 16,500 volumes. It was a better school than the makeshift arrangements in Austin, but it was not the equal of the law school at the University of Texas.

In addition, according to the Court, the law school that was open only to whites had those "qualities which are incapable of objective measurement but which make for greatness in a law school . . . reputation of the faculty, experience of the administration, position and influence of the alumni, standing in the community, traditions and prestige."[19] The Court was concerned with the social isolation imposed upon a law student unable to interact with others who participate in the legal system, and ordered the State of Texas to allow Sweatt to enroll at the University of Texas Law School.

At age 37, Heman Sweatt did just that. He, along with four other black males: Virgil C. Lott of Austin, Texas, George Washington, Jr. of Dallas, Texas, Jacob Hudson Carruthers of Fort Worth, Texas, and Elwin Franklin Jarmon of Columbus, Texas, enrolled in the University of Texas Law School in September 1950. Even before he enrolled, Sweatt suffered from stomach ulcers and, while hospitalized for them, suffered a heart attack. By the time he registered on September 19, 1950, more than four years after he filed suit, he was emotionally and physically exhausted.

Upon arriving on campus, Sweatt was not made welcome. He endured threats, vandalism, and illness, including an appendectomy. Racial slurs came from faculty as well as students. A cross burned for more than fifteen minutes near the Law Building and, after the fire was extinguished, the letters "KKK" were found painted on the building's steps. Sweatt's tires were slashed the morning of his first set of final exams.

Sweatt spent two years at the law school at the University of Texas, then left Texas for Atlanta. He earned a Master's degree in Community Organizing from the Atlanta University Graduate School of Social Work and worked in Cleveland and Atlanta for the NAACP and the National Urban League before retiring. Two of the black students who entered with Sweatt fared better in law school. Virgil C. Lott became the first black graduate of the University of Texas Law School when he finished in January 1953. George Washington, Jr. graduated in January 1954.

*Oklahoma*

Officials in Oklahoma did nothing to establish a law school for blacks within their state for almost two years after they were sued. When Ada Lois Sipuel filed her suit to attend the law school at the State University of Oklahoma at Norman, state officials decided to take no action until she convinced them that she was willing to attend a separate segregated law school. The Justices of the Supreme Court of Oklahoma stated that they saw no reason to establish a new law school unless there was "some ready patronage."[20] Sipuel had not committed to attend any such school. According to the state court, the state had no duty to act because Sipuel had made no demand for legal training upon Langston University, the state university set aside for Oklahoma's black citizens. She had not given the state an opportunity to make "other and proper provision" for her legal training.

Missouri had used a "time to prepare" argument successfully in federal court to avoid Lucile Bluford's admission to the Journalism School at the University of Missouri. The federal court in Bluford's suit required that Bluford give Missouri notice of her desire to obtain a degree in Journalism then give it time to develop an alternative source of instruction before demanding that she be admitted into the University of

Missouri program reserved for whites.[21] The Oklahoma state court's decision in Sipuel's case was consistent with that earlier federal court decision from Missouri.

Similarly, a Tennessee state court held that the state of Tennessee was entitled to reasonable advance notice that a black student wished to obtain instruction in subjects currently offered to white students but not to black students. States would not have to admit blacks to their historically white schools if they acted promptly to provide the requested opportunities for blacks at black state institutions. After six students seeking to begin graduate study at the University of Tennessee filed lawsuits to gain entry, the Tennessee legislature authorized the State Board of Education and the Commissioner of Education "to provide educational training and instruction for negro [sic] citizens of Tennessee equivalent to that provided at the University of Tennessee by the State of Tennessee for white citizens of Tennessee."[22] The court hearing the six suits was comfortable in believing that substantially equal training would soon be available to Tennessee's black citizens. According to that court, the state had, by its recent legislation, "provided a full, adequate and complete method by which Negroes may obtain educational training and instruction equivalent to that provided at the University of Tennessee . . . ."[23] Black students desiring graduate educations could be made to wait until the facilities planned especially for them were ready.

When Ada Sipuel's case reached the United States Supreme Court, Thurgood Marshall was able to evoke from the Court language that put an end to Oklahoma's stalling. In a *per curiam* opinion, the Justices noted that two years had passed since Ms. Sipuel had applied for and was denied admission to the only institution for legal education supported by the state. During that time, white applicants had been afforded an opportunity to study law in Oklahoma. The Court concluded that Ada Sipuel was entitled to a legal education provided by the state as promptly as was any applicant from any other group. On January 12, 1948, it ordered Oklahoma to provide a legal education to Sipuel.[24]

Obedient to the United States Supreme Court, on January 17, 1948, the Supreme Court of Oklahoma directed the Oklahoma Board of Regents:

> to afford plaintiff, and all others similarly situated, an opportunity to commence the study of law at a state institution as soon as citizens of other groups are afforded

174

such opportunity, in conformity with the equal protection clause of the Fourteenth Amendment of the Federal Constitution and with the provisions of the Constitution and statutes of this state requiring segregation of the races in the schools of the state.[25]

On January 22, 1948, the trial court ordered the Board of Regents to "enroll plaintiff, if she is otherwise qualified, in the first-year class of the School of Law of the University of Oklahoma, in which school she will be entitled to remain" unless and until a separate law school for blacks is established and ready to function.[26]

The state of Oklahoma established a separate law school for blacks with amazing speed. On January 24, 1948, the Chairman of the Oklahoma Regents for Higher Education, R.T. Stewart, announced that a separate law school, a division of Langston University, would be open for business and fully operational in two days, a mere two weeks after the U.S. Supreme Court decision ordering Oklahoma to provide a legal education to Sipuel. A dean and two professors were appointed to the faculty of the new law school and space was found for it on the fourth floor of the state capitol. As in Texas, students would use the state law library as their law school library.

As the officials in Oklahoma expected, Ada Sipuel had no plans to attend. In fact, only one student enrolled that spring and the school closed on June 30, 1949, after operating for only a year and a half.

Sipuel sought relief from the United States Supreme Court and was disappointed. In another *per curiam* opinion handed down on February 16, 1948, the Court stated that Oklahoma had done all it was required to do. According to the Court, the state district court correctly understood Oklahoma's options. Oklahoma could admit Sipuel into its existing law school, open a law school for her within the state, or stop offering legal training to its citizens in Oklahoma. The state had chosen an acceptable option when it opened a law school for Sipuel within the state.

In his dissenting opinion, Justice Rutledge noted that "no separate law school could be established elsewhere overnight capable of giving petitioner a legal education equal to that afforded by the state's long-established and well-known law school."[27] Sipuel now had the task of demonstrating to the majority of the Court that Justice Rutledge was right: that the new Langston Law School was not substantially equal to the law school at the University of Oklahoma.

In March 1948, Sipuel filed suit in state district court alleging that the new law school was not equal to the old. Various university regents and prominent local attorneys proclaimed the separate law school equal to the nearly fifty-year-old law school at the University of Oklahoma. Professor Foster, a faculty member at the University of Oklahoma Law School, declared the new law school a fake, fraud and deception. The judge was unmoved by Professor Foster's emotional testimony. Despite testimony from an impressive array of legal and academic authorities to the effect that the two law schools were not equal, the trial court ruled against Sipuel. On August 2, 1948, Judge Hinshaw announced that the new Langston law school was substantially equal to the law school at the University of Oklahoma. Sipuel was expected to enroll in the sham law school organized in just two weeks.

Earlier, in January 1948, six other black students had applied to the University of Oklahoma for admission to graduate programs in six different disciplines. A committee of Deans at the University reported that constructing the physical facilities at Langston for the six programs would cost between ten and twelve million dollars. Annual operating costs would equal at least half a million dollars a year. Oklahoma could not afford to invest in these new schools, so Oklahoma did nothing. It neither constructed facilities for blacks nor admitted them to their white facilities. It waited to be pushed into integrating its schools. Houston and Margold had anticipated this result. In Sipuel's words, "Mr. Jim Crow was becoming too expensive and troublesome to keep around much longer."[28]

In July 1948, Marshall filed suit on behalf of George W. McLaurin, one of the six graduate school applicants rejected by the University of Oklahoma. McLaurin had already earned a master's degree and wanted to enroll in a doctoral program in education. A three-judge federal court instructed Oklahoma to admit McLaurin to its graduate education program or to discontinue the program.

The Board of Regents had acted promptly when the Oklahoma Supreme Court told it to "afford [Sipuel] . . . an opportunity to commence the study of law . . . as soon as citizens of other groups are afforded such opportunity . . ."[29] After stalling for two years, a law school of sorts was up and running in two weeks. Oklahoma could not pretend to develop adequate educational facilities in six different disciplines in so short a period of time. Black students were to be admitted to state educational institutions immediately. The Oklahoma legislature amended its statutes to "permit the admission of Negroes to institutions of higher learning attended by white students, in cases where such institutions offered courses not available in the Negro schools."[30] McLaurin entered graduate school on October 13, 1948, becoming the first black ever to enroll in the University of Oklahoma.

Subsequently, Dr. George Lynn Cross, President of the University of Oklahoma, directed the Office of Admissions to accept Sipuel into the law school. She enrolled the next day, June 17, 1949, 1,251 days after she first applied. She was the only female and the only black in a summer enrollment of 300 law students.

McLaurin was admitted to the University of Oklahoma on a segregated basis. He had to sit apart, in an alcove of the classroom. He had a designated desk in the library and a designated table in the cafeteria. Sipuel was asked to sit behind a portable sign which read "For Colored Only." Her fellow students moved the sign from place to place in the classroom and eventually abandoned its use. At one point, the sign was placed in front of the professor's podium.

The U.S. Supreme Court would later determine that physically separating McLaurin from his classmates handicapped him in his studies. Imposing these conditions of segregation upon McLaurin violated the Fourteenth Amendment.

The Supreme Court handed down the decisions in the *McLaurin* and *Sweatt* cases shortly after Charles Hamilton Houston died on April 22, 1950, at age 54, of an acute coronary thrombosis. His fight to end segregation in graduate and professional schools had been successful. Houston did not live to hear S. Emory Rogers, the attorney representing Clarendon County, South Carolina, in the *Brown II* case, tell the U. S. Supreme Court in oral argument that, "[W]e would not send our white children to the Negro schools."[31] Nor did he live to hear the cruel words of hatred spewing from the mouths of mothers of school age children protesting because a six-year-old walked into a public school in New Orleans. He was not forced to endure the years of litigating school desegregation suits case by case and county by county as the southern states sought to frustrate the rulings of *Gaines* and then both *Brown* decisions. He had set in motion a strategy to effect change then left the venture to be completed by his social engineers.

*Other states*

While Sipuel was trying to get admitted into the University of Oklahoma, Mississippi joined the list of states which offered out-of-state scholarships. In 1948, Mississippi authorized its Board of Trustees of State Institutions of Higher Learning to subsidize out-of-state instruction for its black population at a cost per student no greater than would be the cost to attend school at a state-supported school within the state.[32] The issue of providing graduate and professional education to blacks was squarely before the states.

This pressure to provide equal educational opportunities for blacks in the southern states dovetailed with a movement within those states to maximize their resources through interstate contracts. States with desired facilities would agree to receive students and funding from states without those facilities. Virginia and West Virginia already had such an arrangement whereby fifteen to twenty students per year from the University of West Virginia attended the Medical College of Virginia. Alabama sought to make its School of Veterinary Medicine available to students from other states in this manner. Officials in Alabama reasoned that a larger applicant pool would allow it to choose more highly qualified applicants and that income from other states would help it offset rising costs.

Meharry Medical College, a private medical and dental school in Nashville, Tennessee, was in financial difficulty in 1947. It received no aid from the state and the major grants heretofore supporting the school were ending. It could not raise its enrollment fees without losing significant numbers of its students.

Founded in 1876 as the Meharry Medical Department of Central Tennessee College by the Freedmen's Aid Society of the Methodist Episcopal Church, Meharry Medical College opened October 13, 1876. It gained separate corporate existence in 1915, and now has Schools of Medicine, Dentistry, Graduate Studies and Research, and Allied Health Professions. Meharry estimates that nearly 15 percent of all African American physicians and dentists practicing in the United States are Meharry graduates. In 1948, more than one-half of all such physicians and dentists had completed their training at Meharry.

North Carolina and Alabama were already providing financial support for blacks sent from their states to attend Meharry. Officials at Meharry sought such arrangements with other states. As an alternative

178

they offered the school to the southern states for their joint operation. States still wanting to preserve segregation could establish separate law and graduate schools, but the expense of a duplicate medical school was far too great for any individual state. The joint operation of Meharry would allow the states to share these costs.

Anticipating that ever increasing numbers of black students would apply to attend their segregated medical schools, the governors of fifteen southern states -- Alabama, Arkansas, Florida, Georgia, Kentucky, Louisiana, Maryland, Mississippi, North Carolina, Oklahoma, South Carolina, Tennessee, Texas, Virginia and West Virginia -- agreed to enter into a compact for "cooperative regional education."[33] Under this agreement, Meharry Medical College of Nashville, Tennessee, would be operated as a regional institution for medical, dental and nursing education for blacks. The governors of Kentucky and West Virginia were hesitant to sign the compact. They expressed the fear that the compact would be used to perpetuate racial segregation in higher education.[34] West Virginia had opened its schools to blacks in 1938.

Through this compact, the states created a joint agency called the Board of Control for Southern Regional Education that was to hold title to the facility. The states agreed to finance the operating and expansion expenses of the facility.

The wording of the Compact was driven by the immediate opportunity to acquire and operate Meharry Medical College. The Governors of the signing states agreed that the preservation of an existing medical school was far wiser than incurring the costs of creating a new school. After it was created, the Southern Regional Education Board (SREB), decided against actually owning and operating any institutions. Instead, it defined its role as a broker, identifying the educational needs and resources available within its member states and assisting states to meet their needs through a judicious application of their resources and through interstate cooperation.

From its inception, SREB sought to serve both white and black students. Its first project was to develop an interstate agreement related to veterinary medicine. Four veterinary schools were located in the region: the School of Veterinary Medicine at Alabama Polytechnic Institute, which first offered veterinary medicine courses in 1892 at what is now Auburn University; Tuskegee University School of Veterinary Medicine, established in 1945; the University of Georgia College of Veterinary Medicine, organized in 1946; and Oklahoma A. and M.

179

Veterinary School. Founded in 1948, it is now the College of Veterinary Medicine at Oklahoma State University. Each school pledged to receive a quota of students from designated states and were promised $1,000 per year for those students. Tuskegee agreed to receive black students from any of the Compact states. The SREB assisted its member states to enter into similar agreements related to medical and dental schooling but at a subsidy rate of $1,500. These sums greatly exceeded the small amounts offered by the states to their black citizens who then had to make their own arrangements to attend out of state schools.

SREB describes itself as "founded more than 50 years ago as a way for states to improve and share resources in higher education . . . [and] to provide students with access to graduate and professional programs . . . that were unavailable in their home states."[35] Through its Academic Common Market, students in any of the member states can attend specialized programs in the other member states and pay only the in-state tuition and fees they would pay at their own home state schools. The Southern Regional Education Board continues to work with education agencies in sixteen states. Delaware is now a member. It acts as a clearinghouse for academic information and ideas at all levels, from kindergarten through post graduate work and as a coordinator of efforts to enhance academic standards.

*Louisiana*

Segregation at LSU had been the policy of the Board of Supervisors and a part of the tradition of the school. Kermit Parker applied to LSU Medical School in August 1944 and was denied admission; Alice A. Fassit applied to pursue graduate work in Home Economics in June 1949 and was denied admission, just to give two examples. Despite the June 1950 decisions in *Sweatt* and *McLaurin*, LSU's Board of Supervisors adopted a resolution in September 1950 directing officials at the university to deny admission to twelve students who had recently applied, including Roy Wilson who applied to attend the law school.[36] As in 1868, LSU was committed to maintaining its policy of ethnic exclusion without regard to affirmative law that required desegregation.

In response to Wilson's application, Dean Hebert advised Wilson, just as he had advised Hatfield, that "the State of Louisiana maintains separate schools for its white and colored students . . . Louisiana State

180

University does not admit colored students."[37] Roy Wilson, however, could rely on the newly established precedents of *Sweatt* and *McLaurin* to demand admission to LSU, notwithstanding the presence of a *Gaines* school within the state.

On September 13, 1950, four years after Hatfield's suit and only a few months after the United States Supreme Court's decisions in *Sweatt* and *McLaurin,* Roy S. Wilson sued the Board of Supervisors of LSU for admission to LSU's law school. The U. S. Supreme Court had just told Texas that its new law school, established with five full-time professors and a library of 16,500 volumes, was not substantially equal to its older law school with a nationally recognized full-time faculty of sixteen and 65,000 volumes in its library. In addition, the older law school "possessed to a far greater degree those qualities which are incapable of objective measurement, but which make for greatness in a law school."[38]

In Wilson's case, a three judge court composed of Judge Herbert Christenberry, Judge J. Skelly Wright and Judge Wayne G. Borah, compared the LSU Law School, in existence since 1906 and with 69,224 volumes in its library, to the Southern University Law School, in existence just three years, still housed in the University Library, and with 11,652 volumes. It determined that "the Law School of Southern University does not afford to plaintiff educational advantages equal or substantially equal to those he would receive if admitted to the Department of Law of the Louisiana State University and Agricultural and Mechanical College."[39]

It held that Wilson was "entitled to educational advantages and opportunities available within the state, at the same time, upon the same terms and substantially equal to those which the state provides and makes available to other residents and citizens of the state."[40] The court enjoined LSU Administrators from denying Wilson the right to enter its Department of Law and Roy Wilson became the first student raced black ever to enroll in LSU.[41] On November 11, 1950, Wilson was conditionally admitted to LSU's law school pending review of his qualifications. He attended classes in November and December 1950.

Frustrating those who had worked so hard to get him admitted, Roy Wilson withdrew his application for admission in January 1951 after divulging in a January 3, 1951, deposition his history of violent confrontations with fellow students and co-workers. The LSU Law School did not knowingly graduate a black student until 1954 when Ernest N. "Dutch" Morial, who later became the first black Mayor of

New Orleans, finished law school there. In 1956, Maurice T. Van Hecke, former dean of both the North Carolina University Law School (historically white) and the North Carolina Central Law School (historically black), and President of the Association of American Law Schools, reported that the state-supported law schools at the Universities of Georgia, Mississippi, and South Carolina continued to prohibit blacks from attending.

Roy Wilson's attendance at the LSU Law School did not open the doors of the University's other departments to blacks. LSU followed a policy to reject any application from any black student until directed by a court to accept it. Lutrill Amos Payne was told in a May 5, 1951, letter that, "The University can accept applications for admission from white students only . . . "[42] After Payne filed a lawsuit, Judge Christenberry ordered LSU to admit Payne and Payne registered for graduate school in the 1951 summer session and moved into a dormitory without incident. In October 1951, the Board of Supervisors of LSU voted against the admission of Daryle E. Foister to the Department of Nursing Education at the LSU School of Medicine in New Orleans by a five to four vote. She was forced to sue the school and, on April 1, 1952, Judge J. Skelly Wright issued a permanent injunction requiring the school to admit her. Unlike in Roy Wilson's case, LSU looked but was "unable to find any additional evidence that would tend to disqualify the plaintiff from admission to the School of Medicine . . . "[43] The School of Medicine did not graduate its first black doctor until 1970 when Claude Tellis received his M.D. degree.

In 1953, A.P. Tureaud brought a successful class action seeking admission to the combined six-year course in arts and sciences and law at LSU. Alexander P. Tureaud, Jr., Tureaud's son and named plaintiff in that suit, enrolled in the undergraduate school at LSU in September 1953. Tureaud was isolated by the students and faculty; no one in his classes or in his dormitory would speak to him. He left LSU before the end of the fall term. Ten years would pass before any other black undergraduate would enroll at LSU.

The LSU Board of Supervisors refused to desegregate any of its facilities except under court order. Even after the *Brown* decision, LSU alumni urged school officials to maintain segregation wherever possible. Lutrill Payne was attending graduate school at LSU during the summers. In 1954, when he sought to use the university's swimming pool, the university's retained attorneys advised LSU that Payne ought to be admitted to the pool on the same terms as white students, as required by the *McLaurin* and *Brown* decisions.[44]

Other attorneys practicing in the state disagreed. Their letters urged that the swimming pool be closed down rather than desegregated. Robert Chandler wrote:

> There is nothing in that judgment [*Wilson v. Bd. of Supv. LSU and A and M College*, 92 F. Supp. 986 (1950).] that would require the President of the University or the Board of Supervisors to permit the use of swimming pools at the university by colored students.[45]

Henry C. Sevier wrote:

> I would recommend that the University authorities refuse permission to the negro [sic] or negroes [sic] the use of the swimming pool, and should they persist . . . set one evening aside for their use. . . . Should the court determine negroes [sic] have a simultaneous right . . . I would then close the swimming pool. . . . Swimming is not necessary in obtaining an education.[46]

W. Scott Wilkinson wrote:

> I do not think that L.S.U. nor Louisiana nor any other southern state should acquiesce in the segregation decisions of the Supreme Court except to the extent that they are compelled to do so. . . . No injunction has ever been issued by any court nor has any order ever been issued by any court directed to L.S.U. or any of its officers or agents requiring that they permit Negroes to dance, swim, sleep and consort with white students. . . . If the Board of Supervisors permits indiscriminate social relations between whites and blacks at L.S.U. it will be subject to contempt only from the alumni and others who have supported the university for many, many years.[47]

The firm of L.H. Perez and Sons wrote:

I would further suggest that if any Court would go to such an extreme as to attempt by injunctive order to compel the University authorities to permit negroes [sic] to use the same swimming pool as young white men and white ladies, that the swimming pool ought to be closed and some permanent structure built over it, with a plaque bearing suitable inscription regarding another victory for communist infiltration as the great leveler of human rights to the gutter level.[48]

On September 1, 1956, the LSU Board of Supervisors adopted a resolution concerning the desegregation of its facilities in which it maintained segregation where it could do so without directly violating United States Supreme Court decisions. Black students were "permitted to live in University dormitories on a nonsegregated basis as to rooms, restrooms, classrooms, dining halls, dishes and utensils, including University cafeterias, the Field House Coffee Shop, and seating at athletic events."[49] A campus event that was entertainment could exclude or segregate blacks while those that were educational could not. As an example, although black students were eligible for honor society membership, black students could not attend the organization's annual banquet. At Commencement exercises, graduates could not be seated separately, but their family and friends could be seated in segregated sections.

Hatfield did not attend LSU's Law School. To satisfy the demands of the U.S. Supreme Court, the State of Louisiana established a *Gaines* school at its historically black university. Like Sipuel and Sweatt in their respective states, Hatfield refused to attend the Jim Crow school. He had brought his litigation against LSU to end segregation. He did not want to foster it by acquiescing to it. By 1950, when Roy Wilson attended LSU, Hatfield was teaching in New Orleans.

Notes

1.Speech at 1895 South Carolina Constitutional Convention in MICHAEL L. COOPER, FROM SLAVE TO CIVIL WAR HERO 59 (Lodestar Books 1994).

2.*John Howard Wrighten, III v. Univ. of South Carolina*, 72 F. Supp. 948 (E.D.S.C. 1947). *Heman Marion Sweatt v. Theophilis Shickel Painter, et al. of the Univ of Texas*, 210 S.W.2d 442 (C.Civ. App. 1948), *rev'd* 339 U.S. 629 (1950). *Ada Lois Sipuel v. Board of Regents of the University of Oklahoma*, 199 Okla. 36 (1947), *rev'd per curiam*, 332 U.S. 631, *on* remand, 199 Okla. 586, *aff'd per curiam sub nom. Fisher v. Hurst*, 333 U.S. 147 (1948).

3.1945 South Carolina Acts 223, s. 16.

4.1946 S.C. Acts 601, s. 16, Item 4 (Mar. 13, 1946).

5.1947 S.C. Acts 286, s. 18, Item 2 (May 2, 1947).

6.*Wrighten*, 72 F. Supp. 948, 952.

7.*School Bd. of Norfolk v. Beckett*, 260 F.2d 18 (4th Cir. 1958).

8.Va. Code of 1919 s. 719; Va. Code of 1950, s. 22-221. ("White and colored persons shall not be taught in the same school, but shall be taught in separate schools, under the same general regulations as to management, usefulness and efficiency.") *Davis v. Cty School Bd. of Prince Edward Cty, Va.*, 103 F. Supp. 337, 399 (E.D. Va. 1952).

9.*Davis v. Prince Edward Cty, Va.*, 103 F.Supp. 337, 339.The court found that the newer school buses were not used to transport black students.

10.*Brown v. Bd. of Ed. of Topeka, Kan.*, 98 F.Supp. 797 (D.C. Kan. 1951); *Briggs v. Elliott*, 103 F.Supp. 920 (E.D. S.Caro. 1952); and Gebhart v. Belton, 91 A.2d 137 (Del. 1952).

11.*Brown v. Bd. of Ed. of Topeka, Kan*, 347 U.S. 483, 495 (1954).

12.*Brown v. Bd. of Ed. of Topeka, Kan*, 349 U.S. 294, 301 (1955).

13.*James v. Almond, Gov. of Va.*, 170 F.Supp. 331 (E.D.Va. 1959). (White parents sued the Governor to reopen white high schools that were closed to avoid integration. In some counties the black high schools remained open while white high schools were closed.) *Harrison, Attorney General of Va. v. Day, Comptroller of Va.*, 200 Va. 439, 106 S.E.2nd 636 (1959). (The state denied funding to schools which had integrated in violation of the Constitution of Virginia which requires the state to provide free public schools.)

14.*Wrighten v. Univ. of South Carolina*, 72 F. Supp. 948, 952 (E.D. S.C. 1947).

15.TEXAS CONST. art. VII, s. 7 (1876, repealed 1969), TEXAS CONST. art. VII (1876, amended 1984), s. 14; Tex. Rev. Civ. Stat. arts. 2643b, 2719, 2900 (Vernon, 1925 and Supp.)

16.*Sweatt v. Painter*, 210 S.W.2d 442, 446.

17.1947 Texas Gen. Laws 29 (Mar. 3, 1947).

18.*Sweatt v. Painter*, 210 S.W. 2d 442, 446-447 (1950).

19.*Heman Marion Sweatt v.Theophilis Shickel Painter, et al. of the Univ of Texas*, 339 U.S. 629, 634 (1950).

20.*Ada Lois Sipuel v. Bd. of Regents of Univ. of Oklahoma*, 199 Okla. 36, 38-39 (1947).

21.*Lucile Bluford v. S.W. Canada*, 32 F. Supp. 707, 710-711 (W.D. Mo. 1940).

22.1941 Tenn. Acts 43 (effective Feb. 12, 1941); *Michael v. Witham*, 165 S.W.2d at 380.

23.*Michael v. Witham*, 179 Tenn. 250, 165 S.W.2d 378, 382 (1942).

24.*Sipuel v. Bd. of Regents of Univ. of Oklahoma*, 332 U.S. 631, 633 (1948).

25.*Sipuel v. Bd. of Regents of Univ. of Oklahoma*, 199 Okla 586, 588 (1948).

26.*Fisher v. Hurst,* 333 U.S. 147, 149 (1948) quoting the Oklahoma trial court's unpublished order. Sipuel married Warren W. Fisher March 3, 1944. Her state suit was filed using her maiden name. This subsequent suit was filed using her married name.

27.*Fisher v. Hurst*, 333 U.S. 147, 152 (1948). A *per curiam* opinion is issued by the court as a whole and not by any one particular judge of that court. It is often a brief announcement of the disposition of the case without a written opinion of explanation.

28. ADA FISHER, A MATTER OF BLACK AND WHITE 143 (Univ. of Okla. Press 1996).

29. *Sipuel v. Bd. of Regents of Univ. of Oklahoma*, 199 Okla. 586, 588.

30. *McLaurin v. Oklahoma*, 339 U.S. 637, 639 (1950).

31. PETER IRONS, A PEOPLE'S HISTORY OF THE SUPREME COURT 399 (Viking Press 1999).

32. 1948 Miss. Laws 282 (Apr. 8, 1948).

33. 1948 La. Acts 367 (Jul. 6, 1948).

34. REDDING S. SUGG, JR. AND GEORGE HILTON JONES, THE SOUTHERN REGIONAL EDUCATION BOARD: TEN YEARS OF REGIONAL COOPERATION IN HIGHER EDUCATION 18 (Louisiana State Univ. 1960).

35. SREB Higher Education, http://www.sreb.org/main/HigherEd/higheredindex.asp (visited Oct. 19, 2001).

36. Letter from E. Monnot Lanier, Secretary, to A.P. Tureaud (Sept. 5, 1950), LSU Bd. of Supv. Records, Record Group A0003, Box 8, Folder 316, LSU Archives, LSU Libraries.

37. *Wilson v. LSU*, 92 F. Supp. 986, 987.

38. *Sweatt v. Painter*, 339 U.S. at 634.

39. *Wilson v. Bd. of Supv. LSU and A and M College*, 92 F. Supp. 986, 988 (1950), *aff'd per curiam*, 340 U.S. 909 (1951).

40. *Wilson*, 92 F. Supp. 986, 988.

41. Press release (Jan. 17, 1951). (LSU Bd. of Supv. Records, Record Group A0003, Box 9, Folder 2, LSU Archives.)

42. Letter from R.J. Russell, Dean, to Lutrill Amos Payne (May 14, 1951), LSU Bd. of Supv. Records, Record Group A0003, Box 8, Folder 317, LSU Archives.

43. Letter from James Fuller to Colonel E. Monnot Lanier, Secretary, Board of Supervisors (March 4, 1952), (LSU Bd. of Supv. Records, Record Group A0003, Box 8, Folder 318, LSU Archives.) *Daryle E. Foister v. Board of Supervisors, LSU and A&M College*, No. 937, E.D. La. B.R. div.(Apr. 1, 1952).

44. Letter from James Fuller of Taylor Porter Brooks Fuller and Phillips to Robert Chandler (Aug. 17, 1954), LSU Bd. of Supv. Records, Record Group A0003, Box 8, Folder 315, LSU Archives.

45. Letter from Robert Chandler to M.J. Stewart Slack (Aug. 16, 1954). (LSU Bd. of Supv. Records, Record Group A0003, Box 8, Folder 315, LSU Archives.)

46. Letter from Henry C. Sevier to James R. Fuller (Sept. 17, 1954).( LSU Bd. of Supv. Records, Record Group A0003, Box 8, Folder 315, LSU Archives.)

47. Letter from W. Scott Wilkinson to James Fuller (Aug. 19, 1954). (LSU Bd. of Supv. Records, Record Group A0003, Box 8, Folder 315, LSU Archives.)

48. Letter from L.H. Perez and Sons to Taylor Porter Brooks Fuller and Phillips (Sept. 17, 1954). LSU Bd. of Supv. Records, Record Group A0003, Box 8, Folder 315, LSU Archives.

49. Resolution adopted by Board of Supervisors on recommendation of the Board's attorneys (Sept. 1, 1956), attached to Memo from the President's Office to Members of the Administrative Council (Sept. 6, 1956), of President's Office, Record Group A0001, Drawer 16, Range Z, folder 1127, LSU Archives.

# Part 3.

# Moving On

# Chapter 14.

## Graduate School and Teaching

*I, too sing America.*

*I am the darker brother.*
*They send me to eat in the kitchen*
*When company comes,*
*But I laugh,*
*And eat well,*
*And grow strong.*

*Tomorrow,*
*I'll be at the table*
*When company comes.*
*Nobody'll dare*
*Say to me,*
*"Eat in the kitchen,"*
*Then.*

*Besides,*
*They'll see how beautiful I am*
*And be ashamed –*

*I, too, am America.*

Langston Hughes[1]

While Hatfield's litigation was pending, A.P. Tureaud suggested that Hatfield leave New Orleans. The threats to Hatfield's life posed a real danger. Tureaud feared that Hatfield would be attacked and perhaps killed. Hatfield accepted a teaching fellowship from Atlanta University in Georgia. He began his studies in the spring semester of 1947 and was in the middle of his Master of Arts program when the law school at Southern University opened. Atlanta University's motto, "Find a way or make one," made Hatfield feel that he was in good company. He had sought to make his way into LSU.

At Atlanta University, Hatfield was inspired by the legacy of W.E.B. Dubois, Professor Emeritus. William Edward Burghardt DuBois, 1868-1963, received his Ph.D. from Harvard University in 1895. He taught history and economics at Atlanta University from 1897 to 1910 and was a prolific author, an outspoken advocate for racial equality and a crusader against lynching. He was one of the founders of the Niagara Movement, which led to the formation of the NAACP, and was a staunch supporter of black cultural development. He was director of research and publicity for the NAACP and edited the NAACP's *Crisis* magazine from 1910 to 1934. DuBois is credited with stimulating the cultural outpouring that we know as the Harlem Renaissance.

DuBois encouraged talented blacks to aspire to high academic achievement, to form a cadre of leaders for the less well-educated blacks, and to claim their proper place in society as equals to any others. He is often counterposed to Booker T. Washington, the founder of Tuskegee Institute, who campaigned for industrial and agricultural education for blacks and whose Accommodation Speech at the Cotton States' Exposition in 1895 promised whites that he, and the blacks he represented, would not seek social equality in the near future. Their contrasting positions are portrayed in a poem by Dudley Randall.

> "It seems to me," said Booker T.,
> "It shows a mighty lot of cheek
> To study chemistry and Greek
> When Mister Charlie needs a hand
> To hoe the cotton on his land,
> And when Miss Ann looks for a cook,
> Why stick your nose inside a book?"
>
> "I don't agree," said W.E.B.,

"If I should have the drive to seek
Knowledge of chemistry or Greek,
I'll do it. Charles and Miss can look
Another place for hand or cook.
Some men rejoice in skill of hand,
And some in cultivating land,
But there are others who maintain
The right to cultivate the brain."

"It seems to me," said Booker T.,
"That all you folks have missed the boat
Who shout about the right to vote,
And spend vain days and sleepless nights
In uproar over civil rights.
Just keep your mouths shut, do not grouse,
But work, and save, and buy a house."

"I don't agree," said W.E.B.,
"For what can property avail
If dignity and justice fail.
Unless you help to make the laws,
They'll steal your house with trumped-up clause.
A rope's as tight, a fire as hot,
No matter how much cash you've got.
Speak soft, and try your little plan,
But as for me, Ill be a man."

"It seems to me," said Booker T. –

"I don't agree,"
Said W.E.B.

Dudley Randall[2]

DuBois left an indelible impression on Atlanta University and on
Charles Hatfield. DuBois affirmed Hatfield's efforts to desegregate LSU.
While in Georgia, Hatfield supported himself and his family with
funds from his teaching fellowship and from the G.I. Bill of Rights, the
Servicemen's Readjustment Act of 1944. Under the G.I. Bill, the federal
government paid a monthly stipend to veterans of World War II while

they were enrolled full-time in school. More than two million students attended institutions of higher learning following World War II with support from the G.I. Bill. During the summer session of 1947, Hatfield taught teaching methods and supervised student teaching at Spelman College, a nearby undergraduate school associated with Atlanta University.

Hatfield satisfied the residency requirements for his degree after two semesters and began work on his thesis. He successfully completed thirty semester hours of class work, although only twenty-four hours were needed for graduation. Based on his high scholastic average and on recommendations from his faculty, he was inducted into the Alpha Kappa Delta National Honor Sociology Fraternity.

Hatfield's Master Thesis was entitled: "Social Mobility and Public Housing, A Study of Sixty Low Income Families in the Lafitte Housing Project - New Orleans, La. 1946-47." He wrote about the people in the neighborhood where he lived. Hatfield passed his final examination and had his thesis accepted in May 1948. On Monday, June 7, 1948, Atlanta University conferred upon Charles J. Hatfield the Degree of Master of Arts in Sociology.

Impressed with his excellent performance at Atlanta University, Dr. Ira De A. Reid, Hatfield's advisor and a nationally known sociologist, invited Hatfield to join the faculty of Atlanta University, but Hatfield wanted to return to his family which had remained in Louisiana. He would not consider bringing his family to Atlanta. He had read a sign hanging near a Spelman College dormitory left by a group calling itself the Columbians: "Nigger leave or die." Hatfield didn't know how crazy the people in Atlanta might be. He believed that he knew what he would face in Louisiana.

Dr. Reid sent letters of recommendations on Hatfield's behalf to Ms. Ellen R. Cavanaugh, then Assistant Professor of Education and Critic Teacher at Xavier University, and to Sister M. Francis Dean, also at Xavier, but no job commensurate with his training resulted from these recommendations. Ms. Cavanaugh wrote back that she would have trouble finding Hatfield a job. Sister Dean wrote that she didn't expect to have a place for Hatfield "now or ever." When Dr. Reid received these replies, he posed to Hatfield the question they raised, "What did you do before you left Louisiana?" Hatfield believed that his efforts to enter the law school at LSU made him unattractive as an employee. Hatfield was considered a troublemaker, and anyone who helped him put themselves in jeopardy.

Hatfield did receive one job offer. While Dr. Felton G. Clark was out of town, Hatfield was offered employment at Southern University in Baton Rouge. When Dr. Clark returned to the campus and learned of the offer, Clark refused to hire Hatfield. He wrote to Hatfield that the job Hatfield had been offered had already been filled.

Clark could not hire someone whose act of suing to desegregate LSU threatened the very existence of his Southern University. If LSU opened its doors to blacks a separate Southern University might not be needed. How could Clark argue for continued or increased funding for his school? Who could tell how wide LSU's doors would be opened or if LSU would later close its doors to blacks? What would happen to the higher education of blacks in Louisiana then? Clark did not want Hatfield or his aspirations for desegregation on Southern's campus. Hatfield went back to the Post Office to work.

In addition to his work at the Post Office, Hatfield taught Religion, History, Spanish and English for two years at the Gilbert Academy Senior High School, 1948-1950. He was assigned to teach English because his diction and grammar were so precise. The school's principal, Mrs. Bowen, had initially invited Hatfield to teach at his alma mater beginning in September 1946, but Hatfield had hoped to attend law school. Hatfield also worked as District Superintendent for the St. John the Berchman's Insurance Company, supervising 75 agents and their clericals, 1948-1952.

Hatfield continued to enroll in graduate school courses after he returned to Louisiana. He completed the entire curriculum required for the Bachelor of Education Degree at Xavier and all but one of the courses needed to be certified for high school teaching. He received a Master of Arts Degree in Education from Xavier in 1950, but had done no student teaching. Ms. Cavanaugh, the Xavier professor in charge of placing practice teachers in high school classrooms, could find no suitable place for Hatfield to do his practice work. During spring semester of 1951, Hatfield enrolled at Dilliard University and did his student teaching at Joseph S. Clark High School in New Orleans under the supervision of Mrs. Bernice O. Rann. He received a grade of "Exceptional" in the course, Education 412.

Hatfield later took courses at Southern University and at New Orleans University. He even received course credit from LSU when, in 1956, he completed an LSU extension course for principals, ED 265. In

1964, the American Federation of Teachers awarded Hatfield a summer grant to study at the University of California in Los Angeles. He took two courses: Economics of Public Education in Affluent Society and Collective Bargaining for Teachers. California certified Hatfield to teach in its Junior Colleges.

In 1952, Hatfield was a member of an elite group of schoolteachers. Only 13% of public school teachers throughout Louisiana held the Master degree. Hatfield had earned a Master of Arts degree in Sociology from Atlanta University and a Master of Arts degree in Education from Xavier University. He had taught at both the high school and college levels.

Despite his many years of training and experience, Hatfield had difficulty getting a Louisiana teaching certificate. He believes that Shelby M. Jackson, the elected State Superintendent of Public Education and head of the State Department of Education, was influenced by Ms. Cavanaugh, his education professor at Xavier University, to withhold Hatfield's teaching certificate. Ms. Cavanaugh had warned Hatfield that he would have trouble finding work in Louisiana. Hatfield's advisor in graduate school at Xavier, Professor Michael C. D'Argonne, Ph.D., originally from Belgium, and Professor of Sociology and Director of the School of Social Science, repeatedly told Hatfield that the time had not yet come to integrate the schools in Louisiana. Hatfield was forced to have A.P. Tureaud write a letter on his behalf to Shelby Jackson. The teaching certificate came shortly thereafter.

On March 7, 1952, Hatfield finally received a Type C. (Negro) Teaching Certificate, No. 1623, valid for three years. Shelby M. Jackson signed the certificate and listed on it the subjects Hatfield was certified to teach: Social Science, Spanish, and English. Hatfield immediately applied for work as a teacher and as a substitute teacher in Orleans Parish. He worked as a substitute during the next academic year, was rated good or excellent in all categories, and was hired by the Orleans Parish School Board to teach English and Social Studies, at Joseph S. Clark High School Annex, beginning September 10, 1953. Five years later, Hatfield was transferred to Carver Senior High School when that new school opened. Hatfield remained at Carver from 1958 until he retired in 1979. Hatfield's temporary license was extended for three years, in 1955. His tenure was confirmed on September 10, 1956. He received a Type B (Negro) license, No. 2311, on November 9, 1959, and received a Type A (Negro) Teaching Certificate, No. 4696, valid for life, on October 20,

1965.

At some time in the early 1950s, Father Louis J. Twomey, Regent of Loyola University School of Law in New Orleans, encouraged Hatfield to attend law school there. He offered Hatfield a full scholarship, $2,500.00, plus money for books. Ordained as a Jesuit Catholic Priest on June 21, 1939, Father Twomey actively participated in civil rights and social reform efforts in New Orleans and was anxious to integrate Loyola University to set an example for other schools. Hatfield attended Loyola for three weeks before deciding that his time for attending law school had passed. He needed to continue working full-time to provide for his family and he needed some time to spend with his children. Attending law school would require him to quit one or more of his many jobs, and would leave him no time for his family.

Charles and Beulah Hatfield had three children. Charles, born September 6, 1943, Andrea, the only daughter, born December 18, 1944, and Elliott, born March 19, 1947. Charles' mother, Mary, continued to live with Charles and Beulah until her death in 1954. Mary Douse Hatfield loved to cook, loved to eat and loved her family. Beulah was happy. To her, Hatfield was a very good husband and his mother was a beautiful person.

In 1957, Charles Hatfield started driving a taxi for Johnnie Robertson who owned a local taxi service. Hatfield soon bought his own cab and drove in New Orleans for more than eight years. His most frequent fares were to the Sweggmann's supermarket on St. Claude Avenue. His customers needed to buy groceries, but did not have transportation to the store. Hatfield worked during the day teaching school for $4,300 per year, worked at night at the Post Office, and drove a cab when he could until 1965 when he rented the cab out.

Hatfield had hoped to leave his Post Office job earlier than he did because he found the Post Office to be an obnoxious place in which to work, with neither mercy nor compassion. Only the friendship of a few coworkers made the workplace at all tolerable. There was no spirit of cooperation and no opportunity for advancement. Despotic supervisors would record the most trivial events in an employee's personnel file. The Post Office was filled with Klansmen and supervisors there reminded Hatfield of Simon Legree, a character in Harriet Beecher Stowe's book, *Uncle Tom's Cabin*. In Stowe's story, Legree is described as a mean, low, brutal fellow, an example of the worst of the slave owners. Just before arriving at his plantation, Legree tells his newly purchased slaves:

I don't keep one o' yer cussed overseers; I does my own overseeing; and I tell you things is see to. You's everyone on ye got to toe the mark, I tell ye; quick, - straight, - the moment I speak. That's the way to keep in with me. Ye won't find no soft spot in me, nowhere. So, now, mind yerselves; for I don't show no mercy![3]

Many of the black clerks working at the Post Office joined civil rights organizations to help them combat the endemic discrimination present in their workplace and to provide group support to help them withstand their personal mistreatment by the floor supervisors. Despite his discontent with his work environment and his full-time teaching job, Hatfield remained at the Post Office for eighteen years.

Notes

1. From THE COLLECTED POEMS OF LANGSTON HUGHES by Langston Hughes, copyright ©1994 by The Estate of Langston Hughes. Used by permission of Alfred A. Knopf, a division of Random House, Inc.

2. By permission of Broadside Press

3. HARRIET B. STOWE, UNCLE TOMS CABIN 394-395 (Literary Classics of the U.S., Inc. 1982) (1852).

# Chapter 15.

## *Activism*

*Lamentation*
*If I should live to three score ten,*
*And all this time had been no use to men,*
*Though the earth I enjoyed all this while,*
*'Twould be better had I died before being a child.*

*Charles J. Hatfield, undated*

Shortly after he began teaching in New Orleans, Hatfield became involved in union activity. Ever an opponent of injustice, Hatfield recoiled at the arbitrary treatment of public school teachers. Working conditions for teachers and students were unbelievable to Hatfield. Classes were interrupted at random, teacher assignments were changed without notice, books and materials were in short supply, and faculty were fired if they complained. It seemed as if no one knew about tenure protection.

New Orleans had four nascent teachers' organizations. The National Education Association and the American Federation of Teachers each had separate white and black affiliates in Orleans Parish. Hatfield joined the New Orleans Teachers Union Local 527, the black affiliate of the American Federation of Teachers.

Hatfield worked as the building representative for the union at the Joseph S. Clark High School Annex and at Carver Senior High School when he was transferred there. He mediated disputes between the administration and the faculty, represented teachers at grievance hearings, attended school board meetings, met with local school board officials,

197

and recruited union members. Routinely, 90 per cent of the teachers assigned to Carver belonged to the union, primarily because of Hatfield's leadership.

Hatfield was well respected at Carver by students, faculty members, and the administration. As a spokesman for the other teachers, he confronted the principal when appropriate and spoke his mind freely. He did so in a manner that allowed him to maintain a good working relationship with the principal and, at the same time, effect the changes needed to improve the operation of the school.

Building representatives attended a monthly meeting of the union to which all teachers were invited. Hatfield, out-spoken at these meetings, encouraged teachers to stand together to demand better treatment. He was committed to union work and was devoted to improving the working conditions for teachers in the New Orleans public schools.

Desegregation of the public schools came slowly to New Orleans. In 1954, the United States Supreme Court declared in *Brown v. Board of Education* that segregated public school systems existed in violation of the Fourteenth Amendment of the United States Constitution. That Amendment entitles all citizens to the equal protection of the laws of a state and forbids a state from abridging the privileges and immunities of a United States citizen. In response to the *Brown* case, the Louisiana Legislature enacted statutes requiring public schools to continue to segregate students by skin color: "All public elementary and secondary schools in the State of Louisiana shall be operated separately for white and colored children."[1]

The legislation explained that, "This provision is made in the exercise of the State police power to promote and protect public health, morals, better education and the peace and good order in the State and not because of race." When the Supreme Court ordered, in *Brown II*,[2] a "prompt and reasonable start toward full compliance" with the earlier *Brown* decision, the Louisiana Legislature passed thirteen acts, without a dissenting vote in either the House of Representatives or the Senate, intended to maintain segregation.

To protect local school boards from having to defend suits demanding integration, Act 613 proposed, and the electorate in Louisiana passed, a constitutional amendment to designate local school boards as agencies of the state and to expressly withdraw the state's consent to sue local school boards.[3] Under the doctrine of sovereign immunity, a state can decide by whom and for what it will permit itself or its agencies to be sued. If school boards were agencies of the state, blacks could not sue them to demand admission unless the state granted permission for the suit.

Act 28 permitted parents to refuse to send their children to school "within any public school system and/or private day school wherein integration of the races has been ordered . . ."[4] Act 319 stated that, "Only white teachers shall teach white children in public schools; and only Negro teachers shall teach Negro children in public schools."[5]

To protect colleges and universities from applications that would result in desegregation, Act 15 required each applicant seeking to attend a public college to provide a certificate of eligibility and good moral character signed by both the high school principal and the parish Superintendent of Education, addressed to the institution the applicant sought to attend.[6] To stop high school principals of schools for black students from preparing certificates of eligibility for their students to attend historically white schools, Act 252 made "advocating or in any manner performing any act toward bringing about the integration of the races within the public school system or any public institution of higher learning" a cause for the removal of a permanent teacher.[7] The impact of these statutes was expressed by Arthur D. Smith, a high school principal who refused Miss Arnease Ludley's request for such a letter:

> Your request for a Certificate of Eligibility to attend Louisiana State University is hereby acknowledged. In reply I do not have a form of the Certificate of Eligibility addressed to that institution. If you should get a form and send it to me, I could not sign it, because under a state law I would lose my job for signing the certificate.
>
> I assure you that my refusal to sign the certificate is not intended to cast any unfavorable reflection against your character. I just can not take the risk of losing my job.[8]

A federal court ruled in 1958 that the requirement for a Certificate of Eligibility was unconstitutional because its clear intent was to continue the segregation of public colleges and universities.

The New Orleans public schools began to desegregate only after the resolution of the lawsuit, *Bush v. New Orleans*[9] in 1960. Some school districts in Louisiana, such as East Feliciana Parish, waited until as late as 1970 to begin to desegregate. Segregation suits are still pending in other Parishes. On November 14, 1960, six-year-old Ruby Bridges entered the William Frantz Elementary School escorted by four federal marshals. A mob of screaming women lined the sidewalk where she walked, spitting and throwing fruit at her. A teacher new to New Orleans was hired to teach Ruby because the white teachers at the school refused to have her in their classrooms.

Ruby was the only student in her class because white parents refused to allow their children to attend class with her. Ruby did not play on the playground and did not eat in the cafeteria; her social isolation was as complete as that of A.P. Tureaud, Jr. at LSU. Ruby remained in her class, alone, until the end of the school year. When school resumed in the fall, she started second grade in an integrated classroom.

Hatfield remembered the confusion that accompanied the desegregation of the public schools. He was teaching Spanish and English at George Washington Carver Sr. High School when the *Bush* case was decided. To prevent the local school board from complying with that decision, the state stripped it of its authority, including its authority to write checks. Public school teachers were not paid for three months.

Hatfield's union activities were only indirectly affected by school desegregation. In August 1956, the American Federation of Teachers directed all segregated affiliates to merge with the other race local within the same school district. This directive was in response to the *Brown v. Board of Education* decision and sought to conform union practices to that Supreme Court ruling. The American Federation of Teachers threatened to expel any local chapters which did not admit blacks before the deadline of December 1957. The New Orleans Federation of Teachers Local 353, the white AFT affiliate, gave notice in December 1956 that it would not integrate and asked the AFT to rescind its charter. Although twenty to twenty-five whites joined Local 527, the black AFT affiliate, the majority of the white union members did not.

Hatfield continued to work for the local and served as a delegate to the AFL-CIO state convention in 1964. Over the summer of 1965, Hurricane Betsy damaged the building housing the Carver High School and the school reopened on what was called a platoon basis. Half of the students and faculty attended from 7:00 a.m. to 12 noon; the other half attended from 12 noon to 5:00 p.m. Hatfield worked at the school in the mornings and was free to work for the local in the afternoons. Hatfield, thereby, became the local's first, albeit unpaid, employee. He would be ts only employee until 1967 when Betty Newton was hired as a secretary.

Hatfield served as Secretary-Treasurer of Local 527, American Federation of Teachers. He was elected Vice-President and worked as a legislative lobbyist, seeking raises, benefits, improved tenure and sabbatical leave rules, and better working conditions for state teachers. In Baton Rouge, he worked with Victor Bussie, President of the AFL-CIO in Louisiana, and enjoyed a significant degree of success. For Hatfield, union organizing was dangerous, but he felt that he had faced far greater danger when he applied to attend the law school at LSU.

In 1966, Hatfield and Local 527 began a campaign to persuade the Orleans Parish School Board to grant it collective bargaining privileges. A delegation from the organization presented a petition containing approximately 2,200 signatures to the School Board. Close to half of New Orleans' 5,000 public school employees, including paraprofessionals and clerical staff as well as teachers, black and white, signed the request for collective bargaining election. The five-member parish school board ignored the petition at first, then, on April 27, 1966, voted against the request, four votes to one.

Hatfield, along with Veronica B. Hill, then President of Local 527, and others, led the local in a strike the next morning, the first ever teachers' strike in the South. The other three teachers' organizations in New Orleans were not interested in collective bargaining and did not support the strike. It lasted only three days and attracted only 500 participants. The strike did not achieve its goal, but was a step in a very positive direction. New Orleans voters approved a one cent consumers tax to support the school system and teachers across the South were made aware of the potential intrinsic to a teachers strike for changing working conditions and addressing problems in public education.

Hatfield continued to organize his local and, by 1969, its membership had reached 1,800. In April of that year, the local again petitioned for collective bargaining rights and, again, the school board voted four votes to one to reject its request. The membership decided to strike and, this time, more than 1,000 teachers participated. This strike lasted eleven days, but was eventually unsuccessful at achieving collective bargaining. Local 527 was still without the support of the other teachers organizations in New Orleans.

In 1968, the black and white affiliates of the National Education Association in New Orleans merged with one another to establish the Orleans Educators Association. By 1972, the Orleans Educators

Association had reversed its position on collective bargaining. After negotiations with Nat LaCour, who became President of Local 527 in 1971, the Orleans Educators Association decided to join efforts with Local 527. The two unions formed a new organization, the United Teachers of New Orleans, UTNO. It enjoyed dual affiliation with both the National Education Association and the American Federation of Teachers and was the largest union local in Louisiana. Nathaniel LaCour was elected President. The independent white union that had broken its affiliation with the AFT had gone out of existence.

When the combined unions petitioned for collective bargaining in 1974, four thousand signatures were affixed to the petition. The Board voted in favor of collective bargaining, three votes to two. The union would now negotiate with the Parish School Board to determine salary, health and other benefits, and work duties for teachers. It would help to determine the hours of school operation, the maximum number of hours each teacher would have hall duties, and how often and for what purposes the public address system could interrupt classroom instruction. UTNO's contract went into effect in August 1975 and is believed to be the first teachers union contract with a public school district in the Deep South.

Nathaniel LaCour served as UTNO President until 1999. He was elected Executive Vice President of the American Federation of Teachers in 1998, held both positions in the 1998-1999 school year and left UTNO in 1999. When LaCour left, United Teachers of New Orleans had 5,100 members, 85% of the 6,000 eligible employees in Orleans Parish.

Hatfield pushed employee benefits in a new direction in 1972 when he suggested that the union local establish a federal credit union. Union-run credit unions are rare in the United States. Most school district credit unions are sponsored by the school board rather than by the employees. UTNO's credit union, established and run by union members, had assets amounting to more than twenty million dollars in 1999.

Hatfield retired from teaching on May 30, 1979. He never served as a high school principal and believed that his union activity may have cost him that promotion, but he has no regrets: "I spent thirty years trying to help young minds improve." On April 30, 1983, he was honored by the United Teachers of New Orleans, the local for which he had worked so tirelessly, and presented with its Pioneer Award.

Never one to sit around and let the world go by, Hatfield was as vocal in the greater community as he was in the schools, protesting orally and in writing about the injustices and inequities he witnessed around him. Even before he entered the Army, Hatfield served as a feature writer and editorialist for the *New Orleans Sentinel* and the Louisiana edition of the *Pittsburgh Courier* under its editor, and his friend, John Rousseau. In his articles, Hatfield wrote about the impact of discrimination and the unfairness of unequal treatment. He wrote about the hopelessness of one young soldier who planned to leave the country when the Second World War was over. In his article, the soldier asked:

> What hope do I have? . . . No matter what a man's ability may be or what he does achieve he is still nothing, that is, if he is a Negro. The worst living conditions in the country are offered him and the poorest employment. He is thrown to the rear in every instance and made to accept the worst accommodations. . . . Why should I remain here to accept such insults from the place of my birth?[10]

Hatfield wrote about the plight of a neglected Merchant Marine whose ship had been shot out from under him during World War II. The marine lost an arm and had three ribs crushed. He was losing his sight and was living on the streets. He had spent several months in a marine hospital, then more time in a home for convalescing seamen, then became a homeless beggar. Hatfield wrote that the black man finds, not only thousands of doors closed in his face, but even streets and sidewalks closed.

As a founding member and Executive Secretary of the Gentilly Heights Civic Organization, Hatfield was often in the thick of New Orleans political activity. Hatfield was urged to run for political office, but decided that he was not interested. He was suspicious of politicians, not knowing if scoundrels were attracted to politics or if politics made scoundrels out of good men, although some politicians were his good friends. He never stopped speaking out. Whether through letters to the editors of local newspapers, in editorial columns, at political rallies, or in organization meetings, he worked to effect change.

For his service to his community, Hatfield received a Certificate of Merit from Mayor Morial of New Orleans in May 1978. In October 1997, Hatfield was recognized by the Southern University Law Center during its Fiftieth Anniversary Celebration for the part he played in its creation. On May 11, 2002, he was awarded the Law Center's first ever Honorary Doctor of Jurisprudence degree in a hooding ceremony held during the school's annual graduation. He was able to attend the ceremony and died only a month later, on June 14, 2002.

Charles Hatfield never became a lawyer. He never went to law school at LSU or at Southern University and attended Loyola University School of Law for only a short time. Despite this disappointment, Hatfield's courage and determination in pursuing that dream opened doors of opportunity for many others. Both the out-of-state scholarship program and the law school at Southern University came to fruition when they did because of his courage.

Hatfield never let his disappointment in not attending law school cast a shadow over his life. He became an excellent teacher and an innovative and courageous labor organizer, community leader, and political activist. He changed the laws of Louisiana, not as a lawyer, but as a social engineer nonetheless. Hatfield demonstrated that massive change is brought about by individual acts of defiance. He touched thousands of lives through his efforts to enter LSU and touched thousands more through his teaching and writing. He has been of use to men and has no reason to lament. In Hatfield's words: "I wanted to correct the things that I believed were wrong."

## Notes

1. 1954 La. Acts 555, s. 1 (Jul. 8, 1954).
2. *Brown v. Bd. of Ed. of Topeka, Kan.*, 349 U.S. 294, 300 (1956).
3. 1956 La. Acts 613 (Nov. 6, 1956).
4. 1956 La. Acts 28 (Jun. 21, 1956).
5. 1956 La. Acts 319 (Jul. 13, 1956).
6. 1956 La. Acts 15 (Jun. 20, 1956).
7. 1956 La. Acts 252 (Jul. 8, 1956).
8. *Bd. of Supervisors of LSU v. Ludley*, 252 F.2d 372, 374 (5th Cir. 1958).
9. 364 U.S. 803 (1960).
10. Charles Hatfield, "The Passing Age," in *New Orleans Sentinel* (Sept. 16, 1944).

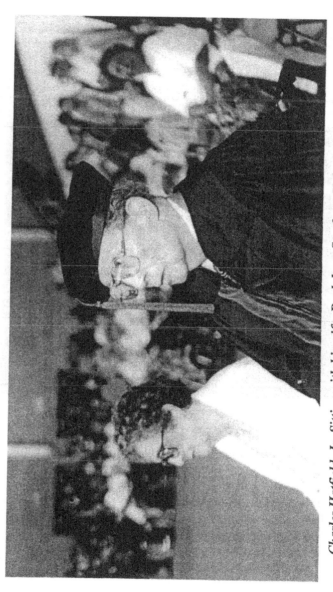

*Charles Hatfield, Jr. Sitting with his wife, Beulah, at Southern University Law Center Commencement Exercises, May 11, 2002*
(photo courtesy of Southern University Law Center)

*Hooding Ceremony*
*for Honorary Doctor of Jurisprudence Degree*

*Chairman of the Southern University Board of Supervisors, John*
*F. K. Belton, and Board member, Tony Clayton, perform the*
*Hooding Ceremony for Charles Hatfield, Jr.*
*Both are graduates of the Southern University Law Center.*
(photo courtesy of Southern University Law Center)

# Bibliography

## Introduction

Earl Ofari, "LET YOUR MOTTO BE RESISTANCE;" THE LIFE AND THOUGHT OF HENRY HIGHLAND GARNET 127 (Beacon Press 1972).
Tureaud Papers, Amistad Research Center, Tulane University.

## Chapter 1.

FORTIER, ALCEE, III A HISTORY OF LOUISIANA (Goupil & Co, Manzi, Joyant & Co., Successors 1904).

CHARLES ARTHUR, HAITI: A GUIDE TO THE PEOPLE, POLITICS & CULTURE (Interlink Books 2002).

Taunya Lovell Banks, *Colorism: A Darker Shade of Pale*, 47 UCLA L.REV. 1705 (2000).

JO ANN CARRIGAN, THE SAFFRON SCOURGE: A HISTORY OF YELLOW FEVER IN LOUISIANA 1796-1905 (Center for Louisiana Studies, Univ. of Southwest Louisiana 1974).

EDWIN ADAMS DAVIS, PLANTATION LIFE IN THE FLORIDA PARISHES OF LOUISIANA, 1836 - 1846 AS REFLECTED IN THE DIARY OF BENNET H. BARROW (AMS Press, Inc. 1967).

Gabriel Debien and Rene' Le Gardeur, *The Saint-Domingue Refugees in Louisiana* in CARL A. BRASSEAUX AND GLENN R. CONRAD, THE ROAD TO LOUISIANA: THE SAINT-DOMINGUE REFUGEES 1792-1809 (Center for Louisiana Studies 1992).

RODOLPHE LUCIEN DESDUNES, OUR PEOPLE AND OUR HISTORY (Louisiana State Univ. Press 1973).

Thomas Fiehrer, *An Unfathomed Legacy* in THE ROAD TO LOUISIANA.

CHARLES GAYARRE, IV, HISTORY OF LOUISIANA (Pelican Publishing Co., 5th ed. 1974).

SISTER MARY FRANCIS BORGIA HART, SSF, VIOLETS IN THE KING'S GARDEN; A HISTORY OF THE HOLY FAMILY OF NEW ORLEANS (self-published Aug. 1976).

ALFRED N. HUNT, HAITI'S INFLUENCE ON ANTEBELLUM AMERICA (Louisiana State Univ. Press 1988).

Mark Jones and John Wertheimer, *Pinkney and Sarah Ross: The Legal Adventures of an Ex-Slave and His (Originally) White Wife on the Carolina Borderlands During Reconstruction*, 103-4 SOUTH CAROLINA HISTORICAL MAGAZINE (October 2002).

Paul F. LaChance, *The Foreign French* in CREOLE NEW ORLEANS: RACE AND AMERICANIZATION (A. Hirsch and J. Logsdon, eds. Louisiana State Univ. Press 1992).

Paul LaChance, *The 1809 Immigration of Saint-Domingue Refugees to New Orleans: Reception, Integration and Impact* in THE ROAD TO LOUISIANA.

PATRICIA MCKISSACK AND FREDERICK MCKISSACK, REBELS AGAINST SLAVERY (Scholastic Inc. 1999).

THOMAS O. OTT, THE HAITIAN REVOLUTION (Univ. of Tenn. Press 1973).

MARTIN ROS, NIGHT OF FIRE (Sarpedon Publ. 1991).

ALBERT THRASHER, ON TO NEW ORLEANS! LOUISIANA'S HEROIC 1811 SLAVE REVOLT (Cypress Press 1995).

N.B. Wood, *Fathers to the Race*, in A NEW NEGRO FOR A NEW CENTURY (J.E. MacBrady, ed. American Publ. House 1900).

MONROE N. WORK, NEGRO YEAR BOOK 1937-1938 (Tuskegee Institute 1937).

**Chapter 2**

GERALD ASTOR, THE RIGHT TO FIGHT: A HISTORY OF AFRICAN AMERICANS IN THE MILITARY (Presidio 1998).

JOHN W. BLASSINGAME, BLACK NEW ORLEANS 1860-1880 (Univ. of Chicago Press 1973).

GERALD MORTIMER CAPERS, OCCUPIED CITY: NEW ORLEANS UNDER THE FEDRALS 1862-1865 67 (Univ. of Kentucky Press 1965).

MARK T. CARLETON, RIVER CAPITAL, AN ILLUSTRATED HISTORY OF BATON ROUGE (Windsor Publications, Inc. 1981).

JO ANN CARRIGAN. THE SAFFRON SCOURGE: A HISTORY OF YELLOW FEVER IN LOUISIANA 1796-1905 (Center for Louisiana Studies, Univ. of Southwest Louisiana 1974).

POWELL A. CASEY, ENCYCLOPEDIA OF FORTS, POSTS, NAMED CAMPS, AND OTHER MILITARY INSTALLATIONS IN LOUISIANA 1700-1981 (Claitor's Publ. Div. 1983).

EDWIN ADAMS DAVIS, LOUISIANA: A NARRATIVE HISTORY (Claitor's Publ. Div., 3rd ed. 1971)

RODOLPHE LUCIEN DESDUNES, OUR PEOPLE AND OUR HISTORY (Louisiana State Univ. Press 1973).

CHARLES GAYARRE, IV HISTORY OF LOUISIANA (Pelican Publ. Co., 5th ed. 1974).

Roland C. McConnell, *Louisiana's Black Military History, 1729-1865* in ROBERT. R. MACDONALD, LOUISIANA'S BLACK HERITAGE (La. State Museum 1979).

C. PETER RIPLEY, SLAVES AND FREEDMEN IN CIVIL WAR LOUISIANA (Louisiana State Univ. Press 1976).

LT. COL. ROBERT N. SCOTT, 15 WAR OF THE REBELLION, OFFICIAL RECORDS OF THE UNION AND CONFEDERATE ARMIES, SERIES I (National Historical Society, Washington Government Printing Office 1886).

EDWARD LAROCQUE TINKER, CREOLE CITY ITS PAST AND ITS PEOPLE (Longmans, Green & Co. 1953).

NOAH ANDRE TRUDEAU, LIKE MEN OF WAR; BLACK TROOPS IN THE CIVIL WAR 1862-1865 (Little, Brown and Co. 1998).

JOHN D. WINTERS, THE CIVIL WAR IN LOUISIANA (Louisiana State Univ. Press 1963).

# Chapter 3

A GRAND ARMY OF BLACK MEN - LETTERS FROM AFRICAN-AMERICAN SOLDIERS IN THE UNION ARMY, 1861-1865 (Edwin S. Redkey, ed. Cambridge Univ. Press 1992).

GERALD ASTOR, THE RIGHT TO FIGHT: A HISTORY OF AFRICAN AMERICANS IN THE MILITARY (Presidio 1998).

JOHN W. BLASSINGAME, BLACK NEW ORLEANS 1860-1880 (Univ. of Chicago Press 1973).

WILLIAM WELLS BROWN, THE NEGRO IN THE AMERICAN REBELLION (Citadel Press 1971).

DUDLEY TAYLOR CORNISH, THE SABLE ARM: BLACK TROOPS IN THE UNION ARMY, 1861-1865 (Univ. Press of Kansas 1987).

JAMES G. DAUPHINE, A QUESTION OF INHERITANCE: RELIGION, EDUCATION, AND LOUISIANA'S CULTURAL BOUNDARY OF 1880-1940 (The Center for Louisiana Studies, Univ. of Southwestern Louisiana 1993).

EDWIN ADAMS DAVIS, I THE STORY OF LOUISIANA (J.F. Hyer Publishing Co. 1960).

RODOLPHE LUCIEN DESDUNES, OUR PEOPLE AND OUR HISTORY (Louisiana State Univ. Press 1973).

DAVID C. EDMONDS, THE GUNS OF PORT HUDSON (Acadiana Press 1984).

ROGER A. FISCHER, THE SEGREGATION STRUGGLE IN LOUISIANA 1862-77 (Univ. of Ill. Press 1974).

SHELBY FOOTE, THE CIVIL WAR, A NARRATIVE: RED RIVER TO APPOMATTOX (Vintage Books 1974).

JOHN HOPE FRANKLIN, RECONSTRUCTION: AFTER THE CIVIL WAR (Univ. of Chicago Press 1961).

GUIDE ON AFRICAN-AMERICANS IN U.S. MILITARY HISTORY, 1526-1900 (Moebs Publ.Co. 1994).

HONDON B. HARGROVE, BLACK UNION SOLDIERS IN THE CIVIL WAR (McFarland & Co., Inc. 1988).

Hatfield Papers, Amistad Research Center, Tulane Univ.

JAMES G. HOLLANDSWORTH, JR., THE LOUISIANA NATIVE GUARDS; THE BLACK MILITARY EXPERIENCE DURING THE CIVIL WAR (Louisiana State Univ. Press 1995).

LANGSTON HUGHES, MILTON MELTZER &C. ERIC LINCOLN, A PICTORIAL HISTORY OF **BLACKAMERICANS** 5th revised ed., Crown Pub., Inc., New York (1983).

HARNETT T. KANE, QUEEN NEW ORLEANS; CITY BY THE RIVER (Bonanza Books 1949).

WILLIAM LOREN KATZ, BREAKING THE CHAINS 163 (Atheneum 1990).

Roland C. McConnell, *Louisiana's Black Military History, 1729-1865* in ROBERT R. MACDONALD, LOUISIANA'S BLACK HERITAGE (La. State Museum 1979).

JAMES MCPHERSON, THE NEGRO'S CIVIL WAR:HOW AMERICAN NEGROES FELT AND ACTED DURING THE WAR FOR THE UNION (Pantheon Books 1965).

BERNARD C. NALTY AND MORRIS J. MACGREGOR, BLACKS IN THE MILITARY; ESSENTIAL DOCUMENTS 32-33 (Scholarly Resources Inc. 1981).

C. PETER RIPLEY, SLAVES AND FREEDMEN IN CIVIL WAR LOUISIANA (Louisiana State

Univ. Press 1976).

Lt. Col. Robert N. Scott, 15 War of the Rebellion, Official Records of the Union and Confederate Armies, Series I (National Historical Society, Washington Government Printing Office 1886).

Supplement to the Official Records of the Union and Confederate Armies, Ser. No. 90, Part II - Record of Events 546 (Janet B. Hewett, ed. Broadfoot Pub. Co. 1998).

Noah Andre Trudeau, Like Men of War; Black Troops in the Civil War 1862-1865 (Little, Brown and Co. 1998).

Charles Vincent, Black Legislators in Louisiana During Reconstruction (Louisiana State Univ. Press 1976).

John D. Winters, The Civil War in Louisiana (Louisiana State Univ. Press 1963).

## Chapter 4

Edwin Adams Davis, Plantation Life in the Florida Parishes of Louisiana, 1836 - 1846 as Reflected in the Diary of Bennet H. Barrow (AMS Press, Inc. 1967).

Rodolphe Lucien Desdunes, Our People and Our History (1911, 1973 translation by Sister Dorothy Olga McCants, Louisiana State Univ. Press).

Mary Gehman, The Free People of Color of New Orleans: An Introduction (Margaret Media, Inc. 1994).

Sister Mary Francis Borgia Hart, SSF, Violets in the King's Garden; A History of the Holy Family of New Orleans (self-published Aug. 1976).

Harnett T. Kane, Queen New Orleans (Bonanza Books 1949).

Frank M. Uter, A History of the Catholic Church in Baton Rouge 1792-1992 (St. Joseph Cathedral, Baton Rouge 1992).

## Chapter 5

Creole New Orleans; Race and Americanization (Arnold R. Hirsch and Joseph Logsdon, eds. Louisiana State Univ. Press 1992).

James G. Dauphine, A Question of Inheritance Religion, Education, and Louisiana's Cultural Boundary, 1880-1940 (Center for Louisiana Studies, Univ. of Southwestern Louisiana 1993).

Virginia R. Dominguez, White by Definition; Social Classification in Creole Louisiana (Rutgers Univ. Press 1986).

Frederick Charles Green, Jean-Jacques Rousseau; A Critical Study of his Life and Writings (Cambridge Univ. Press 1955).

Rebecca H. Gross, Voltaire -Nonconformist (Philosophical Library 1965).

Mary Jacqueline Hebert, Beyond Black and White: The Civil Rights Movement in Baton Rouge, Louisiana, 1945-1972 Doctoral Dissertation (Louisiana State Univ. Dec. 1999).

Negro Year Book 1947 (Jessie Parkhurst Guzman, ed.) Dept. of Records and Research, Tuskegee Institute (1947).

JOE GRAY TAYLOR, LOUISIANA (W.W. Norton & Co. 1976).

VOLTAIRE, CANDIDE (Dover Publications, Inc. 1991).

O. Douglas Weeks, *The White Primary: 1944-1948*, 42 Amer. Pol. Sci. Rev. 500 (1948).

## Chapter 6

Lucile H. Bluford, *The Lloyd Gaines Story*, 32 J. OF ED. SOC. 242 (Feb. 1958).

HAROLD CRUSE, THE CRISIS OF THE NEGRO INTELLECTUAL (William Morrow & Co., Inc. 1967).

RODOLPHE LUCIEN DESDUNES, OUR PEOPLE AND OUR HISTORY (1911, 1973 translation by Sister Dorothy Olga McCants, Louisiana State Univ. Press).

HOLLANDSWORTH, THE LOUISIANA NATIVE GUARDS (Louisiana State Univ. Press 1995).

LANGSTON HUGHES, MILTON MELTZER &C. ERIC LINCOLN, A PICTORIAL HISTORY OF **BLACK AMERICANS** (5th ed., Crown Publishers, Inc. 1983.)

J. CLAY SMITH, JR., EMANCIPATION, THE MAKING OF THE BLACK LAWYER 1844-1944 (Univ. of Pa. Press 1993).

U.S. COMM. ON CIVIL RIGHTS, EQUAL PROTECTION OF THE LAWS IN PUBLIC HIGHER EDUCATION (Greenwood Press 1960).

JUAN WILLIAMS, THURGOOD MARSHALL (Random House 1998).

## Chapter 7

POWELL A. CASEY, ENCYCLOPEDIA OF FORTS, POSTS, NAMED CAMPS, AND OTHER MILITARY INSTALLATIONS IN LOUISIANA, 1700-1981 (Claitor's Publ. Div. 1983).

## Chapter 8

JOHN W. BLASSINGAME, BLACK NEW ORLEANS 1860-1880 (Univ. of Chicago Press 1973).

RODOLPHE LUCIEN DESDUNES, OUR PEOPLE AND OUR HISTORY (1911, 1973 translation by Sister Dorothy Olga McCants, Louisiana State Univ. Press).

Neal Devins, *Government Lawyers and the New Deal,* 96 COLUM. L. REV. 237 (Jan. 1996).

DEVORE AND LOGSDON, CRESCENT CITY SCHOOLS: PUBLIC EDUCATION IN NEW ORLEANS 1841-1991 (Center for La. Studies, Univ. of Southwestern La.1991).

ROGER A. FISCHER, THE SEGREGATION STRUGGLE IN LOUISIANA 1862-77 (Univ. of Ill. Press 1974).

Barry Friedman, The History of the Countermajoritarian Difficulty, Part Four: Law's Politics, 148 U. PA. L. REV. 971 (2000).

THOMAS H. GREER, WHAT ROOSEVELT THOUGHT: THE SOCIAL AND POLITICAL IDEAS OF FRANKLIN D. ROOSEVELT (Michigan State Univ. Press 1958).

KELLY W. HARBISON, THE AMERICAN CONSTITUTION: ITS ORIGINS AND
DEVELOPMENT (4th ed. 1970).
JAMES HASKINS, THE FIRST BLACK GOVERNOR (Africa World Press, Inc. 1973).
PETER IRONS, A PEOPLE'S HISTORY OF THE SUPREME COURT (Viking Penguin 1999).
NATIONAL BAR ASSOCIATION, WHO'S WHO AMONG NEGRO LAWYERS (1945).
J.W. PELTASON, 58 LONELY MEN: SOUTHERN FEDERAL JUDGES AND SCHOOL
DESEGREGATION (Univ. of Illinois Press 1974).
JOE GRAY TAYLOR, LOUISIANA (W.W. Norton & Co., Inc. 1976).
Tureaud Papers, Amistad Research Center, Tulane University.
U.S. COMM. ON CIVIL RIGHTS, EQUAL PROTECTION OF THE LAWS IN PUBLIC HIGHER
EDUCATION 1960 (Greenwood Press 1968.)
CHARLES VINCENT, A CENTENNIAL HISTORY 1880-1980 (Southern Univ. 1981).

## Chapter 9

ADA FISHER, A MATTER OF BLACK AND WHITE (Univ. of Oklahoma Press 1996).
MARY JACQUELINE HEBERT, BEYOND BLACK AND WHITE: THE CIVIL RIGHTS
MOVEMENT IN BATON ROUGE, LOUISIANA, 1945-1972 (Doctoral
Dissertation, Louisiana State Univ. 1999).
LSU Bd. of Supv. Records, LSU Archives, LSU Libraries, Louisiana State Univ.
GENNA RAE MCNEIL, GROUNDWORK (Univ. of Pa. Press 1983).
Tureaud Papers, Amistad Research Center, Tulane University.
CHARLES VINCENT, A CENTENNIAL HISTORY OF SOUTHERN UNIVERSITY (Southern
Univ. 1981).

## Chapter 10

V.L. BEDSOLE AND OSCAR RICHARD, EDS., LOUISIANA STATE UNIVERSITY; A
PICTORIAL RECORD OF THE FIRST HUNDRED YEARS (Louisiana State Univ.
Press 1959).
JOHN W. BLASSINGAME, BLACK NEW ORLEANS 1860-1880 (Univ. of Chicago Press
1973).
Bluford, *The Lloyd Gaines Story,* 32-6 J. OF ED. SOC. 242-244 (Feb. 1958).
EDWIN ADAMS DAVIS, THE STORY OF LOUISIANA (J.F. Hyer Publishing Co. 1960).
ROGER A FISCHER, THE SEGREGATION STRUGGLE IN LOUISIANA 1862-77 (Univ. of
Ill. Press 1974).
WALTER FLEMING, LOUISIANA STATE UNIVERSITY (Louisiana State Univ. Press
1936).
MICHAEL AND JUDY NEWTON, THE KU KLUX KLAN; AN ENCYCLOPEDIA (Garland
Publ., Inc. 1991).
Joe M. Richardson, *The American Missionary Association and Black Education in
Louisiana, 1862-1878* in Robert R. MACDONALD, LOUISIANA'S BLACK
HERITAGE (La. State Museum 1979).
Joe Gray Taylor, *Louisiana, An Impossible Task* in RECONSTRUCTION AND
REDEMPTION IN THE SOUTH (Louisiana State Univ. Press 1980).
CHARLES VINCENT, A CENTENNIAL HISTORY OF SOUTHERN UNIVERSITY AND A&M
COLLEGE (Southern Univ. 1981).

Charles Vincent, *Black Louisianians During the Civil War and Reconstruction: Aspects of Their Struggles and Achievements* in ROBERT R. MACDONALD, LOUISIANA BLACK HERITAGE(La. State Museum 1979).

MARCUS M. WILKERSON, THOMAS DUCKETT BOYD, THE STORY OF A SOUTHERN EDUCATOR (Louisiana State Univ. Press 1935).

## Chapter 11

Lucile H. Bluford, *The Lloyd Gaines Story*, 32 J. OF ED. SOC. 242 (Feb. 1958).

JOHN P. DYER, TULANE: THE BIOGRAPHY OF A UNIVERSITY 1834-1965 (Harper & Row Publi. 1966).

40 SOUTHERN UNIVERSITY BULLETIN - THE SCHOOL OF LAW (Aug. 1953)

Dean A.A. Lenoir, *Historical Sketch of the Southern University Law School*, 245 La. 157 (1964).

LSU Bd. of Supv. Records, LSU Archives, LSU Libraries, Louisiana State Univ.

JAMES HAWKINS, THE FIRST BLACK GOVERNOR, PINCKNEY BENTON STEWART PINCHBACK (Africa World Press, Inc. 1973.)

OPINIONS AND REPORTS OF THE ATTORNEY GENERAL OF THE STATE OF LOUISIANA APRIL 1, 1946 - APRIL 1, 1948. FRED S. LeBLANC, ATTORNEY GENERAL

Joe M. Richardson, *The American Missionary Association and Black Education in Louisiana, 1862-1878* in ROBERT R. MACDONALD, LOUISIANA'S BLACK HERITAGE. (La. State Museum 1979)

J. CLAY SMITH, JR., EMANCIPATION, THE MAKING OF THE BLACK LAWYER 1844-1944 (Univ. of Pa. Press 1993).

Action by the Southern University Board of Supervisors, June 29, 1985. *See*, letter from Joe Terrell, Chairman of Board of Supervisors, to William Arseneaux, Commissioner of Higher Education (Jul. 8, 1985).

Southern University School of Law Annual Report for 1955-1957 (Jul. 1957).

Southern University School of Law Report of the Dean for: June, 1951 to July, 1954, (Jul. 1954).

A.P. Tureaud, *The Negro at the Louisiana Bar* (Nov. 12, 1959) (Tureaud Papers, Amistad Research Center, Tulane Univ.)

Alexander P. Tureaud, Paper presented at National Bar Association Meeting, New Orleans, La. (Aug. 1953) (Tureaud Papers, Amistad Research Center, Tulane Univ.).

H. Washington, *History and Role of Black Law Schools*, 18 How. L.J. 385 (1974).

## Chapter 12

NAT BRANDT, THE TOWN THAT STARTED THE CIVIL WAR (Syracuse Univ. Press 1990).

DARK SYMPHONY, NEGRO LITERATURE IN AMERICA (James A. Emanuel and Theodore L. Gross, eds. The Free Press 1968).

ADA FISHER, A MATTER OF BLACK AND WHITE(Univ. of Oklahoma Press 1996).

JESSIE PARKHURST GUZMAN, ED., NEGRO YEAR BOOK 1941-1946 (Tuskegee Institute 1947).

Lawrence V. Jordan, *Educational Integration in West Virginia - One Year*

*Afterward*, 24-8 J. of Negro Ed. 371 (1955).
LSU Bd. of Supv. Records, LSU Archives, LSU Libraries, Louisiana State Univ.
FRED MCCUISTION, GRADUATE INSTRUCTION FOR NEGROES IN THE UNITED STATES (George Peabody College for Teachers, Nashville, Tn. 1939).
GENNA RAE MCNEIL, GROUNDWORK (Univ. of Pennsylvania Press 1983).
Constance Baker Motley, *The Historical Setting of Brown and its Impact on the Supreme Court's Decision,* 61 FORDHAM L. REV. 9 (Oct. 1992).
SEGAL, BLACKS IN THE LAW (Univ. of Penn. Press 1983).
U.S. COMMISSION ON CIVIL RIGHTS, EQUAL PROTECTION OF THE LAWS IN PUBLIC HIGHER EDUCATION: 1960 (Greenwood Press 1968).
Washington, *History and Role of Black Law Schools*, 18 How. L.J. 385 (1974).
JUAN WILLIAMS, THURGOOD MARSHALL (Random House 1998).

## Chapter 13

*Austin American-Statesman*, April 14, 2000, at A15.
Donald P. Baker, *Shame of a Nation: The Lessons and Legacy of the Prince Edward School Closings* 7 Washington Post, Mar. 4, 2001, p. W08.
Bill Brands, Oral History Interview with Dean W. Page Keeton, 2nd interview 18 (Jun. 2, 1986) (Tarlton Law Library, The University of Texas at Austin www.law.du.edu/russell/ih/sweatt/docs/koh.htm)
Bracey Campbell, Director of Communications, SREB (Telephone interview Oct. 23, 2001).
*Daily Texan*, Oct. 18, 1950.
ADA FISHER, A MATTER OF BLACK AND WHITE (Univ. of Okla. Press 1996).
Herb Frazier, Post and Courier, Oct. 4, 1996, at B3 (Charleston, SC).
Michael Gillette, *One person can be a catalyst for change*, DALLAS MORNING NEWS, Jun. 12, 2000, at 13A.
FLETCHER MELVIN GREEN, *Resurgent Southern Sectionalism, 1933 - 1955* in DEMOCRACY IN THE OLD SOUTH AND OTHER ESSAYS (Vanderbilt Univ. Press 1969).
The Handbook of Texas Online: Sweatt, Heman Marion (visited Apr. 2, 2001).
MARY JACQUELINE HEBERT, BEYOND BLACK AND WHITE: THE CIVIL RIGHTS MOVEMENT IN BATON ROUGE, LOUISIANA, 1945-1972 Doctoral Dissertation (Louisiana State Univ. Dec. 1999).
PETER IRONS, A PEOPLE'S HISTORY OF THE SUPREME COURT (Viking Press 1999).
LSU Bd. of Supv. Records, LSU Archives, LSU Libraries, Louisiana State Univ.
GENNA RAE MCNEIL, GROUNDWORK (Univ. of Pennsylvania Press 1983).
*Peregrinus Yearbooks*, 1950-1960, and University of Texas commencement programs, "Minutes & Documents of the School of Law," 1952-1958, LS141-LS147, Tarlton Law Library, School of Law, University of Texas at Austin.
Edward Rogoff and Derryl Zimmerman, *The Trials of Black Lawyers* 5-4 AMERICAN LEGACY 50 (Winter 2000).
REDDING S. SUGG, JR. AND GEORGE HILTON JONES, THE SOUTHERN REGIONAL EDUCATION BOARD: TEN YEARS OF REGIONAL COOPERATION IN HIGHER EDUCATION (Louisiana State Univ. 1960).

*Texas Lawyer*, Oct.4, 1999, at 2.

Steven L. Turner, History of the Civil Rights Movement in Prince Edward County (1951-1964) (Longwood College Library www.lwc.edu/administrative/library/turner1.ht visited Jul. 9, 2001).

Maurice T. Van Hecke, *Racial Desegregation in the Law Schools*, 9 J. L. Ed. 283 (1956).

Denise Wallace-Haymore, *Black Law Schools: The Continuing Need*, 16 So. Univ. L.R. 249 (1989).

Washington, *History and Role of Black Law Schools*, 18 How. L.J. 385 (1974).

JUAN WILLIAMS, THURGOOD MARSHALL (Random House 1998).

## Chapter 14

H. BABBIDGE AND R. ROSENZWEIG, THE FEDERAL INTEREST IN HIGHER EDUCATION (McGraw-Hill Book Company, Inc. 1962).

*Biographical Note*. Louis J. Twomey, S.J., Papers, Loyola University Library, Department of Special Collections and Archives, New Orleans, La. (1999).

COLUMBUS SALLEY, THE BLACK 100; A RANKING OF THE MOST INFLUENTIAL AFRICAN-AMERICANS, PAST AND PRESENT (Citadel Press 1999).

Made in the USA
Coppell, TX
07 February 2022

73107130R10128